RECLAIMING EVERYDAY PEACE

Bringing armed conflicts to an end is difficult; restoring a lasting peace can be considerably harder. *Reclaiming Everyday Peace* addresses the effectiveness and impact of local level interventions on communities affected by war. Using an innovative methodology to generate participatory numbers, Pamina Firchow finds that communities saturated with external interventions after war do not have substantively higher levels of peacefulness according to community-defined indicators of peace than those with lower levels of interventions. These findings suggest that current international peacebuilding efforts are not very effective at achieving peace by local standards because disproportionate attention is paid to reconstruction, governance and development assistance with little attention paid to community ties and healing. Firchow argues that a more bottom-up approach to measuring the effectiveness of peacebuilding is required. By finding ways to effectively communicate local community needs and priorities to the international community, efforts to create an atmosphere for an enduring peace are possible.

Pamina Firchow is Assistant Professor of Conflict Analysis and Resolution at George Mason University. She has published widely on the effectiveness of international aid after conflict. Specifically, she studies the international accompaniment of communities affected by mass violence, primarily in sub-Saharan Africa and Latin America. Professor Firchow has received support for her research from the United States Institute of Peace, the Carnegie Corporation of New York, the Rotary Foundation, the Kellogg Institute for International Studies and the University of Geneva. She has been working in the peacebuilding sector as a scholar–practitioner for non-governmental organizations and universities since 1999.

Reclaiming Everyday Peace

LOCAL VOICES IN MEASUREMENT AND EVALUATION AFTER WAR

PAMINA FIRCHOW

George Mason University

CAMBRIDGE
UNIVERSITY PRESS

University Printing House, Cambridge, CB2 8BS, United Kingdom

One Liberty Plaza, 20th Floor, New York, NY 10006, USA

477 Williamstown Road, Port Melbourne, VIC 3207, Australia

314–321, 3rd Floor, Plot 3, Splendor Forum, Jasola District Centre, New Delhi – 110025, India

79 Anson Road, #06-04/06, Singapore 079906

Cambridge University Press is part of the University of Cambridge.

It furthers the University's mission by disseminating knowledge in the pursuit of education, learning, and research at the highest international levels of excellence.

www.cambridge.org
Information on this title: www.cambridge.org/9781108416252
DOI: 10.1017/9781108236140

© Pamina Firchow 2018

This publication is in copyright. Subject to statutory exception and to the provisions of relevant collective licensing agreements, no reproduction of any part may take place without the written permission of Cambridge University Press.

First published 2018

Printed in the United States of America by Sheridan Books, Inc.

A catalogue record for this publication is available from the British Library.

Library of Congress Cataloging-in-Publication Data

Names: Firchow, Pamina, author.
Title: Reclaiming everyday peace: local voices in measurement and evaluation after war / Pamina Firchow.
Description: Cambridge, United Kingdom; New York, NY : Cambridge University Press, 2018. | Includes bibliographical references and index.
Identifiers: LCCN 2018011570| ISBN 9781108416252 (hardback : alk. paper) | ISBN 9781108402767 (pbk. : alk. paper)
Subjects: LCSH: Peace-building—Case studies. | Peace. | Conflict management.
Classification: LCC JZ5538 .F569 2018 | DDC 303.6/6--dc23
LC record available at https://lccn.loc.gov/2018011570

ISBN 978-1-108-41625-2 Hardback
ISBN 978-1-108-40276-7 Paperback

Cambridge University Press has no responsibility for the persistence or accuracy of URLs for external or third-party internet websites referred to in this publication and does not guarantee that any content on such websites is, or will remain, accurate or appropriate.

To the memory of my father, Peter Edgerly Firchow

Contents

List of Figures	page ix
List of Tables	xi
Acknowledgments	xiii
List of Abbreviations	xvii
Introduction	1

PART I UNDERSTANDING EVERYDAY PEACE

1	Measuring Peace	29
2	Who Counts in the Measurement of Peace?	54
3	A New Approach to Measuring Peace	68

PART II EVALUATING EVERYDAY PEACE

4	Everyday Peace in Uganda and Colombia	87
5	The Multidimensionality of Everyday Peace	108
6	Why Do Local Level Interventions Fail and Why Do They Succeed?	127

Conclusion	147
Appendices	159
Bibliography	175
Index	187

Figures

3.1.	Verification Focus Group participants and lists in Odek, Uganda.	*page* 72
4.1.	Map of 2005 presence of INGOs, NGOs, IOs and UN agencies	99
5.1.	Percentage of peace indicators by category in Odek and Atiak	116
5.2.	Percentage of indicators by dimension in Odek and Atiak	117
5.3.	Percentage of peace indicators by category in El Salado and Don Gabriel	119
5.4.	Percentage of indicators by dimension in El Salado and Don Gabriel	119
5.5.	Dimensions of everyday indicators in five countries	123
6.1.	Dimensional analysis of survey results – El Salado	131
6.2.	Dimensional analysis of survey results – Don Gabriel	131
6.3.	Category analysis of survey results – El Salado	132
6.4.	Category analysis of survey results – Don Gabriel	132
6.5.	El Salado average survey responses – peace indicators	133
6.6.	Don Gabriel average survey responses – peace indicators	135
6.7.	Peace perception by dimension – Atiak	139
6.8.	Peace perception by dimension – Odek	139
6.9.	Odek average survey responses – peace indicators	142
6.10.	Atiak average survey responses – peace indicators	143
6.11.	Peace perception by category – Atiak	144
6.12.	Peace perception by category – Odek	145

Tables

1.1.	SDG 16 targets and indicators	*page* 44
5.1.	Everyday peace indicators in Uganda by community and category	112
5.2.	Everyday peace indicators in Colombia by community and category	113

Acknowledgments

This book tackles two important questions encountered by the international community in conflict-affected contexts: How do we know what interventions work best for sustainable peace at a local level? And, how can we measure effectively in a way that reflects the priorities and needs of the population we strive to serve? These are questions that have fascinated me since I began my career in peacebuilding almost twenty years ago, and they are in large part what led me to become a scholar, in the hope that I might contribute to the collective effort of answering them. In this book, I present a different approach to measurement that addresses many of the concerns elaborated upon by peacebuilding scholars and practitioners. I use the everyday indicators to answer questions about local level peacebuilding effectiveness and demonstrate how we need to change our thinking and doing to reorient ourselves to a more participatory and inclusive approach. I demonstrate how this is possible using both qualitative and quantitative data.

I have several goals for this book. First, I hope that this introduction and demonstration of the everyday indicator approach helps to address some of the concerns and further the debates about the reliability of measurement equivalence across contexts and experiences. Valid measurement is mostly about ensuring that what you are measuring means the same thing to everyone who is being measured. That means ensuring the concepts you use are adequately defined for everyone. I hope to contribute, in whatever small way, to these important discussions about the role of concepts in measurement. It is said that statistics are like sausages: the more you know about them the less appetizing they are. My hope is that with this book, and the everyday indicator approach presented in it, the potential and possibility for the measurement of difficult-to-define concepts such as peace will become a little more appealing and, ultimately, more valid.

Many people have helped me write this book. First and foremost, I am indebted to the community members of Atiak and Odek, Uganda and El Salado and Don Gabriel, Colombia who participated in this project, as well as staff at the Justice and Reconciliation Project and the Fundación Semana. In particular, I am grateful to Rosario Arias Callejas, Maria Cabal Londono, Oryem Nyeko, Evelyn Akullo, Patrick Odong and Grace Achan. I am, also, deeply indebted to several colleagues and friends for their generous engagement with and support of my work. Gary Goertz, Ernesto Verdeja, Tom Scherer and Agnieszka Pazynska provided helpful feedback on the entire manuscript. Their comments and critiques helped me to bring together many ideas and thoughts into what I hope is a coherent whole. Solon Simmons, Thomas Flores, Charles Martin Shields, Peter Wallensteen, Roger Mac Ginty, Adam Moore, Henk-Jan Brinkman, Andy Carl, Melanie Greenberg, Allard Duursma, Chris Mitchell and, in particular, Naomi Levy gave valuable feedback on specific chapters of the manuscript. Their feedback helped improve individual chapters within their own areas of expertise. Montserrat López, José (Pepe) Saldaña, Nilofar Sakhi, Lindsay McClain Opiyo, Luis Felipe Botero, Michael English and Shannon Golden provided much needed editing, research and program management assistance. Kristen Wall's practical and theoretical knowledge of the field, as well as her excellent editing skills, were indispensable in putting this book together.

The United States Institute of Peace and the Carnegie Corporation of New York provided the funding necessary to research and write this book. However, their support has not only been financial. Working with individuals within these organizations has given me the encouragement necessary to continue to work on this project and believe in its potential. In particular, I would like to thank Steve Del Rosso, Aaron Stanley, Lili Cole, Eliza Urwin, Belquis Ahmadi, Gigi Lopez, Noel Dickover, Ruben Grangaard, Andy Blum and Ginny Bouvier, who did not live to see this book published, but whose help will never be forgotten.

Many other colleagues helped by providing feedback on the proposal, opening doors, providing moral support and brainstorming ideas. All of these people are too numerous to thank by name, but some stand out. Mark Goodale and Séverine Autesserre provided valuable feedback on the proposal when I was just beginning to think about writing the book. Many of my colleagues at the School for Conflict Analysis and Resolution gave useful advice and feedback on ideas, both in formal and informal gatherings. In particular, I am grateful to Kevin Avruch who advocated on my behalf to give me the time off from teaching to write this book. Susan St. Ville, George Lopez, Gay Seidman, Isabelle Schulte-Tenckhoff, Eric Selbin, Isabelle Lange, Danielle Reiff, Nanette Svenson, Jan Nemecek and Chavanne Peercy have continuously provided moral support and a springboard for discussion when I had questions about their experiences or research. I have also benefited from participating in and presenting my work at workshops and conferences at universities, government agencies, NGOs, international organizations and academic conferences that are too numerous to list here. My students have also provided helpful feedback and discussion on the book manuscript, in particular my monitoring and evaluation class at Eastern Mennonite University's Summer Peacebuilding Institute stands out. Last, but definitely not least, I thank my collaborator and friend, and the pioneer of the Everyday Peace Indicators, Roger Mac Ginty, for his support, guidance and great sense of humor. This book, and indeed this project, would not exist if it weren't for his keen childhood observations in Northern Ireland of shopkeepers replacing boarded-up window frames with glass panes once they believed there was less risk of bombings.

Most importantly, I would like to thank my family for the steadfast support they have given me since the beginning of this project. In particular, my husband, Fabrizio, who has cheerfully and willingly taken on more than his share of rearing our three children to allow me the time and space to write this book and pursue my research. He has been relentless in his support of me and without him this book would not have been possible. I am truly grateful for his love and dedication. Fabrizio, along with my children, Marta, Chiara and Isaia, have accompanied me on research trips and explored faraway lands with interest and a sense of adventure. They drive me to do more, to do it better and to go further.

Finally, my father passed away ten years ago, but his guidance, patience and influence on my life guide me daily and will always stay close to my heart. This book is dedicated to him.

Abbreviations

ADP	Area Development Program
CNRR	Comisión Nacional de Reparación y Reconciliación
CORE	Community Reconciliation team
DME	Design, Monitoring and Evaluation
DPS	Departamento para la Prosperidad Social
EPI	Everyday Peace Indicators
FDI	Foreign Direct Investment
GPI	Global Peace Index
g7+	Group of Seven Plus
HDI	Human Development Index
HTS	Human Terrain Systems
ITK	Indigenous Technical Knowledge
IMPACT	Initiative to Measure Peace and Conflict Outcomes
IEP	Institute for Economics and Peace
INCODER	Instituto Colombiano de Desarrollo Rural
PIRC	Integrated Plan of Collective Reparations
IDPs	Internally Displaced Persons
ICD	International Crimes Division
ICC	International Criminal Court
INGOs	International Non-Governmental Organizations
IOs	International Organizations
JRP	Justice and Reconciliation Project
LRA	Lord's Resistance Army
MEL	Monitoring, Evaluation and Learning
MDGs	Millennium Development Goals
M&E	Monitoring and Evaluation

MSC	Most Significant Change
CNRR	National Reparations and Reconciliation Commission
NRA	National Resistance Army
NGOs	Non-Governmental Organizations
NAVCO	Nonviolent and Violent Conflict Outcomes
OECD	Organization for Economic Cooperation and Development
PAR	Participatory Action Research
PRA	Participatory Rural Appraisal
PRDP	Peace Recovery and Development Plan
PSGs	Peacebuilding and Statebuilding Goals
UPDF	Peoples' Defence Forces
RCTs	Randomized Control Trials
RRA	Rapid Rural Appraisal
RFPs	Requests for Proposals
FARC	Revolutionary Armed Forces of Colombia
SFCG	Search for Common Ground
SMEs	Subject Matter Experts
SDGs	Sustainable Development Goals
SCORE	The Social Cohesion and Reconciliation Index
DFID	United Kingdom Department for International Development
UN	United Nations
UNICEF	United Nations Children's Fund
UNDP	United Nations Development Program
UNHCR	United Nations High Commissioner for Refugees
IAEG-SDG	United Nations Inter-Agency Expert Group
UNOCHA	United Nations Office for Coordination of Humanitarian Affairs
UNODC	United Nations Office on Drugs and Crime
UNOPS	United Nations Office for Project Services
TST	United Nations Technical Support Team
AUC	United Self-Defense Forces
USAID	United States Agency for International Development
USIP	United States Institute of Peace
UCDP	Uppsala Conflict Data Program
VGFs	Verification Focus Groups
PRT	Workers Revolutionary Party of Colombia
WFP	World Food Program

Introduction

Although the wounds had healed years ago, you could still visibly see the machete marks indented in his skull, on his forehead and across his ear. This man and the other community members I spoke with, all Tutsi survivors of the Rwandan genocide, had taken part in an internationally funded peacebuilding and reconciliation project I had been hired to externally evaluate. They lived in an urban part of Kigali where other international programs assisted and supported peacebuilding and human rights efforts at a local level, and they had participated in this project that brought together micro-lending, dialogue and psycho-social support for seven years. In this particular meeting, I sat with some of the project participants to discuss their lives in the community and the project's impact on their recovery from the Rwandan genocide more than twenty years earlier. Yet, when I asked this man about the impact the programs had had on him specifically he was not very optimistic: "I do not have the strength to take part, so I do not participate in any savings and loans programs," he told me. "For me I do not see anything worthwhile to invest in my community that can be productive." But, when I turned to a woman in the group, she indicated that things indeed had improved for her after participating in the program. "Before this program I had a house of nine iron sheets, now I have a house of thirty iron sheets," she told me. Their responses, along with those of many others in their group, were often contradictory and confusing to me. It was difficult to ascertain how impactful the programming had been.[1]

It was my job to determine whether these internationally funded programs had helped participating Rwandans improve their situations after they had been ravaged by genocide, war and misery more than twenty years ago.[2] How could I judge, and

---

[1] All of these interviews were conducted by the author in Kigali and the Southern and Western provinces of Rwanda in December 2015.
[2] For more on the role humanitarian organizations played in the Rwandan genocide, see Uvin 1998 and Rieff 2003.

according to what standards? It was clear that the tools available were not sufficient to make concrete assessments about peoples' experiences. I was given neither the time, nor the close contact with the communities to be able to make confident judgments about their situations. The only standards I could apply to help guide me were developed by outsiders and not sufficient to parse the local context and nuance necessary to understand the impact of programming in communities dealing with very unique problems.

This book addresses the challenges that I wrestled with while conducting evaluations in Rwanda and elsewhere. It makes the argument that beneficiaries are best placed to not only determine the effectiveness of external interventions – policies, programs, and projects – designed to benefit them, but also should be included in the design of the measurement tools used to evaluate them. It also proposes a new and innovative methodology based on inductive, everyday indicators that bridges the divide between quantitative and qualitative approaches to measurement. Using people's own indicators of peace in communities affected by violence is an innovative alternative to existing measurement systems and addresses several of the unanswered questions and criticisms posed by scholars on how the international community can more effectively support localities emerging from conflict to work toward peace. It recognizes the difficulty and often inherent contradictions presented by qualitative assessments done in short timeframes and based on interviews and focus groups, as well as the limitations of the more rigid, quantitative approaches to measurement that attempt to capture complex concepts through simplified quantifiable measures. The study uses mixed methods and participatory frameworks to generate data with the complexity and depth of qualitative findings and the replicability and clarity of quantitative research.

The findings presented here suggest that communities saturated with external interventions after war do not have substantively higher levels of peacefulness than those with lower levels of interventions, according to community-defined indicators of peace. Through the analysis of everyday indicators of peace generated by communities, the study concludes that everyday peace is multidimensional, varies across contexts, and is dynamic and evolving, which is why interventions that address peacebuilding concerns must also share the same characteristics. Therefore, I argue that more intervention is not necessarily better and that more attention must be directed toward the constituent parts and distribution of interventions, and their approach, content and quality, rather than an increase in the size and number of projects. In particular, my findings suggest that conflict-affected communities with large amounts of assistance in reconstruction and development require more interventions pertaining to social cohesion and community social relations than those with little to no assistance.

The study also finds that international and local organizations must develop transparency and coordination among themselves in order to work toward more comprehensive peacebuilding. Currently, communication among intervening organizations is insufficient due to the competitive nature of funding schemes. I concur with other assessments that donors should incentivize organizations to work together in order to increase the likelihood of success. In addition, local authorities and government officials should be consulted in project implementation where appropriate.

Most importantly, however, I argue that the first step toward determining what works best is to actively include communities not only in the evaluation, and monitoring of external interventions, but also in programming design. By analyzing community-generated indicators and comparing them to existing indicators used by international agencies, I suggest that beneficiaries define peacebuilding effectiveness differently than external interveners and that exogenous and indigenous indicators need to be harmonized in order to more effectively design projects and determine peacebuilding effectiveness at the local and national level.

Most indicators upon which measurement systems rely are designed by researchers and policymakers in capital cities of developing countries in the Global North, and purport to measure communities' progress according to standards that are defined and developed by community outsiders.[3] This is not surprising, considering that communities receiving aid are often left in the dark regarding aspects of decision-making from above and have little understanding of the logic and reasoning behind what they are receiving, or the origin of the services and goods.[4] As I discuss in more detail below, studies have shown that local and international perceptions often differ greatly on whether or not interventions have been successful.[5] Studies have also shown that developing countries implementing reforms often suffer from "isomorphic mimicry," the tendency to introduce reforms that enhance external legitimacy and support in order to ensure external financing. Scholars argue that isomorphic mimicry creates capability traps by focusing implementers on external standards rather than internal impact, ultimately resulting in failed programming.[6] These kinds of dangers could be circumvented by using participatory and community-generated impact indicators that are representative of grassroots concerns.

Everyday peace indicators are the signs we look to in our daily lives to determine whether we are more or less at peace. These are indicators everyone, whether from the Global North or South, subconsciously uses and collects everyday. They can be used as a hermeneutic tool of indigenous technical knowledge to measure and analyze daily life. Everyday indicators are usually quite simple and deal with various aspects of our lives depending on the community we live in.[7] Indicators can vary from hearing barking dogs at night, to the coroner removing dead bodies from the street in a timely fashion, to being attended promptly by a doctor when you are sick, or being

---

[3] Merry et al. 2015b: 17.
[4] Branch 2008; de Waal 1997; Finnström 2008.
[5] Mac Ginty 2011b; Moore 2013; Autesserre 2014; Richmond 2005.
[6] Andrews et al. 2013: 234.
[7] Mac Ginty 2013a.

able to attend a village festival. By using everyday indicators, I demonstrate the utility of finding ways of including affected populations' voices into more global standards and measurement systems, thereby addressing some of the seemingly innocuous, but often insidious, politics behind existing global systems of knowledge production. By allowing people and communities to decide what indicators determine impact and peace, we shift the inherent power imbalance away from international interveners and researchers to allow the beneficiaries of international interventions to make important decisions for themselves about what constitutes peace. By encapsulating local knowledge within indicators, we are still able to communicate effectiveness in a technical language the international community can comprehend.[8]

This chapter is meant to give a brief introduction to the chapters of the book where many of the arguments and issues presented here are elaborated upon in more detail. I start with a summary of the challenges scholars and practitioners confront when defining difficult to measure concepts such as peace and give an overview of my *big-P* and *small-p* peacebuilding distinctions, which attempt to provide some nuance in the efforts to define peacebuilding. I then proceed to discuss the role and importance of indicators in measurement and the conceptual debates and divisions surrounding the issue of indicators. I move on to give an overview of the methodology and research design for the study and analysis on local level peacebuilding effectiveness illustrated in this book. The overview of methodology and research design is only a brief summary of Chapters 3 and 4, which provide much more detail. I then summarize the main arguments presented in the book based on the analysis of the everyday indicators and survey results in the matched case research design discussed in Chapters 5 and 6. I then elaborate on how these results relate to the literature and theory on peacebuilding effectiveness. I continue by explaining why we need local standards and why a reevaluation of our approach to traditional top-down measurement and indicators developed by outsiders is particularly urgent now. I conclude by discussing terminology used in the book and give a summary of each chapter.

I.1. THE DIFFICULTIES OF DEFINING PEACE

While I was in Rwanda, I was also confronted with the challenges involved in measuring and making judgments about encompassing concepts such as peace and reconciliation. When I asked groups of survivors in Rwanda about their relationships with neighbors and with those that had killed their family members, the responses were varied. Initially, people would respond, "No problem, everything here is fine," and usually they would go on to say, "We are reconciled, maybe not 100 percent, but we are okay. There is no genocide ideology here." Yet, once I dug a little deeper,

---

[8] See Uvin 2013: 51 for more about how locals and the international community prioritize the same things, but are unable to communicate these to each other effectively.

it was clear tensions still existed. For example, a woman in the same survivor group in Kigali explained to me that when she went home to the place where her family was killed, she would interact and greet her neighbors during the day. But, later she admitted that fear continues to pervade her community. "I trust them during the day, but at night I am afraid. You cannot see inside someone's heart."[9]

Scholars and practitioners have long recognized that reconciliation and peace are difficult to measure. The terms may change depending on multiple variables such as context, culture, language, education and history. It is difficult to map the levels of these kinds of basic variables because they change according to context. Experts thus have difficulty arriving at decisive definitions of what exactly the terms mean and what needs to be measured in order to make claims about them.[10] Qualitative researchers are especially concerned with conceptual validity, or capturing the diverse dimensions of a concept, and are often critical of quantitative indicators that can fail to represent all dimensions of a concept.[11] Measurement is difficult because big concepts such as peace and reconciliation are multifaceted and varied by context and they may contain elements, such as feelings and relationships, which are not easily quantifiable.

Such difficulties are especially prevalent in monitoring and evaluation efforts, where implementers are required to establish indicators to assess the impact of their work, but also in more overarching efforts to measure peace such as producing indices and barometers. Indicators are usually determined by literature reviews and an assessment of already established indicators created by experts, instead of by consulting communities directly. Most organizations and measurement systems continue to use externally developed indicators despite the fact that scholars have found that there are significant differences between local and international actor's narratives and definitions of peace.[12]

Admittedly, part of the problem is that there is little consensus on what peacebuilding actually is.[13] Moreover, there is no existing consensus on peacebuilding effectiveness or what constitutes success or failure, although this issue is being actively pursued by researchers and practitioners.[14] By turning to local communities to elicit their own indicators, the innovative approach presented here allows us to obtain a clearer picture of local understandings of the impact of interventions concerned with normative goals of "peace" and "reconciliation," and helps us understand differing conceptions of these mercurial terms.

---

[9] This was only the beginning of what would be a very difficult evaluation of reconciliation programming in a complex society with rigid ideas about victimhood and historical memory. For more discussion on the complexity of reconciliation in Rwanda, see Thomson 2013; Davenport and Stam 2009.
[10] Diehl and Druckman 2010: 113; Esser and Vanderkamp 2013.
[11] Goertz and Mahoney 2012: 130.
[12] Autesserre 2014; Richmond 2005; Mac Ginty and Firchow 2016.
[13] Barnett et al. 2007.
[14] Diehl and Druckman 2010: 93–133.

This study distinguishes between *big-P* Peacebuilding and *small-p* peacebuilding. *Big-P* Peacebuilding encompasses all community-level interventions, from humanitarian assistance received immediately after war to longer-term assistance in economic development, health and education, governance reform, conflict resolution, rule of law, transitional justice and security – essentially, everything that purports to work toward a normative goal of peace. In contrast to *big-P* Peacebuilding, the *small-p* approach to peacebuilding is one that is focused, often at a more local level, on agency and the transformation or building of relationships with normative goals of peace.[15]

The book addresses a dilemma raised by scholars and practitioners alike over the challenge of harmonizing "the local" and "the international." It demonstrates that there are ways in which peace can be measured at local levels that are globally transferable. It also investigates the ways in which the international human rights and peacebuilding communities grapple with issues of measurement, monitoring, and data collection and information sharing, and explores the consequences of current monitoring and evaluation practices for the beneficiaries of peacebuilding and development programs. It is fundamentally an academic inquiry into peacebuilding effectiveness at the local level, but deals intricately with methods and methodology since it presents a new approach to establishing peacebuilding effectiveness. In sum, it critically examines questions of power and agency in the threading together of local, state and international needs.

I.2. THE POWER OF INDICATORS

Indicators are powerful tools that wield significant authority in international politics.[16] Global indicators are often designed to name and shame by boycotting and benchmarking states that rank low on indices that measure everything from corruption to human trafficking, or by relegating projects and institutions as delinquent if they do not measure up. They can also keep states, institutions or programs in check by monitoring their progress and behaviors over time.[17] Indicators are a simplified form of a concept and are generated in order to move from a concept to concrete data that can be quantified.[18] Merry et al. (2015b) define indicators as

> a named collection of rank-ordered data that purports to represent the past or projected performance of different units. The data are generated through a process that simplifies raw data about a complex social phenomenon. The data, in this simplified and processed form, are capable of being used to compare particular units of analysis (such as countries or institutions or corporations), synchronically or over time, and to evaluate their performance by reference to one or more standards.[19]

---

[15] For more of my discussion on this distinction, see Chapter 1.
[16] Kelley and Simmons 2015; Merry et al. 2015; Broome and Quirk 2015.
[17] Kelley and Simmons 2015: 68.
[18] Goertz and Mahoney 2012.
[19] Merry et al. 2015b: 4.

Indicators wield significant power and they are of crucial importance for the procurement of resources, funding, prestige and livelihoods. Indicators can be used to gather qualitative data, but are mostly used in generating quantitative measurement tools. Qualitative indicators typically deal with feelings or intangible issues that cannot be counted.

Gary Goertz and James Mahoney explain the tensions in concepts and measurement efforts between qualitative and quantitative approaches.[20] Qualitative approaches typically resist over-simplification and are concerned with conceptual validity. The failure of indicators to represent all dimensions of a concept is problematic for qualitative researchers because they are concerned with all attributes of a concept.[21] As Goertz and Mahoney put it clearly: "They [qualitative researchers] believe that concepts must be defined independently of data considerations. The definition of a concept should not be driven by the data that are available to measure that concept."[22] Quantitative approaches, however, are driven by data considerations as well as conceptual validity, therefore indicators can be discarded if there is no data available to measure them. Quantitative research is less concerned with measurement error to do with the definition and structure of concepts and instead more concerned with the operationalization and use of indicators, because measurement must be uniform across cases.[23] Although quantitative researchers are concerned with measurement equivalence, or the comparability of measured attributes across populations, obtaining truly uniform data across populations is rare and extremely challenging.[24] Therefore, measurement error for quantitative research occurs at the level of indicators and not at the level of concepts (as it does for qualitative researchers). In fact, some quantitative researchers go as far as claiming that a concept is defined by the indicators used to measure it.[25]

Since indicators are typically data-driven, they can obscure and erase certain elements of the concepts that are being measured. Anthropologists Sally Engle Merry and Susan Wood demonstrate an example using children's rights indicators in Tanzania.[26] They outline a "paradox of measurement," in which they illustrate the tensions between qualitative and quantitative research. Merry and Wood take issue with the fact that what is being measured by indicators is "already recognized as measureable," while other elements of a concept that may be obscured are therefore immeasurable.[27] They give the example of the "right to play" indicator used by the UN Committee on the Rights of the Child and demonstrate how this indicator cannot be measured the same way in industrial contexts as it is in developing contexts like Tanzania since what constitutes "children playing" for us may not apply

[20] Goertz and Mahoney 2012; Mahoney and Goertz 2006.
[21] Goertz and Mahoney 2012: 130.
[22] Ibid.
[23] Mahoney and Goertz 2006: 244; Sartori 1970.
[24] Davidov et al. 2014: 55–61.
[25] Ibid.
[26] Merry and Wood 2015: 206.
[27] Merry and Wood 2015: 207.

the same way in other places. Merry and Wood question whether this indicator adequately captures the reality of families with children in Tanzania and whether there is a common understanding of play across cultural contexts. They conclude that in order to generate data comparable at the international level, researchers were forced to forge ahead with indicators that were not culturally appropriate.[28] In other words, top-down approaches to designing measurement tools only include indicators that are accessible or exposed to experts and researchers because they have already been discovered by the literature or other studies. Merry and Wood demonstrate, through their case study, that the use of indicators requires interpretation or "translation" and these translations pose challenges to measuring phenomena not previously counted. Therefore, issues are obscured, and hence immeasurable, since it is impossible to measure what you don't know is there. Their frustration with the data-driven approach is exactly what Goertz and Mahoney identify as the tension between quantitative and qualitative approaches in concepts and measurement.

The paradox of measurement is a problem particularly for those attempting to measure at a local level using indicators developed by outsiders, because these indicators may only represent certain issues within the community that are either already being measured or are typically measured to ascertain the effectiveness of programming (e.g. morbidity or infant mortality). This paradox is also illustrated by the difficulties presented to researchers in accurately reflecting gendered interests and problems. Gendered indicators – such as life expectancy, average wages and access to resources – often neglect issues of specific importance to women (or to men) because they do not take into account their specific circumstances or the relevance and meaning of these existing indicators to their wellbeing.[29] In addition, such top-down approaches often only include indicators that are easily measurable or already measured, discarding indicators without existing data or where data collection is too difficult.

The paradox of measurement is also fundamentally a clash between positivist and interpretivist approaches. Fred Schaffer explains how positivist social scientists find ways to reconstruct everyday words to meet their research needs, which require measurement, comparison and generalization.[30] He shows that positivists strip everyday language from its sometimes vague, multidimensional meanings in order to generate a specialized, technical language that allows for tangible results and analysis. For example, the term democracy may have a very fixed and engineered meaning for positivist social scientists that could mean something entirely different for people experiencing democracy in practice or in a foreign context. Andre Broome and Joel Quirk similarly demonstrate that this is done in global benchmarking efforts through what they call reification or the

---

[28] Merry and Wood 2015: 214–15.
[29] Austen, Jefferson and Thein 2003: 2.
[30] Schaffer 2016: 5.

translation of complex phenomena into observable and quantifiable conceptual categories that are presumed to be universally applicable irrespective of cultural or historical context. Reification effectively stabilizes the meaning of complex and highly contested categories, such as democracy, freedom and stability.[31]

In other words, in order to measure a concept, social scientists need to be able to pin down exactly what it is and which elements belong in the conceptual data container to be measured.[32] This involves making important decisions about what belongs and what does not, as well as generalizing significantly in order to make the indicators universally applicable.

Regardless of the empirical approach, concepts of interest need to be defined and a method for making systematic observations developed. However, in the case of interpretivist scholarship, the primary conceptual task is to elucidate shared meanings and interrogate the relationship between social science language and everyday meanings,[33] or the distinction made by Clifford Geertz between experience-distant and experience-near concepts.[34] Geertz distinguished between these two concepts in order to demonstrate how social science creates abstractions in order to study phenomena from a distance. Experience-near concepts encompass the ways in which those directly experiencing phenomena might describe them. For example, referring to democracy as "the majority of people who voted for something won." Interpretivist social scientists also must construct concepts, but use inductive methods to glean the applicability of a concept to a particular place or culture. Both interpretivist and positivist scholars say things about concepts they have made decisions about and create experience-distant concepts to analyze and communicate the experience-near. Both approaches have their strengths and weaknesses. Because of their interest in good numerical measures, positivists are able to make claims about how large populations view their constructed concepts, whereas interpretivists are able to construct concepts for smaller populations, which makes them more concerned about substantively valid concepts.[35] Scholars using a combination of methods are often the most effective because they are able to give context to generalizability.

It is the dynamic debate between qualitative and quantitative and positivist and interpretivist approaches that I address here and is one of the main areas where this book makes a contribution to the literature.[36] Just as Schaffer calls for "an approach that provides people opportunities to articulate the connections that they themselves

---

[31] Broome and Quirk 2015: 828.
[32] Sartori 1970: 1052.
[33] Schaffer 2016: 10.
[34] Schaffer 2016: 2; Similar to emic and etic understandings of sociocultural phenomena. See more discussion on emic and etic approaches to understanding culture, in Avruch 1998: 60–5.
[35] Goertz 2005: 2.
[36] I am in agreement with Schaffer's caution that these categories are not fixed and inflexible, but are illustrative of the overarching methodological approaches scholars tend to fall into. See footnote 1 in Schaffer 2014 for more on this.

make between meanings, the complexities that they themselves grapple with, and the conceptual puzzles that they themselves have not been able to solve,"[37] I argue that quantitative and positivist approaches can and must take concepts more seriously and find ways to integrate more comprehensive, democratic and participatory elements into measurement and monitoring.

Doing so is crucial precisely because of the political, "soft" power wielded by indicators, especially with the onset of the data revolution and the inordinate dissemination of information globally. The data revolution has made an enormous amount of information available to researchers. With the radical increase in the availability of information, indicators should now work alongside concepts to offer more holistic representations of social phenomena since they are no longer as restricted by data availability. Indicators are the metrics that increasingly matter in a world of new public management and technocracy. A change in the design of indicators is particularly urgent since increasing numbers of policy outcomes are influenced by indicators. Access to indicator-based data allows policy-makers to quickly scan results rather than read underlying reports, which can take weeks.[38] This increased dependency on indicators to guide policy outcomes makes the generation of concept-rich indicators more urgent than ever.

1.3. A FEW WORDS ON RESEARCH DESIGN AND METHODOLOGY

This study employs a matched case research design[39] and uses mixed methods in two very different contexts to investigate whether interventions after war indicates effects on community-generated indicators of peace.[40] The study uses an innovative methodology that allows researchers and others to measure impact according to the ways individuals themselves measure peace in their communities. Instead of drawing on indicators of success developed by "experts" and "scholars" – often in the Global North with data collected in the Global South – researchers ask communities themselves to establish their own indicators of peace, which are then measured longitudinally through surveys. The resulting everyday indicators articulate, translate and vernacularize the measurement of local data in ways that traditional measurement systems cannot. The conclusions of this book are based on survey data from 2,038 surveys in four communities in Uganda and Colombia.[41] The study uses the matched case research design in four communities supplemented by over one-hundred interviews with community members in the villages, local and national elites in

---

[37] Schaffer 2014: 328.
[38] Kelley and Simmons 2015: 57.
[39] Maclean 2010: 32.
[40] See Chapters 3 and 4 for much more detail on research design and methodology.
[41] Indicators of peace and reconciliation were collected in Colombia. The analysis in this book presented in Chapters 5 and 6 is based solely on the indicators of peace.

I.3. A Few Words on Research Design and Methodology 11

both countries, United Nations staff in New York, and international peacebuilders working in the monitoring and evaluation sector in Washington, DC.[42] In addition, results of the study are complemented by insights from a pilot of the Everyday Peace Indicator approach in three other sub-Saharan contexts (South Sudan, Zimbabwe and South Africa) and the author's own experiences working as an external evaluator for international peacebuilding organizations.[43]

Data from the communities demonstrates the utility of the indicators by measuring peace within communities that are demographically similar, with similar histories of violence and displacement, but that have significantly different levels of external intervention.[44] The contrast in communities with different degrees of interventions allows us to see the cumulative impact of interventions and to make some conclusions about cumulative local peacebuilding successes and failures according to community measures.[45] It also allows us to look at individual programming success and failure by isolating individual interventions after a baseline assessment is conducted. By conducting a baseline and then tracking events and interventions in a community over time, the longitudinal survey data indicates the effect of current events on community-generated indicators of peace.

Finally, many of the people interviewed for this book requested to be anonymous, out of professional or safety concerns. In most cases I have therefore cited only the dates and places of these interviews and a general description of their role with the understanding that any more specificity may allow identification of the informant. For those publicly available interviews or interviews that were not requested to be anonymous, I have included full citations with name and location. Almost all of my interviews were conducted in English or Spanish without a translator. A minority of interviews were conducted in Luo (the language used by the Acholi) and required a translator.[46]

In both Uganda and Colombia the villages selected have been seriously affected by war, causing massive displacement and death. El Salado and Don Gabriel in the Montes de Maria region of Colombia are both relatively similar villages. They are primarily *mestizo* and Christian, approximately the same distances from their municipalities, and are mostly dedicated to agricultural work such as farming and cattle ranching. These communities were also ravished by the paramilitary violence that beset the region in the early 2000s and consequently displaced, and both were victims of the leftist guerrilla groups prior to and during that time. However, El Salado was singled out by a Bogota-based foundation as an example

---

[42] See Appendix 2 for a list of interviews.
[43] See everydaypeaceindicators.org for more information on the approach and other sub-Saharan pilots.
[44] See Dunning 2012 for more information on natural experiments and quasi-natural experiments.
[45] The matched case research design used in this study cannot account for preexisting differences between the communities. As a result, my statistical findings cannot guarantee a causal relationship.
[46] See Appendix 2 for list of interviews conducted for this study.

of an emblematic case of the violence in the region and the foundation helped return internally displaced people (IDPs) to the village. Through various high-profile campaigns, the Fundación Semana was able to draw international attention to the community, which resulted in an enormous influx of funding, projects and external intervention after 2009.

Similarly, in Uganda, the sub-counties of Odek and Atiak, which are located in Acholiland in the northern region of Uganda, were devastated by war and displacement in the early 2000s. Here the communities were targeted by the Lord's Resistance Army (LRA) and then forced into displacement camps by the government. The situation was aggravated in 2003 when President Museveni referred members of the LRA to the International Criminal Court (ICC) in the first attempt by the ICC at bringing "global justice" to the victims of human rights abuses. As Susan Hirsch demonstrates, the ICC assumed that local victims wanted international justice when this may not have been in their best interests.[47] It certainly was not in the best interest of the peace process, which floundered in large part due to the indictments.

Both communities chosen in Uganda are demographically similar and were birthplaces of LRA leaders (Vincent Otti in the case of Atiak and Joseph Kony in the case of Odek), although Atiak's location along a dirt road which became a highway to South Sudan in 2016 raised the profile of the sub-county and exposed the community to more interventions and external aid than Odek. Odek, on the other hand, was neglected for many years in part due to its distance from Gulu, the capital of Acholiland, and in part because of the high-profile stigma of being the birthplace of Joseph Kony, the leader of the LRA and only remaining at-large group member indicted by the ICC. Kony organized his first raids in Odek and used Awere Hill in Odek as his ceremonial and strategic headquarters.[48]

I.4. THE ARGUMENT IN BRIEF

The quality and effectiveness of community interventions is something that not only concerns community-based organizations, but also those who fund interventions, such as international donors, multi-lateral and bilateral organizations, and governments. When projects are implemented in communities, funders expect implementing organizations to demonstrate that their money is being well spent and that the results are illustratable. Measurement and evaluation can be relatively easy for concrete development projects that are designed to produce a certain outcome with a particular impact – for example, agricultural programs that aim to introduce a new technique to increase the yearly crop, or economic programs with goals of increasing

---

[47] Hirsch 2010.
[48] See Chapter 4 for more detail of the community selection and background of the conflicts in Uganda and Colombia.

the number of businesses and the average income for a community. In such cases, deliverables can be relatively easily counted – crops can be weighed and counted, numbers of businesses can be calculated, and average income can be measured. However, when dealing with more intangible issues such as governance or peace, that deal primarily with relationships and processes between individuals, groups and institutions, counting and measuring becomes more difficult. Organizations implementing such projects often have significant difficulty in demonstrating their impacts and instead focus on accountability, outputs and implementation processes or less rigorous forms of evaluation designs.[49]

In most cases, impact or outcomes are less frequently measured, because measuring impact is often seen as costly and relatively ineffective (since establishing concrete findings can be difficult). When impact is measured, it is extremely difficult to make claims or prove causality because of multiple factors discussed in more detail in Chapter 1. Therefore, organizations often make decisions and evaluate programs based on theories of change. Theories of change are theories or models organizations use to develop programming or, simply put, "an explanation of how and why a set of activities will bring about the changes a project's designers seek to achieve."[50] For example, a theory of change based on the contact hypothesis would state something like: "*If* we bring groups A&B together, **then** they will be able to resolve their conflict *because* they will have contact with one another." These theories are intentionally broad and are based on assumptions about "how the world works."[51] Embedded assumptions are often not tried or tested and allow organizations and implementers to make "if-then-because" statements in order to organize their project logic. Theories of change are easy tools to allow project implementers to organize their assumptions and ideas about a particular program or topic. Yet, they often lack testing and rigor and rely on the knowledge and experience of the project implementers rather than communities themselves or the rigorous analysis of empirical data.[52]

In addition, since organizations lack transparency and often have little idea of what other projects are happening concurrently in the communities in which they operate, there is little communication about what works and what does not, or even what is being done by different organizations working in the same community. Therefore project implementers frequently create theories of change with impartial or incorrect information. In post-war contexts specifically, organizations working in communities are sometimes unaware of whether or not the specific issues confronting a community that has experienced violence and loss have been addressed. The difficulty of determining what ails a community is specific to war-affected contexts

---

[49] Firchow and Tilton 2018.
[50] Lederach et al. 2007: 25.
[51] Ibid.
[52] Blum 2016: Three things left to do: #3, A Stronger Theory of Change; Firchow and Tilton 2018.

because of the complexity and insecurity these situations generate and the fast pace at which things change for them. Unless an organization or an evaluator has had sustained contact within the community, a diagnosis is particularly difficult to ascertain within a short amount of time and with little intimate knowledge of the context.

Given the myriad factors preventing accurate assessment of impact, and the difficulty of measuring impact, it is perhaps not surprising that the data collected and analyzed from the everyday indicators in Uganda and Colombia generated disappointing conclusions. As discussed further in Chapter 6, external interventions did not have significant substantive impacts on those issues identified in Chapter 5 as priorities in locally generated indicators of peace, therefore demonstrating a weakness in the ways interventions are implemented at a local level after war. This finding supports Adam Moore's rejection of the capacity argument put forward by Michael Doyle and Nicholas Sambanis.[53] Doyle and Sambanis assert that an increase in international assistance at the national level has a positive effect on sustainable peace.[54] My findings suggest that there is much more complexity required than just an increase in aid and personnel to ensure sustainable peace at the local level, at least according to the communities themselves. In fact, my findings suggest that when there is an increase in aid and personnel for reconstruction and development, this must be accompanied by *small-p* peacebuilding mechanisms such as programs that attend to social cohesion and relationships in communities.

Disaggregating for dimensions of peace – development, social relations, security, and human rights – suggests a more checkered record of success. Communities with little intervention across the study perceive more security than those with a lot of intervention. In other dimensions of peace such as development, the communities that have received high levels of assistance report significantly higher levels of development. These results indicate that development interventions have an effect on community perceived changes. However, they also suggest that development comes at the cost of higher perceived insecurity among residents. This indicates that the extra attention provided to communities, as well as additional infrastructure (such as roads) leads to additional complexity that may not exist in communities with little intervention.

So, why would well-intentioned external interventions lead to counterintuitive or underwhelming results? The reasons are fleshed out in the analysis of the everyday indicators presented in Chapter 5, where I find that peace at a local level is multi-dimensional, context-dependent, and evolving. In other words, people look to multiple indicators to measure their everyday peace, including positive and negative measures of peace (or indicators that refer to violence reduction versus improved welfare). This multi-dimensionality in defining peace consequently requires local level interventions to also be multi-dimensional, which is frequently not the case. The community-generated indicators confirm other research that shows that people use

---

[53] Moore 2013.
[54] Doyle and Sambanis 2006: 4.

different measures than do international actors to determine peace.⁵⁵ Community-generated indicators are highly localized and dependent on context. Each unique set of circumstances confronting communities requires a different set of indicators to measure peace and the effectiveness of post-war interventions. Therefore, a template approach to peacebuilding effectiveness is problematic in that it does not take into account the specific issues confronting a community at any given time. The tendency of the international community to prioritize technical skills – for instance in agricultural development or governance reform – over cultural and political knowledge of an area when designing and staffing development programs, results in a mismatch in terms of priorities on the international and local levels.⁵⁶ Finally, community definitions of peace change over time depending on the distance from active conflict. Communities closer to violence prioritize security. As time passes, communities look more to measures of development and social cohesion to evaluate their degree of peacefulness. Communities with higher levels of intervention have higher levels of perceived insecurity perhaps because the influx of external actors and projects decreases the need for social cohesion and inter-community reliance.

I consider two primary reasons – constituents and distribution – to explain why communities saturated with interventions may have arrived at similar overall levels of (locally defined) peacefulness as those with little intervention. In contemporary peacebuilding practice, the constituents, or the kinds of interventions implemented in communities, are highly variable and fluid. Interventions are dependent in some cases on the needs identified by communities themselves, but rely heavily on funding priorities determined by donors.⁵⁷ Often, the overarching approaches or theories of change of an organization are prioritized over a concerted and planned peacebuilding strategy or much attendance to community needs or priorities. Activities focused on peace and reconciliation are typically given significantly less priority by funders than programming focused on economic and agricultural development and the physical rebuilding of a community. Interventions, therefore, often lack the multi-dimensional aspects necessary to address the holistic peacebuilding approach required and demonstrated by the multidimensionality of the everyday indicators. The lack of planning and attention paid to the variance of priorities and needs from community to community in a post-war context contribute to uneven consequences.

Even when there is attention paid to developing a holistic approach to post-war recovery efforts, little thought is given to the distribution of interventions to community groups and members. Clearly, in the immediate aftermath of war, humanitarian needs such as medical attention, food and shelter must be tended to. However, not enough thought is put into how these assistance programs are distributed to members of the community. Often, programs do not adequately assess what is needed by a

---

[55] Richmond 2005; Autesserre 2014.
[56] Autesserre 2014; Mac Ginty 2012; de Waal 1997.
[57] This argument is also made by other scholars such as Heideman 2013.

community, and instead implement programming based on the needs and priorities of funders and implementers. In other words, community needs are given a backseat to funding trends and implementer specializations. As communities rebuild after war, different needs develop at different times, and the order and distribution of reforms can impact peacebuilding successfulness. For example, Adam Moore found that specific sequencing of peacebuilding reforms, in particular political and economic liberalization, led to a more sustainable peace in Bosnian communities.[58] Additionally, some dimensions of interventions are neglected – attention to psychosocial factors is often left unpaid, to be dealt with at a later date (which sometimes never happens). Organizations functioning in the same communities, frequently funded by the same donors, have little coordination and discussion regarding the sequencing or distribution of their interventions and the priorities given to certain kinds of projects and certain kinds of beneficiaries. Decisions surrounding who receives which benefits can be detrimental in the peacebuilding process and sometimes cause more harm than good.

Many of the issues confronted in the implementation of projects and interventions at the community level are due to the lack of communication and transparency between donors, organizations and communities. The organizations themselves are usually the least at fault for this lack of transparency. Funding schemes and donor demands create an environment where organizations are discouraged from communicating and cooperating for fear of losing funding to a competing organization or being exposed to criticism if a project has failed or not performed. Donors also often determine what it is an organization is going to do – organizations and communities may have to fight to apply their own approaches, and their knowledge is not always respected. Many donors have a strategy for the constituents of interventions, but donors often do not coordinate among themselves, or share the information with communities and implementing organizations. While donors are often better placed and funded to conduct broader evaluations and foster increased coordination, intervention strategies should be shared with and informed by the community of donors and implementing organizations as well as communities. Greater transparency and coordination among donors, organizations and communities is needed to leverage the essential contributions of each and to achieve multidimensional and contextually appropriate interventions that meet community needs.

I.5. CURRENT THEORETICAL EXPLANATIONS OF INTERNATIONAL PEACEBUILDING EFFECTIVENESS

The findings presented in this book are part of a larger conversation about the successes and failures of peacebuilding interventions. Studies that evaluate peacebuilding efforts primarily focus on macro-level dynamics pertaining to post-conflict

---

[58] Moore 2013: 102–3.

I.5. Current Theoretical Explanations of International Peacebuilding Effectiveness 17

reconstruction, security sector reform, rule of law and economic factors to do with peace processes. In addition, empirical and scholarly studies almost exclusively focus on UN peacebuilding and peacekeeping operations and largely ignore local efforts and actors such as civil society organizations, who frequently implement projects contracted out by international organizations such as the United Nations, the World Bank, the United States Agency for International Development (USAID) and the United Kingdom's Department for International Development (DFID).[59] Importantly, many existing studies assume that elite-level peace processes will impact local level peace, but the opposite has been found to be true by scholars studying local level dynamics.[60] And, in most cases, conflict analysis at the national level does not draw upon local voices. Therefore, this study fills a much-needed gap on peacebuilding successes and failures at the community level.

Many recent, cogent studies on peacebuilding effectiveness use the state and/or elite actors as their unit of analysis. Page Fortna demonstrates that peacekeeping, which she considers a part of peacebuilding efforts, is effective at sustaining the support of decision-makers within the government and rebel organizations for peace agreements (*peacekept*).[61] Doyle and Sambanis also demonstrate that peacekeeping has a positive effect by supporting new actors committed to the peace, building governing institutions, and monitoring and policing the implementation of peace settlements.[62] In *Why Peace Fails*, Chuck Call demonstrates that the inclusion of former opponents in postwar governance is the most important factor for achieving sustainable peace.[63] Most recently, Peter Wallensteen argues that a *Quality Peace* must meet three conditions: a losing party must retain its dignity; security and the rule of law must be ensured for all; and the time horizon for a peace settlement must be long enough to ensure a sense of normalcy.[64] All of these studies contribute meaningful findings about the effectiveness of peacebuilding efforts on national-level dynamics.

However, these findings do not necessarily apply at the local or community level, nor does state-level peacebuilding effectiveness necessarily have a trickle down effect. Critical peace scholars argue that peacebuilding is often ineffective at the local level because it is based on liberal and Western notions of peace that are state-centric.[65] Others argue that a bias among external interveners for the macro-level can be detrimental to peacebuilding effectiveness.[66] Séverine Autesserre demonstrates that

---

[59] See, among many others, Autesserre 2014, 2010; Barnett 2002; Call 2012; Doyle and Sambanis 2006; Fortna 2008; Paris 2004; Richmond 2014; Wallensteen 2015.
[60] Autesserre 2014; Richmond 2005.
[61] Fortna 2008.
[62] Doyle and Sambanis 2006.
[63] Call 2012.
[64] Wallensteen 2015.
[65] Richmond 2012; Mac Ginty 2011b.
[66] Autesserre 2014.

the structure and approach of the UN in the Democratic Republic of Congo was such that only macro-level interventions were seen as legitimate and that local level peacebuilding was deemed unimportant in building sustainable peace.[67]

Autesserre and other scholars contend that subnational dynamics are fundamental to peacebuilding success and that only a combination of top-down and bottom-up efforts can build and, particularly, sustain peace. This hybrid approach has been put forth by scholars such as Oliver Richmond and Roger Mac Ginty, who operationalize the concept of hybridity to demonstrate the negotiation between bottom-up and top-down actors.[68] They argue that the dance between international, national and local actors contributes to what ultimately becomes a negotiated peace. Others, such as Adam Branch, dismiss intervention entirely and advocate for "disintervention."[69] Branch conducts an extensive ethnography of Western intervention in northern Uganda during and immediately after the war. He concludes that this form of intervention does not work and that resources and energy would be best spent on making policy changes at home. Therefore, he advocates an approach where privilege and power on the part of Western interveners is abdicated by ensuring they also have to live with the consequences of their actions by acting at home, not just Africans living with the consequences of Western intervention (or others in the global south). Ultimately, Branch proposes that, if left alone, communities are more inclined to advocate and rise up for themselves, something they are unable to do now because they are given too much external support. That external support sometimes discourages communities from revolting out of fear that they will no longer receive outside support. He argues that in the long term this is not healthy for societies emerging out of conflict. This is similar to my finding that communities with little support are more resilient in finding ways to build social ties by themselves.

What constitutes success and failure of peacebuilding efforts also varies widely depending on how researchers define success and failure. For example, is the reduction of violence, or "negative peace," sufficient to merit a determination of peacebuilding success? Or should the root causes and factors of structural violence or "improved welfare" also be addressed to affirmatively determine success? Scholars have used multiple measures to determine effectiveness. These can be separated into structural measures such as peace processes and agreements,[70] peacekeeping mandates,[71] economic conditions,[72] the length of time without recurrence of war,[73]

---

[67] Autesserre 2010.
[68] Richmond 2009; Mac Ginty 2011b.
[69] Branch 2011a: 247.
[70] Walter 2002.
[71] Doyle and Sambanis 2006; Howard 2008.
[72] Collier 2008; Paris 2004.
[73] Fortna 2008.

I.5. Current Theoretical Explanations of International Peacebuilding Effectiveness 19

effective state building,[74] justice[75] and democratic governance.[76] There are also human agency-focused measures such as incentives to join rebel groups,[77] popular opinion,[78] reconciliation[79] and dignity.[80] This study does not choose a particular indicator or measure of success and instead uses community-defined indicators to define peacebuilding success for each individual community. These community-generated indicators demonstrate that peace at the local level is a multidimensional concept that varies from community to community and over time, and that communities choose both positive and negative peace indicators when measuring everyday peace.

Fewer studies choose the local beneficiaries of external interventions as their unit of analysis when discussing peacebuilding effectiveness and the dominant practitioner lens looks at programs and projects. However, one macro study conducted by Mary Anderson, Dayna Brown and Isabella Jean (2012) from CDA Collaborative Learning Project's listening program explores the ways in which beneficiaries of international aid efforts perceive their impact.[81] Through interviews with nearly 6,000 people in 20 countries, many of which are conflict-affected, Anderson, Brown, and Jean argue that interventions have not met local expectations and that the system of international aid is deeply flawed. They demonstrate the importance of listening to beneficiaries and the people most directly affected by external interventions. While their study harnesses an enormous amount of information with succinct analysis, it does not offer insights (whether critical or not) into alternative ways of measuring peacebuilding interventions. It is also not specific to post-conflict contexts, nor does it provide new approaches to communicating beneficiary acumen to the international community.

Another community-level study by Adam Moore examines two Bosnian communities, one mired with problems and emblematic of the failure of international efforts to overcome deep divisions, and the other a model case of successful Bosnian peacebuilding. Through a grounded analysis of localized peacebuilding dynamics, Moore finds that the design of political institutions, the sequencing of political and economic reforms, local and regional legacies from the war and the practice and organization of international peacebuilding efforts explain the contrasts in outcomes in the two towns.[82] Moore's approach is similar to my own in that he compares and contrasts two communities with different peacebuilding outcomes. However, his study is entirely qualitative and not cross-culturally comparative. In

---

[74] Richmond 2014; Paris 2004.
[75] Sriam et al. 2012.
[76] Doyle and Sambanis 2006; Call 2008a; Zürcher et al. 2013.
[77] Walter 2004; Daly 2012.
[78] Autesserre 2014.
[79] Lederach 2005.
[80] Wallensteen 2015.
[81] Anderson et al. 2012.
[82] Moore 2013: 4.

addition, his case study selection is of two communities that have had "intensive and lengthy international peacebuilding intervention in the postwar period."[83] He seeks to answer the question of why these interventions have been successful in one community and not in the other. This is a valuable approach, but different from my study, which examines communities with different levels of peacebuilding intervention.

Last, just as researchers have found that local and subnational conflicts often motivate larger scale violence,[84] community-level peace has an impact on macro-level peace. When communities are stable and strong, there is less likelihood that they will be adversely affected by war and violence.[85] For example, Ami Carpenter found that key factors such as the organization of non-sectarian self-defense groups, place attachment, collective efficacy, active intervention to de-escalate tensions, and also the presence of local religious leaders who forbid sectarian attacks, prevented sectarian attitudes and behaviors from taking hold in a number of multi-ethnic neighborhoods in Baghdad. Therefore, it is important to be able to measure peacefulness at a local and community level in order to establish their resilience to future conflict.

Although several of the macro studies use quantitative approaches to measure effectiveness, local-level studies are typically qualitative and ethnographic. There may be good reasons for this since local studies recognize the importance of participation and inclusion in telling the stories of individual communities. The present study accomplishes both qualitative and quantitative analysis through a mixed method approach that is also participatory and inclusive. This approach is not only innovative, but also important for measuring peacebuilding effectiveness because it does not rely on external definitions of peace and success – widely recognized obstacles to measuring peacebuilding effectiveness.[86] In addition, a method of gleaning everyday acumen from local communities avoids the risks of relying on the views and perspectives of a narrow cross section of society (e.g. community or capital-based elites).

1.6. WHY DO WE NEED LOCAL STANDARDS?

Since most research focuses on macro-level peace variables, there is a gap in understanding what defines and contributes to community-level (or local-level) peace as well as in finding viable approaches to facilitate the integration of micro- and macro-approaches. International organizations have recognized this need and called for more effective ways of making their work more people-centered.[87] When evaluating

---

[83] Ibid.
[84] Kalyvas 2006; Autesserre 2010; Justino et al. 2013.
[85] Carpenter 2014; Van Metre 2016.
[86] Autesserre 2014.
[87] For example, see the Report of the High-level Panel on Peace Operations (HIPPO), United Nations Doc. a/70/95-s/2015/446, June 17, 2015, page 10, which lists as one of its four "essential shifts" for the

community-based interventions, there are many reasons to use local standards. In what follows, I will discuss four of what I believe are the most important.

First, and perhaps most obviously, it is important to understand the consequences of international actions for communities on the receiving end of often well-intentioned, but sometimes harmful, interventions. As Arturo Escobar puts it: "[t]he remaking of development must start by examining local constructions, to the extent that they are the life and history of the people, that is, the conditions for and of change."[88] Just as professors ask students to fill out evaluations at the end of the semester or restaurants ask patrons to fill out comment cards, it is important to understand how the everyday recipients of development projects receive external interventions that purport to serve them. There is a normative argument that attributing impact without getting feedback from an affected population robs them of agency, voice, and self-determination. It dehumanizes communities by treating them as objects rather than as subjects. As peacebuilding aims to foster agency and voice, measuring impact in a way that negates these qualities is counterproductive, as well as morally problematic.

Second, local standards contribute to the richness and accuracy of defining and measuring peace and peacebuilding effectiveness. Context matters. Taking the restaurant example again for a moment, if a researcher were to look at global tipping behaviors as an indicator of satisfaction with service and not consider context and cultural habits of a particular place, then they would come to some very erroneous conclusions quite quickly. Considering the obligatory nature of gratuities in the United States in comparison to Europe and other cultures, an analysis without contextual knowledge would be useless and invalid since the conclusions would most likely lead the researcher to argue that the US has a far superior service to other cultures. Similarly, external researchers and interveners need more contextual knowledge to interpret local experiences and dynamics. Community-level measures of peace that are cognizant of local level dynamics and meanings are needed to guide efforts to achieve sustainable peace.

Bottom-up indicators can also reveal sub-state variations in data. One aspect of national-level data is that it flattens out sub-state experiences to produce a generalized account of a phenomenon. Community-level, bottom-up data shows how a national account of peace or conflict can be unrepresentative of localized experiences. Bottom-up indicators are able to add more texture and finer-grained detail that is not available at the national level. By their nature, national-level indicators rely on abstraction and generalization. Their advantage is in their ability to aggregate an impossibly diverse story into comprehensible data. Bottom-up indicators, depending on their nature and the categorizations they employ, may be able to

future design and delivery of United Nations peace operations the need to become more field-focused and people-centered.
[88] Escobar 2011: 98.

supplement the generalizations of top-down indicators with the particularity of localism, thereby ensuring content validation, which "assesses the degree to which an indicator represents the universe of content entailed in the systematized concept being measured."[89] Comparing local and national measures could have a significant impact on the approach and indicators included in existing measures of peace, potentially transforming the way indicators are used for measurement.[90]

Third, indicators wield a lot of power. It is in the interest of those concerned with community needs to see that community measures are included in the creation of national and global indicators that are used to pressure states. Indicators not only set the agenda of what is measured, but are also significant tools of soft power, or "the ability to get desired outcomes because others want what you want."[91] Indicators, measurement and monitoring all belong in the international soft power toolbox, and pressure states to bend to certain standards and institutions in order to avoid being perceived unfavorably by others, as well as to set agendas and ensure that everyone is working toward similar goals.[92] Some states are sensitive to their rating in indices and are often competitive when compared to their neighbors. Integrating community perspectives into top-down indicators will help foster greater accountability for community needs at the national and international levels.

The fourth reason is that community-level approaches need to be negotiated and harmonized with macro-approaches in order to more effectively measure peace. Bottom-up indicators may be able to reinforce or contradict the validity of international policy and academic priorities. If communities in conflict-affected areas identify issues of concern that are not on the international or national policy radar, then that suggests that international and local priorities are mismatched. This is additionally exacerbated if communities are excluded from the problem definition and agenda-setting inherent in these knowledge creation systems. Therefore, there is a need for complementarity of localized indicators with more macro- and generalized indices such as the Human Development Index or the Global Peace Index. Amartya Sen explains the balance between "internal" versus "external" views of health and discusses the tensions in evaluations based on the two. He advocates for a combined approach in evaluation that integrates both "internal," or a patient's perceptions, and "external," or observations by doctors and pathologists. Without this integration, a complete picture of the problem is impossible. As he puts it, "a good practitioner would be interested in both."[93] If we apply Sen's idea to the peacebuilding sector, there are currently many "external" evaluation structures, but not many "internal" ones. A more balanced version is necessary to give a complete picture of the plight

---

[89] Adcock and Collier 2001: 537.
[90] Duursma et al. 2018
[91] Keohane and Nye 1998: 86.
[92] Kelley and Simmons 2015.
[93] Sen 2002: 860–1.

of a particular community. Therefore, the everyday indicators can be seen as an advocacy tool for those interested in representing the interests of communities in more effective ways.

I.7. ORGANIZATION OF THE BOOK

Throughout this book, I will employ terms such as post-war or post-conflict, peace-building, community, indigenous, local, or Western and scientific without the use of quotation marks. These terms remain, however, deeply problematic for many reasons, including their generality. I use them without a simultaneous textual indication of their questionable nature only to prevent awkwardness and promote fluency in reading. At this point it seems prudent to discuss in more detail what is meant by the terms local and community, which are used ubiquitously in this book.

Studies indicate that people use their physical locations as well as shared experiences and joint activities as the primary ways of identifying their communities.[94] A community here is defined by its locus or as a neighborhood in an urban setting, or a village, or consortium of villages, such as a sub-county, in a rural setting. Jens Friis Lund makes the point that local people are often referred to as communities in the literature on international development.[95] For the purposes of this study, local will be used in the same manner to refer to the same villages and sub-counties encompassed in my definition of community. These communities are clearly diverse and composed of people directly affected by violence, as well as those that are directly affected by a myriad of factors, including loss or harm of a loved one, witnessing traumatic events, experiencing the aftermath and forced displacement for various reasons.

When we think about the consequences and aftermath of mass violence and massacres and how best to deal with these at a community level, it is important to recognize how violent events affect the collective differently than the individual. When any community is affected by violence, particularly widespread violence, it can affect relationships among members of that group, especially in terms of social cohesion, social ties, and trust. Suddenly, a whole series of new relationships emerge that relate, directly and indirectly, to the trauma experienced by a collective and the individual roles played within that collective. Relationships among neighbors, friends and church groups are affected, but also those between individuals and the state. Political trust is a direct casualty of violent conflict, especially in contexts where those relationships are already quite fragile.[96] New labels emerge as well, in particular those of victim and perpetrator, and community members begin to align themselves vis-à-vis their relationship to either side. Therefore, the effects of violent events should not be seen in isolation, and focusing solely on the victim or perpetrator

---

[94] MacQueen et al. 2001.
[95] Lund 2013: 104.
[96] De Juan & Pierskalla 2014.

when evaluating impact does not provide a complete picture of the effects of conflict in a community.

The way in which communities experience collective harm varies, but typically they share characteristics with more traditional collective harm cases such as problems of climate change, overpopulation, and poverty, in that many actions taken together cause a certain outcome, but no action alone causes that outcome.[97] Discussions of what constitutes collective harm are not adequately addressed in the literature, even though the concept is used regularly when defining peacebuilding measures and outcomes.[98] Whether or not there is a collective harm beyond that suffered by individuals and whether that requires a collective response requires a more profound and informed understanding of collective victimhood. What is inherently difficult to determine in the concepts of collective harm and collective victimhood is the identification of the collective. When an act of collective harm such as displacement or mass violence occurs in a community such as a village, who can claim the status of collective victimhood? Is it only those who are direct victims of the violence, or is the entire village an indirect victim of the collective harm? When we think about interventions after war in these communities, who do we talk to in order to determine whether or not they have been effective and if the concerns of the victims have been addressed? This book grapples with such questions and suggests some strategies to for addressing them.

The ensuing chapters are split into two sections: the first chapters are conceptual, dealing with the debates around and challenges to measuring and understanding the effectiveness of external interventions. The second section seeks to establish causality about local level peacebuilding effectiveness and is concerned with the outcomes and results of this study.

Chapter 1 takes on the critiques of measurement and discusses the challenges of current attempts to measure peace. It weighs the benefits and drawbacks of measurement systems and discusses the ethics of evaluation. Importantly, it discusses some of the ethical and political challenges inherent in the distillation of peace into short, measurable units of indicators and measurement tools used to quickly assess the impact of interventions. It offers reflections upon whether the everyday indicators are able to more accurately uncover some of the hidden and unmeasurable issues that traditional indicator systems often obscure. The chapter also looks at the contemporary challenges outlined by scholars and practitioners surrounding the effective evaluation of local level programming, including issues of potential elite capture, transparency, institutional memory, lack of accountability and the challenges of measuring peace. It highlights the difficulties in effectively monitoring and evaluating at a project and process level, as well as the difficulties of determining

---

[97] Kagan 2011.
[98] UN Human Rights Council 2013, Rosenfeld 2010.

overall impact. It is informed by interviews at the country and international level with peacebuilding professionals.

Chapter 2 discusses the dynamic relationship between international interveners and the communities they hope to serve. It presents the tensions between elite actors and the disenfranchised groups and how these groups interact in a push and pull, hybrid relationship to negotiate a local and contextualized peace. This different epistemological perspective allows us to more effectively address some of the flaws raised in the previous chapter of current efforts at measuring peace. The chapter further discusses the conceptual challenges in the measurement of difficult concepts such as peace, and demonstrates why it is necessary to include communities in the design of measurement and evaluation tools, as well as in the planning of peacebuilding interventions. In sum, the chapter provides the theoretical grounding for the everyday indicators approach and gives background on participatory numbers and the everyday indicators framework as a technology of Indigenous Technical Knowledge (ITK).

Chapter 3 presents a new approach to measuring peace, outlines the everyday indicators methodology, and demonstrates its utility for measuring peace. Creating direct and less subjective ties to everyday beneficiaries of external interventions is important to improve measurement systems that determine the effectiveness of external interventions. Most importantly, it allows us to have a broader picture of the impact of external interventions on communities affected by violent conflict according to their own measures. In addition, concerns from skeptics of local level indicators about the commensurability of these kinds of indicator systems are addressed.

Chapter 4 gives background and justification for the case study selection used in Uganda and Colombia. The conclusions of this study are based on 2,038 surveys in four communities in Uganda and Colombia. The study uses a rigorous matched case research design in these four communities supplemented by over one-hundred interviews with community members, local elites and national elites in both countries and with international peacebuilders working in the monitoring and evaluation sector in Washington, DC. Data from the comparative study demonstrates the utility of the indicators by measuring peace in communities that are demographically similar, with similar histories of violence, but that have different levels of external intervention. Case studies from two significantly different contexts allow for comparison and provide information about how experiences vary across contexts.

Chapter 5 presents the analysis of the everyday indicators. The everyday indicators differ from existing measurement systems in that they not only measure impact, but also allow us to analyze the indicators themselves to give more detailed context and meaning to what communities perceive and experience when conceptualizing peace. Here the findings are presented that everyday peace is a multidimensional concept that reflects both negative and positive peace. These findings indicates *how* interveners are often disconnected from community needs. In addition, the chapter demonstrates that everyday indicators of peace are highly variable and dependent on context, which has significant implications for peacebuilding design and implementation. The categorization of indicators shows in what ways communities are similar or different in the ways they define peace and whether or not they look more toward security, development, human rights, etc. to determine whether or not they are more or less peaceful. The analysis finds that communities currently or recently experiencing violence are more likely to choose security-related indicators to measure peace than those further away from violent events, which are more likely to use social cohesion or development-related indicators. The priorities of local communities are again compared to the kinds of interventions being externally implemented in the communities to determine peacebuilding successes and failures.

Chapter 6 presents statistical analysis of survey data from the matched case research design and offers insights into why local level interventions fail or succeed in achieving peace in communities. It suggests that external interventions after conflict have not had a substantial impact on community-defined peace in the communities studied. From the comparative case studies in Colombia and Uganda, results indicate that more intervention in communities does not necessarily result in better outcomes. As discussed earlier, this result means that more focus is needed on the constituents and distribution of interventions. Most clearly, and as demonstrated by the indicators, there is a need for more attention to be paid to the psychological and social aspects of community healing and cohesion after war. This is especially acute in communities that are receiving significant external assistance in other areas such as development, humanitarian assistance and reconstruction, which might exacerbate tensions between members of the community.

The book concludes by summarizing the findings of this study on local level peacebuilding effectiveness and discussing the way forward for local level peacebuilding. It also offers recommendations about more effective ways of connecting local, state and international peacebuilding efforts in order to better meet the needs of brave and resilient communities emerging from violent conflict and seeking a better future.

PART I

Understanding Everyday Peace

1

Measuring Peace

INTRODUCTION

The big data revolution is upon us. Every purchase we make, every doctor's visit we schedule, every Google search we input, every movement we make with our mobile phone, is stored as a piece of data. As more data is created, the potential it presents for policymaking has sparked enormous efforts to index and catalog it. There is now, at least in highly developed countries, an overwhelming amount of data available about daily human life. For many policymakers and scholars, the growing amount of data presents unprecedented opportunities to analyze trends and test the effects of policy in human activity across fields. The new availability of large quantities of data about everyday habits and life contributes to a growing embrace of quantitative standards to measure, compare and evaluate a range of phenomena, from daily human health, to global weather patterns, to peace. Interest is high because policymaking based on quantitative data employing multiple cases is more acceptable to many policymakers and scholars than using individual case studies. Growing interest in quantitative evaluation is apparent across sectors, including public health, education and global governance.

The growing impetus for data-informed policymaking is increasingly felt in the fields of international peacebuilding and related fields of development, human rights and humanitarian intervention.[1] With increased pressures from donors and constituencies, an "evidence-based" approach is now necessary to prove that international interventions in countries affected by war are effective at achieving planned outputs and outcomes, as well as making an impact. Policymakers have decided that quantitative evaluation matters for accountability, and that it matters for assessing cost and impact effectiveness of interventions after war.

Yet, there are many limitations to evaluation that can result from quantitative measurement of intervention effectiveness, some of which have been documented

---

[1] Natsios 2011.

in detail by scholars.[2] Numbers, as it turns out, are not neutral, accurate reflections of fact. Nuance and the ability to accurately interpret results are often lost in the rush to measure.[3] Challenges of commensuration and translation arise when identical measurement systems are applied to uniquely different social and political circumstances facing communities around the world.[4] For example, a decrease in violence in one conflict-affected region may reflect the success of interventions in that context, but may signal the exact opposite in another context if repressive armed groups have assumed power. Such challenges are particularly pronounced in contexts affected by conflict, where interventions have complex, normative and indeterminate goals for peace, justice and reconciliation. National-level statistics can average out sub-state variations; for example, masking evidence that violence occurs primarily in a particular region of a nation state. Additionally, government agencies, whose budgets rely on performance, have incentives to fabricate or massage official statistics, or may rely too heavily on estimates or outdated benchmarks.[5]

Technical and universal, one-size-fits-all, evaluation approaches, that often do not even work from a context specific conflict analysis, risk missing the underlying root causes of the failure of postwar interventions. They often inspire a superficial "problem-solving" approach that tweaks accepted approaches to interventions rather than questioning the assumptions and postcolonial legacies that undergird the practice and design of these interventions.[6] In addition, many project evaluations of peacebuilding efforts such as democracy building or economic development implicitly assume that the effectiveness of their interventions will lead to peace because their intervention fits into the commonly accepted liberal peace model. Such evaluations may measure the success of democratization interventions but fail to measure peace or changes in levels of peacefulness. Importantly, too much of evaluation practice is focused at the input_output level and too little is known about how systemic (behavioral, cultural, structural, attitudinal) change dynamics in conflict contexts actually work and how they can be influenced and affected by deliberate interventions. As a result, too little is known about what makes peacebuilding interventions succeed or fail.

Although many of the challenges to peacebuilding and the evaluation and monitoring of postwar interventions have been identified by scholars and practitioners in the evaluation field, not enough attention has been paid to the conceptual underpinnings of fundamental – and notoriously controversial – concepts such as "peace" and "reconciliation." Not enough thought has been given to including the input of beneficiary populations (as well as nonbeneficiary populations) in defining or evaluating peace through participatory approaches. Until beneficiaries at the local

---

[2] Merry 2016; Willis 2017; Andreas and Greenhill 2010; Davidov et al. 2014; O'Neil 2016.
[3] Merry 2016.
[4] Davidov et al. 2014: 56.
[5] For an example of this see Thiessen 2017.
[6] Pugh 2013.

level are included in the process of defining peace, I argue that the international community will find it difficult, if not impossible, to build peace. This is for three main reasons: first, including communities in defining their own peace helps clarify peacebuilding goals. Peace in most postconflict situations lacks adequate conceptual definition and is often highly politicized, making the goal of peace a moving political target. Including local communities grounds concepts of peace in local, everyday experiences. Second, locals have knowledge that outsiders do not have about community traditions, practices and dynamics that can help build peace, which leads to more effective interventions. Finally, beneficiary definitions and indicators of peace should be prioritized for the effectiveness of peacebuilding efforts since these should attend to local needs and demands rather than exclusively catering to national or elite level power dynamics.[7] Skeptics may point out that elite level power dynamics are equally, if not more, important for conflict resolution and peacebuilding. And in practice, stabilizing "fragile" partner states is the dominant priority in international development. However, many of the issues present at elite-level negotiations, such as national transportation systems, electric grids or national elections impact and affect local communities. Therefore, it is arguable on grounds of accountability that what is negotiated and monitored at the elite level must have proper representation from constituents. Local cooperation is also essential for the success of any peace plan; cooperation is much more likely if policies are derived from and responsive to local needs.[8]

In their report on local ownership in evaluation, Carlisle Levine and Laia Griñó state that, "International assistance remains something done to people rather than *with* them."[9] The same can be said of measurement and evaluation, which continue to measure impact and progress according to standards external to those being measured. This chapter begins by giving an overview of the current peacebuilding landscape, based on a liberal peace model that includes local civil society, international organizations and governments from local to international levels. It is important to understand how different actors view peacebuilding in order to understand better how they measure and evaluate peace. The chapter discusses the current challenges and problems of evaluation and measurement and gives historical background on the measurement of peace and the evaluation of peacebuilding interventions.

THE LIBERAL PEACE MODEL

Current-day interventions with normative goals of creating, strengthening or solidifying peace – which is generally called peacebuilding – are primarily based on a top-down, liberal peace peacebuilding model. The liberal peace has become

---

[7] Autesserre 2014; Richmond 2005.
[8] O'Reilly et al. 2015.
[9] Levine and Griñó 2015: 5.

synonymous with Western and postcolonial impositions of external models that support the international financial architecture, state sovereignty and the international *status quo,* which includes upholding internationally agreed upon rules and standards.[10] The assumptions underlying the liberal peace model are rooted in Immanuel Kant's democratic peace thesis that free markets and trade cannot coexist with war and therefore the establishment of societies based on the ideals of democracy and individual rights will secure peace. Proponents of the liberal peace prescribe three core areas of intervention in conflict-affected societies: the establishment of democratic processes, universal and individual human rights and market-led economic models. It is assumed by proponents of the liberal peace that if initiatives fit within the prescriptions of the core areas of the liberal peace, then they will eventually lead to building a sustainable peace. In implementing the liberal peacebuilding and statebuilding architecture, liberal peace actors impose and promote a top-down, external version of peace on societies affected by conflict. Interventions assume that reforms will be adopted without resistance and in similar ways to those in which they are present in the Global North. I argue that within the liberal peace model there are two main forms of approaching and defining peacebuilding. For the purposes of clarification, I will refer to these kinds of approaches as *big-P* and *small-p* peacebuilding.[11]

Big-P *Peacebuilding*

The United Nations (UN) (and other international organizations such as the Organisation for Economic Cooperation and Development [OECD], World Bank or the g7+) takes what Cheyanne Church calls the "big tent" approach to peacebuilding in a postwar context, this approach essentially includes the kitchen sink of efforts to address postwar contexts.[12] Akin to statebuilding, *big-P* Peacebuilding is primarily an endeavor of the international community to transform a conflict-affected country based on a liberal model of peacebuilding and typically includes political processes, safety and security, rule of law and human rights, social services, core government functions and economic revitalization and livelihoods.[13] Scholars making the distinction between statebuilding and peacebuilding have demonstrated that the two also have very different sets of intended outcomes – state coherence

---

[10] Mac Ginty 2008: 143.
[11] I recognize that the *big-P* and *small-p* peacebuilding categories are not static and there are individuals in both *big-P* and *small-p* contexts that advocate for different approaches. There are clearly many overlaps and the two are interrelated in many ways; however, I find that it is helpful to distinguish the two in order to understand what is meant by peacebuilding efforts when discussed by different actors and by different scholars studying interventions after war.
[12] Scharbatke-Church 2011: 463.
[13] What does "Sustaining Peace" mean? https://undg.org/wp-content/uploads/2017/01/Guidance-on-Sustaining-Peace.170117.final_.pdf (accessed March 28, 2018).

in the case of statebuilding and depth of peace in the case of peacebuilding.[14] The UN includes most programming and interventions in the immediate and extended aftermath of war in their definition of peacebuilding programming, or what they call their "sustaining peace" approach.[15] Frequently, the focus is on peacebuilding in the context of peacekeeping missions, but in the case of the UN, it also includes contexts with UN Country Teams or settings where there are small political missions, often called Peacebuilding Missions (e.g. in Sierra Leone). Political science and international relations scholars typically study *big-P* Peacebuilding and statebuilding.

The *big-P* approach is generally focused on the structural and technical elements of peacebuilding and statebuilding, such as security, governance reform, rule of law and democracy promotion, and is rooted in the liberal peace model based on Western liberalist ideals. It is, therefore, also traditionally less concerned with social issues found in local or community-based peacebuilding.[16] Big-P Peacebuilding projects do not necessarily need to have clear normative goals of peace that are based on beneficiary perceptions of peace. It is assumed that because their interventions (e.g., institutional reform, elections, justice, development programs) fit into the liberal peace model, they will lead to sustained peace.

Big-P programming is often conflict-sensitive, but not peace-sensitive. The difference between the two is significant. Peacebuilding has as a general goal the transformation of conflict into sustainable, positive peace. In contrast, conflict sensitivity's primary goal is to allow conflict analysis to inform development and humanitarian work in order to do no harm or avoid exacerbating the current context, while not requiring them to have explicit and deliberate prevention and peacebuilding goals.[17] When organizations or researchers aim to be conflict-sensitive, they are less concerned about working toward the normative goal of peace and using standards to track the achievement of peace.

Small-p *Peacebuilding*

In contrast to *big-P* Peacebuilding, there are other more relationship-based definitions of what peacebuilding means within the relatively small peacebuilding NGO

---

[14] Barma et al. 2017.
[15] What does "Sustaining Peace" mean? https://undg.org/wp-content/uploads/2017/01/Guidance-on-Sustaining-Peace.170117.final_.pdf (accessed March 28, 2018). The UN has expanded their approach to peacebuilding by adopting resolutions S/RES/2282 and A/RES/70/262. In April of 2016, the Security Council and the General Assembly expanded peacebuilding from a post-conflict process to "activities aimed at preventing the outbreak, escalation, continuation and recurrence of conflict" which "should flow through all three pillars of the UN's engagement at all stages of conflict."
[16] Autesserre 2014.
[17] Rogers et al. 2010: 7.

and INGO community.[18] I will call these *small-p* peacebuilding interventions.[19] In contrast to *big-P* Peacebuilding, the *small-p* approach to peacebuilding is one that is focused on agency and the transformation or building of relationships with normative goals of peace. Akin to Lederach's identification of the "Process-Structure Gap," *small-p* peacebuilding recognizes the importance of relationship building as constitutive to more structural efforts such as peace agreements or infrastructure assistance.[20] As one peacebuilding NGO evaluation staff member explained to me that she understood peacebuilding "[a]s any opportunity to bring groups that are divided together to find common ground and to improve relationships."[21] *Small-p* peacebuilding is long-term, extending beyond just the immediate aftermath of war, to two or even three decades after the cessation of war. Groups such as Search for Common Ground (SFCG) stress their local and long-term frameworks that posit that peace is a process that requires "a continuous presence to develop relationships on all sides of the conflict, understand the deep concerns of all parties and gain the trust needed to enable a shift toward safe, constructive, and creative problem-solving."[22] Peacebuilding NGOs that take a *small-p* approach distinguish themselves from development and human rights organizations by focusing on issues of conflict prevention, transformation and resolution, and reconciliation at a local and community-level in villages or neighborhoods. Those in the *small-p* peacebuilding community claim that successful interventions depend on designing programs that are responsive to local needs, and enable local ownership and local solutions that are less technocratic, universal and template based. Although *small-p* peacebuilding can address a myriad of concerns from security to health, its approach is always less focused on state-society interactions than *big-P* Peacebuilding and more focused on inclusiveness and relationship building.[23]

Though *small-p* peacebuilding focuses on relationships rather than more formal structural reforms or stabilization, for the most part it still falls within the liberal peacebuilding paradigm, for two reasons. First, organizations implementing *small-p* peacebuilding programs are dependent on outside funding from donors working within a liberal peace framework that have related goals and priorities, which often

---

[18] Although some UN agencies, such as the UNDP and UN Women, also conduct *small-p* peacebuilding activities.

[19] Stephan Hopgood distinguishes between Human Rights and human rights in his 2013 book "The End times of Human Rights." My distinction between *small-p* and *big-P* Peacebuilding is not related to Hopgood's, although there are apparent overlaps. I was made aware of Hopgood's framework after presenting a paper on a chapter of this book at the International Studies Association meeting in Baltimore in 2017.

[20] Lederach 1999.

[21] Interview, Washington, DC, January 19, 2016.

[22] Why it works #1, www.sfcg.org/about-us/core-principles/ (accessed September 27, 2017).

[23] Examples of *small-p* peacebuilding in different sectors can be found in: Building Peace Together, page 18 www.qcea.org/wp-content/uploads/2018/03/Building-Peace-Together.pdf (accessed March 28, 2018).

have little to do with communities at the receiving end of that funding. Second, though locally informed peacebuilding is held as a standard, the organizations primarily responsible for implementation are usually INGOs that function in top-down ways while implementing projects in communities, as do some of their local partners. Although many NGOs and INGOs claim to be participatory and inclusive, their operating structures, project design procedures and evaluation systems are significantly top-down. Terms such as "mobilizations" (signaling an effort to recruit people to join a project to meet program goals), and "sensitizations" (signaling an effort to educate people about a topic), come up often in NGO terminology to signal top-down ways of implementing projects. Often, participation and inclusion mean relying on local partners for input or doing a focus group or an interview to gauge community needs or opinions about an already established project. Crucially, everyday citizens are rarely included in designing or implementing a program and are mainly relied upon as sources of information when it comes time to evaluate programs. Elite capture can be an issue – many organizations are staffed by local elites from a different social class or ethnic group than the project beneficiaries. Local NGO staff can be either disconnected from the needs of the majority population or have preestablished ideas about "what they need." Yet many INGOs establish programming based on the recommendations of local elites and rely on them to represent the local, rather than focusing on what Oliver Richmond terms the really existing "local-local" or the everyday people of a society.[24] INGOs often base their decisions on an artificially constructed civil society removed from on-the-ground realities, needs and priorities.

THE PROBLEM OF EVALUATION

Billions are spent annually on peacebuilding programs.[25] Yet determining whether such programs are systematically effective proves to be extraordinarily difficult. As in any endeavor, there must be a means of evaluating whether success has been achieved. Measuring and evaluating peace turns out to be a deeply fraught endeavor.

I argue in this section that a trend toward the quantification of peace has yielded methods of measuring and evaluating both *big-P* and *small-p* peacebuilding effectiveness that are deeply flawed. As a result, we often simply don't know whether peacebuilding has been successful. And worse, it is possible that flawed evaluation methods that depend on quantification provoke us to set and pursue the wrong goals and targets, thus leading us astray during planning and undermining peacebuilding efforts. However, qualitative approaches are insufficient for large-N analyses that allow for robust macro-level analyses. Therefore, new thinking is needed to accurately measure the effectiveness of peace-related work in conflict-affected contexts.

[24] Richmond 2009.
[25] Luengo-Cabrera and Butler 2017.

Two broad approaches to measurement and evaluation in conflict-affected contexts have developed over recent decades. One emphasizes bottom-up and more human-faced approaches to research and evaluation. Influenced by anthropology and sociology, practitioners and scholars often use case study methodologies that focus on contextual factors and include local views. Such an approach is used mostly in *small-p* peacebuilding or by scholars working from an interpretivist perspective. Although it is recognized as a valuable source of evaluation, it is often undermined by quantitative approaches that are able to provide short analyses that are easier to read and digest.

The other approach to evaluation emphasizes scientific rigor and is influenced by the natural sciences. This vein of evaluation follows broader trends in the social sciences and policy circles that have attached a premium to studies that seem to be replicable and methodologically robust. A powerful political economy has encouraged many scholars and practitioners to adopt more quantitative approaches to their research and presentation of findings. Changes to the way major funding agencies, such as the National Science Foundation, distribute funding to social scientists has pushed researchers toward the use of quantitative methods. The result has been extra incentives for universities to hire scholars working from a positivist perspective and a proliferation of the use of quantitative methods in social science. Social scientists increasingly see quantitative methods as the "right" way to do rigorous research. And because many development and peacebuilding practitioners are trained by these social scientists, this perspective is passed on to them.

A focus on quantitative evaluation has grown as peacebuilding, like many other types of international intervention, has undergone a technocratic turn in recent years.[26] Technical expertise and skills of external, often Western, experts are frequently preferred over local and context-specific knowledge. A bureaucratic imperative focusing on the accounting and standardization of interventions after war and humanitarian disasters has assumed a significant role in the norms, practices and worldviews of organizations that work in peacebuilding, development, human rights and disaster relief.[27] Many current peacebuilding practices and norms have been imported from the business world, and manifest themselves in the "businessification" and professionalization of peacebuilding organizations as they adopt the financial reporting systems and vernacular that are often associated with commercial enterprises. "Benchmarking," "audit trail" and other terms from New Public Management have become commonplace in the reports of NGOs and international organizations.[28] Advocates of technocracy stress that it is objective, "modern" and evidence-led.

---

[26] Goetschel 2009; Mac Ginty 2012b.
[27] de Waal 1997.
[28] New Public Management is a broad label used for a set of administrative doctrines that dominated the bureaucratic reform agenda in many OECD countries in the late 1970s and 1980s. For more, see Hood 1991.

Technocratic approaches attach a premium to forms of information that are regarded as scientific, objective, robust and replicable. Such a perspective favors econometric measurements and reinforces quantitative, purportedly more "scientific" ways of collecting and reporting information to donors and publics. A reliance on the use of New Public Management strategies results in a generation of indicators that are measurable and demonstrable, but not necessarily relevant or valid.

In addition, political pressures on donors to show results to those sceptical of peacebuilding have encouraged greater reliance on quantitative reporting from recipients.[29] Governments are under pressure from their electorates and taxpayers to show transparency and value-for-money in their foreign aid expenditures. As a result, donors increasingly demand measureable evidence of the impact of their programs. Cost accountability and output reporting mechanisms that depend on quantitative measurements can be quickly summed up, but are often missing the nuance necessary to understand and interpret results. Donor pressure was often cited by NGO personnel interviewed for this book as a barrier to experimentation and creativity in measurement and evaluation, since implementing organizations are often under pressure to deliver very specific evaluation metrics. Even donors reported feeling the restrictions that audit requirements place on innovative approaches to measurement, such as the EPI approach discussed here.[30]

Indicators of Peace

The indicator is the heart of the quantitative evaluation system. It is the central mechanism used to track progress and determine success. As evaluation has taken a quantitative turn, indicators of peace have become increasingly important as a tool to evaluate peacebuilding and development effectiveness. Indicators can measure for impact (outcome indicators that represent achievement of goals), accountability (output indicators marking completion of promised activities or results) or process. A standard is a range or fixed point on the indicator's scale that is an acceptable number for that particular indicator. Targets and goals typically exceed standards. Indicators determine what needs to be measured in order to monitor goals and targets, which aim to achieve intervention objectives.[31] Indicators help to define and restrict any given concept's meaning, once that concept has been sharpened and constructed.[32] Measurement at both the universal (global) and relative or custom (local) levels generally involves gathering information to establish accountability

---

[29] de Coning and Romita 2009: 6–8.
[30] Natsios 2011; Operationalizing Bottom-up Indicators Workshop, United States Institute of Peace, May 27, 2016.
[31] Merry 2016: 12.
[32] Sartori 1970: 1046.

based on previously established indicators and standards that together should produce progress toward a certain outcome such as "peace" or "gender equality."[33]

Indicators can also serve different functions depending on the goals of the measurement system and the objectives for establishing them. For instance, advocates working in civil society may use indicators to make problems visible, whereas international organizations and governments may use them to monitor and control institutional behavior.[34] Therefore, indicators can have political as well as utilitarian goals.

Current measurement by the international community to determine impact and progress of external interventions happens at global and local (custom) levels. Goals of global and local measurement systems are intrinsically different, although often interlinked. The standards or indicators used to measure progress at each level can differ significantly, as does the purpose of the measurement. Global standards aim to compare progress of countries or regions in a given conceptual category, such as economic development, whereas custom measurement and evaluation is typically project-focused and tracks program activities and achievement of local program goals, for instance for programs to train farmers in new agricultural techniques. In many cases, attempts to measure peace at the country or macro-level may completely obscure regional or local realities that disappear in overall averages and scores represented in indices and other efforts at generating national averages. In the next sections, I take an in-depth look at current practices in global and project level (custom) evaluation systems, and identify key weaknesses.

Measuring Global Peace

Within the last half-century, momentum has grown to set global standards of peacefulness. The majority of early efforts to measure peace measured violence, armed conflict and war – all measures of negative peace – since it is easier to count the presence or absence of war and violent death than it is to establish measures of positive peace. We can see that the concept of peace has been historically difficult to pin down and that peace research is primarily "concerned with the question of violence."[35] Although Jan Gotlib Block was a pioneer of the statistical analysis of war as early as the 1890s, the origins of the scientific analysis of conflict are usually attributed to the groundbreaking statistical work in the 1930s and 40s by social scientists such as Lewis Fry Richardson, Pitirim Sorokin and Quincy Wright, as well as the more conceptual work done by Kenneth Boulding and Adam Curle in the 1950s and 60s. Subsequently, related databases emerged, such as the efforts by the Correlates of War project in the mid-1960s and the Uppsala Conflict Data Program in 1978.

---

[33] Development and peacebuilding indicators are usually established at the global or universal levels so that they can be compared. However, certain "custom" indicators can be developed at the national or local level, although this is usually discouraged. Interview, Former Office of US Foreign Assistance Resources Staff member, Washington, DC, November 5, 2016.

[34] Merry 2016: 13.

[35] Wallensteen 2011: 15.

The first attempt to measure peace in international relations was made by sociologist Dean Babst in 1964.[36] Babst was the first of many subsequent scholars in the social sciences to statistically study what is now called the democratic peace theory.[37] The study of the democratic peace theory was developed further in the 1970s, 80s and 90s and continues to be of interest to political scientists today. However, as with many earlier measures that purportedly measured peace, the statistical study of the democratic peace theory is arguably more a study of war (or the absence of war) and negative peace than it is of positive peace. Its dependent variable is war (nonrecurrence of war or years without war/durability) and researchers do not look past the cessation of violence to determine peace.

Another early effort to measure peace was spearheaded by Matthew Melko in his work on peaceful societies in the 1970s.[38] Melko defines peaceful societies as the absence of large-scale physical violence within the borders of the society for at least a century. This definition yielded fifty-two cases since 2560 BC. He went on to compare them in terms of their government, diplomacy, political attitudes and style in order to try to find common attributes or indicators of peacefulness. Similarly, in 1978 David Fabbro published a study on the social preconditions of peace based on societies that shared five criteria of peacefulness.[39] Although his study was qualitative and involved only seven case studies, along with Melko's work it provided the basis of the systematic study and categorization of peaceful societies and cultures of peace. However, the systematic study of the social preconditions of peace has not moved much beyond these early efforts,[40] although there have been some studies dedicated to determining what regime types offer the most stability after war.[41]

More recent efforts to catalog, index and measure peace-related events began in the 1990s with a focus on peace agreements. INCORE's database on peace agreements and Uppsala's Conflict Termination Dataset were among the first.[42] These initiatives began the quantitative analysis of peace agreements, as well as recordkeeping and accountability mechanisms for the implementation of peace accords. More recently, the University of Notre Dame's Kroc Institute has developed the Peace Accords Matrix (PAM) and the Political Settlements Research Programme at the University of Edinburgh the Peace Agreements Database, PA-X.[43] Reconciliation barometers began in 2003 with the South African Barometer Survey and are being used in South Africa, Cyprus, Nepal, Colombia, Ukraine, Liberia, Australia, Rwanda, the

---

[36] Babst 1964.
[37] The democratic peace theory posits that democracies do not go to war with one another.
[38] Melko 1971; 1973.
[39] Fabbro 1978.
[40] Bonta 1996 is one of the few other studies of categorizing cultures of peace.
[41] Hegre 2001; Although a group of researchers associated with the Earth Institute at Columbia University are working on a project that models the core dynamics of sustainably peaceful societies.
[42] Kreutz 2010; Wallensteen and Axel 1994; Bell and O'Rourke 2009; Harbom et al. 2006.
[43] Joshi et al. 2015. For more see: www.peaceaccords.nd.edu and www.peaceagreements.org (accessed March 6, 2018). Also see the UN's Peace Agreements Database Search: https://peacemaker.un.org/document-search (accessed March 28, 2018).

Balkans, among others. They draw upon methodological approaches developed by regional public opinion data collection projects known as the Afrobarometer, Asian Barometer, Latinobarometro, Arab Barometer and Eurasia Barometer, which have partnered to form a Global Barometer Network. But, unlike the various regional barometers, which collect data on a range of social, political and economic factors over time, reconciliation barometers are distinguished by a focus on gathering data on factors that are connected to the preceding period of conflict and recovery in the post-conflict period.[44]

Although it does not claim to measure peace directly, the Human Development Index (HDI) is widely considered a measure of peace since economic and social development are often taken as proxy indicators for peace. Indeed, an immense academic and policy literature stresses the correlation between conflict on the one hand and economic decline and bad governance on the other.[45] More recent initiatives such as the Global Peace Index (GPI), the Fragile States Index and the OECD's States of Fragility Report and the World Happiness Report produced by the United Nations Sustainable Development Solutions Network have also attempted to conceptualize and measure peace. In addition, several efforts at measuring Sustainable Development Goal 16 exist and are elaborated upon in the next section.

Two additional scholarly efforts to measure peace-related activities are worth mentioning here. Erica Chenoweth leads a dataset initiative on civil resistance developed from her initial work, together with Maria Stephan, on the statistical measurement of civil resistance, presented in the book *Why Civil Resistance Works*. Various iterations have now been released of the Nonviolent and Violent Conflict Outcomes (NAVCO) dataset to study civil resistance, versions 1.0 (2008), 1.1 (2011) and 2.0 (2013).[46] Another database, the WomenStats Project, was initially developed for the book *Sex and World Peace* in which the authors move forward the democratic peace theory to include women.[47] They argue that the security of women is a vital factor in the security of the state and its incidence of conflict and war. The ongoing database initiative explores the relationship between the situation and security of women, and the dynamics between security, stability, and behavior of the state.

Most of the more recent initiatives to index peace use a mixture of data sources to create statistical measures of peacefulness, happiness or reconciliation based on pre-established sets of indicators. The data used in these measures are typically a combination of events-based data, such as incidents of armed conflict usually tracked

---

[44] Cole and Firchow 2018; Reconciliation Barometer Workshop, USIP, Washington, DC, September 7–9. See for example: www.scoreforpeace.org (accessed September 27, 2017) and reconciliationbarometer.org (accessed March 6, 2017).

[45] World Bank 2011: 2.

[46] Chenoweth and Stephan 2011; Navco Data Project, www.du.edu/korbel/sie/research/chenow_navco_data.html (accessed September 27, 2017).

[47] Hudson et al. 2013; WomanStats Project, www.womanstats.org/index.htm (accessed September 27, 2017).

by the Uppsala Conflict Data Program's datasets;[48] statistics collected by national statistics agencies on indicators encompassing a range of data from gender equality to governance reform measures; and, primarily for the barometers, national opinion polls such as the Afrobarometer or the tailor-made reconciliation barometers.[49] The indicators themselves vary significantly depending on the index or barometer, as well as the concept they are trying to measure (e.g., nonviolence, reconciliation or positive versus negative peace).

Information collected at the global level is driven by universal sets of indicators developed by researchers and experts for each individual measurement system. At the global level, criteria for indicator selection are not always clear, nor are they the same for each measurement system. In most cases, criteria include universal application to all contexts, data availability, and relevance to the target, goal or concept being measured.[50] Yet, relevance is sacrificed for the other criteria when it is inconvenient to collect data or the data are not generalizable.[51] Indicators are often chosen by the researchers developing the index themselves, sometimes in consultation with an expert panel and gleaned from scholarly literature, and rarely in consultation with local populations.[52] Using the same sets of indicators across different countries or regions allows for general comparison across cases. However, missing data or variation in data reporting across governments necessitates imputation, replacing missing data with substituted values. Most global indexes impute data when it is not available or ascribe data asterisks with disclaimers in order to comprehensively produce their global peace and reconciliation-related indices.[53] Indicators can also have multiple levels representing a category or dimension (e.g., intergroup anxiety) and then the actual observed items (e.g., whether a person is anxious, threatened, calm).[54]

---

[48] The Uppsala Conflict Data Program, www.pcr.uu.se/research/ucdp/datasets/ (accessed September 27, 2017).
[49] Cole and Firchow 2018.
[50] For examples of criteria, see Score Methodology page 29 or Annex B (p. 23) The New Deal: Achieving Better Results and Shaping the Global Agenda, www.pbsbdialogue.org/media/filer_public/a1/52/a152494f-0bb0-4ff3-8908-14bb007abd25/psg_indicators_en.pdf (accessed September 27, 2017).
[51] Interview, Former IEP Staff member, Washington, DC, July 20, 2016.
[52] The GPI, for example, selected its indicators in 2007 with the help of an expert panel. The indicators are revisited on an annual basis, although the original list has not changed since 2007. The Score Index and Colombian Reconciliation barometers use focus groups to establish indicator relevance in some cases.
[53] Interview, Former IEP Staff member, Washington, DC, July 20, 2016; Reconciliation Barometer Workshop, USIP, Washington, DC, September 7–9; Also see page 98 of the 2016 GPI Report and page 30 of the SCORE Index methodology; However, the UCDP has a policy against imputation and data that can only be verified by several sources is included, see codebook for UCDP's georeferenced dataset, http://ucdp.uu.se/downloads/ged/ucdp-ged-50-codebook.pdf (accessed September 27, 2017) Of course, this does not prevent others using UCDP data to impute where they cannot find adequate data to populate their indicators.
[54] A nice diagram explaining this can be found on page 28 of Score's methodology, www.scoreforpeace.org/app/webroot/files/general/files/methodology%20of%20score.pdf (accessed September 27, 2017).

As discussed, standards developed by outsiders do not always reflect the lived reality of those being measured or adequately represent the concept being measured. Sometimes indicators unintentionally measure the opposite of what they mean to. Without the contextual meaning of data, quantitative measurements can easily be misinterpreted. Data that suggests social goals have been achieved may in fact mean something very different. A good illustration of the challenges inherent in using universal standards to measure peace and security is provided by Graham Denyer Willis in his ethnographic study on homicides in São Paulo, Brazil.[55] He presents convincing evidence that the decline in homicide statistics since the 1990s in São Paulo is not attributable to an increase in government accountability or police effectiveness, as was touted by some, but to the fact that gangs and cartels now control large sectors of the city's justice and security mechanisms through a system of informal tribunals and punishment schemes. He demonstrates that these gangs are not only the protagonists of violence, but also its regulators and therefore the statistical decrease in homicides does not reflect an increase in state control and autonomy. Deaths by homicide, an indicator often used to demonstrate peace through improved governance, did not accurately reflect the deeper concept that it was meant to measure. In addition, he argues that the monopoly on violence that cartels maintain in São Paulo (and elsewhere in Brazil and Latin America for that matter) is in the interest of government authorities that can benefit "from the numbers."[56] Following Willis' argument, a decrease in homicide statistics in São Paulo would also mean a subsequent decrease in governance, state control and security. However, analysts using universal indicators designed to measure governance and peace globally would attribute a drop in homicides to an increase in peacefulness and stability.[57] Willis provides one of many good examples of why we should heed warnings about an overreliance on universal and top-down approaches to measuring peace.

Goal 16: The First Global Goal for Peace

The challenges facing quantitative efforts to measure peace are evident in the development of the latest and most ambitious global attempt to measure peace. In September 2015, the UN approved seventeen SDGs, setting its development agenda for the ensuing fifteen years. The SDGs are significant and worth mentioning in detail because they set the tone for future international funding and programming inside and outside of the UN system. The SDGs fall under five main thematic areas: People, Planet, Prosperity, Peace and Partnership. The seventeen SDGs have 169 targets, or subgoals, each of which in turn has dozens more indicators that if

---

[55] Willis 2015; 2017.
[56] Willis 2016a: 44.
[57] See Goertz et al. 2016: 28 for more discussion on the conceptual understandings and use of peace in international relations.

reached signal the achievement of the SDGs. The goals and targets encompassed under the five "P"s must be measured on a yearly basis by member states in order to demonstrate progress (or nonfeasance).

For the first time in history, the UN has decided to include peace as a global development goal. SDG 16 is dedicated to the promotion of peaceful and inclusive societies for sustainable development, the provision of access to justice for all, and building effective, accountable institutions at all levels. It marks the UN's first attempt to include a goal that requires measurement of peace, justice and strong institutions (or governance). Goal 16 has sixteen targets that are measured by 23 indicators (see Table 1.1).[58]

The SDG targets comprise, to a large extent, indicators that are universal and outcome-based. The indicators were chosen by the Inter-Agency Expert Group (IAEG-SDG) on SDG Indicators, comprising member states (primarily national statistical officers), and including regional and international agencies as observers.[59] This represents a major divergence from the prior Millennium Development Goal (MDG) indicator selection and monitoring, which was mainly conducted by UN entities and not by member states. The spearheading of the indicator selection process by member states also made the process significantly more political than the MDG monitoring process.[60] In addition, data collected to populate the indicators will be the responsibility of member states and their national statistics offices, with some limited data validation and harmonization, as well as support in capacity development, provided by international organizations and experts.

The criteria for SDG indicator selection were based on the SMART criteria – an acronym for Specific, Measurable, Available/achievable in a cost effective way, Relevant for the program and available in a Timely manner[61] – developed for project and human resources management.[62] Indicators were chosen by member states and were initially ranked from A to C according to feasibility, suitability and relevance. An indicator rated "AAA" would be considered (by a majority of national statistical offices, i.e., 60 percent or more) easily feasible, suitable and very relevant to measure the respective target for which it was proposed.[63] This ranking system

---

[58] This is subject to change. Tier III indicators 16.1, 16.3 and 16.10 are still being reviewed and additional indicators may be added or slightly changed, but none will be eliminated. This is similar to the MDG process, which began with 48 indicators and ended with 60 indicators to measure the MDGs because of fine-tuning and the addition of three targets. Interview, Henk-Jan Brinkman, New York, March 10, 2017.

[59] http://unstats.un.org/sdgs/iaeg-sdgs (accessed September 27, 2017).

[60] Interview, Henk-Jan Brinkman, New York, March 10, 2017.

[61] Doran 1981.

[62] Economic & Council 2015.

[63] United Nations Statistical Commission (2015). Technical report by the Bureau of the United Nations Statistical Commission on the process of the development of an indicator framework for the goals and targets of the Post-2015 Development Agenda. New York. Retrieved July 23, 2015.

TABLE 1.1. SDG 16 targets and indicators. Source: UNDP

Promote peaceful and inclusive societies for sustainable development, provide access to justice for all and build effective, accountable and inclusive institutions at all levels

10 Targets	23 Indicators	Tier
16.1 Significantly reduce all forms of violence and related death rates everywhere	16.1.1 Number of victims of international homicide per 100,000 population, by sex and age	1
	16.1.2 Conflict-related deaths per 100,000 population, by sex, age and cause	3
	16.1.3 Proportion of population subjected to physical, psychological or sexual violence in the previous twelve months	2
	16.1.14 Proportion of population that feel safe walking alone around the area they live	2
16.2 End abuse, exploitation, trafficking and all forms of violence against and torture of children	16.2.1 Proportion of children aged 1–17 years who experienced any physical punishment and/or psychological aggression by caregivers in the past month	3
	16.2.2 Number of victims of human trafficking per 100,000 population, by sex, age and form of exploitation	2
	16.2.3 Proportion of young women and men aged 18–29 years who experienced sexual violence by age eighteen	2
16.3 Promote the rule of law at the national and international levels and ensure equal access to justice for all	16.3.1 Proportion of victims of violence in the previous twelve months who reported their victimization to competent authorities or other officially recognized conflict resolution mechanisms	2
	16.3.2 Unsentenced detainees as a proportion of overall prison population	1
16.4 By 2030, significantly reduce illicit financial and arms flows, strengthen the recovery and return of stolen assets and combat all forms of organized crime	16.4.1 Total value of inward and outward illicit financial flows (in current United States dollars)	3
	16.4.2 Proportion of seized small arms and light weapons that are recorded and traced, in accordance with international standards and legal instruments	2
16.5 Substantially reduce corruption and bribery in all their forms	16.5.1 Proportion of persons who had at least one contact with a public official and who paid a bribe to a public official, or were asked for a bribe by those public officials, during the previous twelve months	2
	16.5.2 Proportion of businesses that had at least one contact with a public official and that paid a bribe to a public official, or were asked for a bribe by those public officials during the previous twelve months	2
16.6 Develop effective, accountable and transparent institutions at all levels	16.6.1 Primary government expenditures as a proportion of original approved budget, by sector (or by budget codes or similar)	1
	16.6.2 Proportion of the population satisfied with their last experience of public services	3

TABLE 1.1. *(continued)*

Promote peaceful and inclusive societies for sustainable development, provide access to justice for all and build effective, accountable and inclusive institutions at all levels

10 Targets	23 Indicators	Tier
16.7 Ensure responsive, inclusive, participatory and representative decision-making at all levels	16.7.1 Proportions of positions (by sex, age, persons with disabilities and population groups) in public institutions (national and local legislatures, public service and judiciary) compared to national distributions	3
	16.7.2 Proportion of population who believe decision-making is inclusive and responsive, by sex, age, disability and population group	3
16.8 Broaden and strengthen the participation of developing countries in the institutions of global governance	16.8.1 Proportion of members and voting rights of developing countries in international organizations	1
16.9 By 2030, provide legal identity for all, including birth registration	16.9.1 Proportion of children under five years of age whose births have been registered with a civil authority, by age	1
16.10 Ensure public access to information and protect fundamental freedoms, in accordance with national legislation and international agreements	16.10.1 Number of verified cases of killing, kidnapping, enforced disappearance, arbitrary detention and torture of journalists, associated media personnel, trade unionists and human rights advocates in the previous twelve months	3
	16.10.2 Number of countries that adopt and implement constitutional, statutory and/or policy guarantees for public access to information	2
16.a Strengthen relevant national institutions, including through international cooperation, for building capacity at all levels, in particular in developing countries, to prevent violence and combat terrorism and crime	16.a.1 Existence of independent national human rights institutions in compliance with the Paris Principles	1
16.b Promote and enforce nondiscriminatory laws and policies for sustainable development	16.b.1 Proportion of population reporting having personally felt discriminated against or harassed in the previous twelve months on the basis of a ground of discrimination prohibited under international human rights law	3

Note: Tier classification	Indicators
1: Indicator conceptually clear, established methodology and standards available and data regularly produced by countries	6
2: Indicator conceptually clear, established methodology and standards available but data are not regularly produced by countries	9
3: Indicator for which there are no established methodology and standards or methodology/standards are being developed/tested	8

was eventually transformed into a Tier system from I to III, with Tier I indicators being the most feasible and easy to measure with existing data and methodologies and Tier III indicators being the least feasible, requiring significant development of methodologies and data collection efforts.

Recommendations for Goal 16 indicators were provided by the Technical Support Team (TST), staffed by experts from the UN system and cochaired by the Peacebuilding Support Office, the United Nations Development Program, The United Nations Office on Drugs and Crime and the Rule of Law Unit. Another effort to buttress the indicator selection process was provided by the Virtual Network for the Development of Indicators for Goal 16 in a report entitled "The Indicators We Want," which was the outcome of "a discussion among many experts who were actively engaged in the design of a top-notch global monitoring framework for Goal 16."[64] In addition, experts from civil society groups also had influence through The New Deal for Engagement in Fragile States.[65,66] For example, a frequently used indicator by barometers of peacefulness or insecurity, "walking alone at night," was also included in the measurement of SDG 16, building on the New Deal's peacebuilding and statebuilding indicator generation process. This indicator was also the only overlapping one with the SDG 16 indicators that was also chosen frequently by participants in the Everyday Peace Indicators project.

The Institute for Economics and Peace (IEP), which produces the GPI, presented a comprehensive analysis of the challenges of measuring SDG 16 in its 2016 report. In it, they demonstrate that only two of the twenty-three indicators can be

---

[64] The Virtual Network for the Development of Indicators for Goal 16 brought together governance experts, development practitioners, statisticians, UN agencies and civil society organizations to advise on the best possible set of indicators for measuring governance, justice, peace and security in the Post-2015 development framework (p. 5). www.undp.org/content/dam/undp/library/Democratic%20Governance/Virtual%20Network%20on%20Goal%2016%20indicators%20-%20Indicators%20we%20want%20Report.pdf (accessed September 27, 2017).

[65] Referred to as the "New Deal," www.cspps.org/documents/130616042/130793247/CSPPS+statement+post-2015+indicators+and+New+Deal+Lessons+-+25+Feb+2015.pdf/2c009db9-aadf-44c3-8f34-06bab1d3a689 (accessed September 27, 2017).

[66] In 2011, conflict-affected governments calling themselves the g7+, international donors and civil society adopted The New Deal. In some ways the precursor to SDG 16, the New Deal participants developed five Peacebuilding and Statebuilding Goals (PSGs) – legitimate (inclusive) politics, security, justice, economic foundations, and revenues and services. Perhaps for the first time, international civil society and governments spent significant time, money and energy on thinking together about how to measure these goals. They developed a set of 34 "common indicators," that applied globally, while countries piloting the New Deal also developed "national indicators" to measure these goals. Participants in the process found that a balance between universal (global) and national (country specific) indicators is necessary for the measurement of peacebuilding and state building, but they did not go on to investigate whether sub-national indicators were necessary. In addition, they found that no single indicator could adequately capture the five goals and therefore combinations of many indicators are necessary. However, their process for choosing standards and indicators was still a significantly top-down process based primarily on the input of international donors and national government and civil society leaders.

fully measured with currently available data. Thirteen indicators can be measured with significant gaps and the rest will need to rely entirely on proxy indicators if additional measurement methodologies are not developed.[67] Additionally, the IEP finds four methodological issues with Goal 16. The first concerns the availability of data – some of the data measured may not be relevant to the indicator or may not be disaggregated at the level necessary. Second, some targets are not fully measured by the chosen indicators, which therefore do not adequately cover the full ambition of the targets. Third, there are perception challenges relating to the objectivity and capacity of many national offices, which necessitate some form of independent analysis to establish the veracity of official reporting. Finally, there are certain concepts that cannot be accurately measured by using only a few indicators; in some cases indicators are not actual measures of a concept, but rather proxies that are not able to fully encompass what is being measured.[68]

In the cases where information is not available to measure an indicator, the UN is looking for alternatives to existing national statistics and conducting baselines to be able to collect its own data.[69] Efforts at creating a methodology to address so-called Tier III indicators that do not currently have data collection available are the responsibility of the IAEG-SDG. Additionally, the SDG 16 Data initiative, a collective project by a consortium of organizations (including the IEP) to support the open tracking of the global commitments made by countries for SDG 16, has tried to compensate for some of these challenges by suggesting complementary indicators that may provide additional insight for targets, and also suggesting additional data sources to track indicators.[70]

Although SDG 16 represents significant advances in prioritizing peacebuilding efforts by the UN community, Goal 16 does not ultimately intend to measure peace comprehensively. It complements other SDGs that measure other conceptual dimensions of peace such as poverty and education, and is more a measure of violence, corruption, rule of law and inclusive governance. As Henk-Jan Brinkman from the UN Peacebuilding Support Office explains, "For violent death you just need a dead body … So, I've always argued that that aspect of goal 16 is so much easier to measure than others."[71] Yet, the goal also puts peacebuilding on the map for international assistance and is fundamental for organizations interested in the building of peace, not just the reduction of violence.[72] Although the establishment of a peace goal has been quite an accomplishment for the UN, the conceptual confusion around SDG 16, and whether or not it is a goal for the reduction of violence

---

[67] http://visionofhumanity.org/app/uploads/2017/09/SDG16-Progress-Report-2017.pdf (accessed September 27, 2017).
[68] Institute for Economics & Peace 2016: 91–3.
[69] https://sustainabledevelopment.un.org/topics/indicators (accessed September 27, 2017).
[70] www.sdg16.org/data/ (accessed September 27, 2017).
[71] http://dmeforpeace.org/learn/me-thursday-talk-measuring-goal-16 (accessed September 29, 2016).
[72] Interview with UNDP staff member 1, New York March 10, 2017.

or a goal for peace more broadly, is problematic and demonstrates the political challenges involved in capturing a difficult and multi-faceted concept such as peace.[73]

EVALUATING PROJECT IMPACT ON PEACE

Efforts to measure the impact of local peacebuilding projects on peace face many challenges as well. Since most *small-p* peacebuilding work by NGOs occurs at the project level, the measurement of peace at the *small-p* peacebuilding level is mostly project-based. Indicators at the project level are developed or chosen in the project design phase. In some cases, indicators are based on global standards and evaluators look to global indicators to evaluate projects, or organizations are required to choose from a suite of indicators given to them by donors.[74] These indicators are usually developed by experts within the donor network, typically technical experts and scholars. For example, the F-indicators (Standard Foreign Assistance Indicators) used by USAID and the State Department are developed by Subject Matter Experts (SMEs) within USAID and the State Department, with occasional outside advisers. The process is significantly expensive since "all of these people are doctors, experts and people in the field with decades of experience who are ... ensuring that things are defined in the way they should be."[75] Sometimes program staff are able to choose local, program-relevant (custom) indicators at the outset of a program or when applying for grant funding. Custom indicators are generally discouraged, but accepted if field staff feel there is a need for context-specific indicators. Typically such indicators are tied in some way to the project's theory of change and are chosen by project staff because they are deemed to be a good measure by the organization. Beneficiaries are rarely, indeed in most cases never, consulted in the selection and/or generation of indicators for project evaluation.

Evaluations are either conducted internally by the organization being evaluated,[76] usually by internal M&E staff, or externally by an independent consultant, often an academic or professional evaluator. Common evaluation and measurement practice includes a review of program documents and reports followed by a short field visit, and a write-up of an evaluation report.[77] *Small-p* peacebuilding projects are typically evaluated for outcome, relevance or accountability; they are measured by their success in following a promised process and achieving promised outputs. Evaluation is

---

[73] See Richmond 2014 for more on the evolution of the concept of peace over time and ideological spaces, as well as discussion on the difficulties in conceptualizing peace.
[74] See for example, the State Department's F indicators, www.state.gov/f/indicators/ (accessed September 27, 2017).
[75] Interview, Former Office of US Foreign Assistance Resources Staff member, November 5, 2016.
[76] The term *evaluand* is used in the evaluation literature to refer to the organization or project being evaluated.
[77] Blum 2011: 6.

seen (by evaluators at least) to be closely intertwined with design in interventions, the two informing each other in a complementary fashion.[78]

Peacebuilding evaluations can serve multiple functions. Most evaluations serve promotional purposes such as to fundraise, to help with public relations or to justify programming or predetermined decisions.[79] This may not be stated explicitly, but the purpose of the evaluation becomes clear by reading between the lines: the types of questions in the Terms of Reference given to external evaluators, guidance given by the evaluation manager, interest in the evaluation by the country team and feedback received on the draft report.[80] The use of evaluations in promoting programs is one reason why evaluators and organizations are reluctant to demonstrate failures. Reports of failures in peacebuilding projects are rare, and publicly available evaluation reports even more so.[81] Unfortunately, a minority of evaluation reports are commissioned for organizational learning. In these rare cases, the organization (or donor) wants to evaluate whether a project is working effectively and to learn how to improve it, as well as whether or not the promised deliverables have been delivered.

Many commissioned evaluations are impact evaluations, often in the form of randomized control trials (RCTs).[82] Determining causality or attribution is the aim of impact evaluation,[83] yet it is also one of the main challenges of impact evaluations identified by evaluation scholars.[84] The so-called attribution contribution challenge reflects the difficulty of isolating the causal impact of *small-p* peacebuilding interventions within a wider spectrum of postwar assistance. Impact evaluations aim to determine whether a peacebuilding intervention can be given pure attribution, partial attribution or contribution for the intended outcome.[85] Debates about attribution and contribution surround *small-p* peacebuilding effectiveness. Many question whether seeking sole attribution is a meaningful exercise in peacebuilding.[86]

Peacebuilding evaluators are encouraged to use mixed methods to bring a more holistic and rigorous approach to evaluation.[87] It is argued that using mixed methods to triangulate data allows for evaluators to view interventions from multiple

---

[78] Scharbatke-Church 2011: 471.
[79] Scharbatke-Church 2011: 476.
[80] Ibid.
[81] One example of an exception is an evaluation of some of Peace Direct's work in the Democratic Republic of Congo. This publicly available document lists the project's successes, but also discusses its "challenges." See: www.peacedirect.org/us/peacebuilders/drcongo/monitoring-and-evaluation/ (accessed September 27, 2017).
[82] Rogers 2012: 13.
[83] Rogers 2012: 2; Chigas et al. 2014 also make the point that impact evaluation is interpreted in different ways and that it is important to specify the variables involved in the causality equation. In other words, is the dependent variable the specific outcomes of the intervention, the drivers of the conflict or the longer-term situation?
[84] Scharbatke-Church 2011; Rogers 2012; Chigas et al. 2014.
[85] Chigas et al. 2014: 20.
[86] Chigas et al. 2014: 21.
[87] Scharbatke-Church 2011; Blum 2011; Rogers 2012; Chigas et al. 2014.

perspectives. Similar to empirical methods in the social sciences, evaluations take the form of experimental or quasi-experimental designs, theory-based or case-based designs or participatory approaches.[88] However, there are fundamental differences in the purpose, standards of data collection and forms of analysis and deliverables of evaluations in comparison to social science research projects.[89] For example, experimental or quasi-experimental designs can be very costly and difficult to conduct in conflict-affected contexts due to high levels of volatility and change. These may be more feasible for scholars who work with different time and budgetary restrictions.[90]

Peacebuilding monitoring and evaluation faces many challenges, from the politics involved and often unhelpful, latent intentions of evaluations, to issues of methodological rigor and attribution, short timelines and low budgets. Perhaps because of such challenges, programming and evaluation rarely comprehensively include the actual beneficiaries of interventions in their design and implementation.[91] As stated earlier, impact evaluations rarely (if ever) actively involve beneficiaries of peacebuilding projects beyond calling on them as sources of information in interviews and surveys, even though this has been found to be of great value in the development and humanitarian sectors.[92] When beneficiaries are included, it is often only to provide feedback such as whether or not sensitization workshops have worked to convince them of the benefits of participating in a program, or information on the success of mobilizations to get community support to implement an activity.[93]

When participatory evaluations are pursued, they can take different qualitative and quantitative forms that vary in their level of participation, but are typically not seen to focus on causal explanations, except for in the rare cases in peacebuilding that they are participatory impact assessments.[94] Instead, they are perceived by evaluators to focus on accountability to stakeholders and joint learning to improve intervention strategies.[95] Chigas et al. outline two forms of the so-called participatory techniques currently used in peacebuilding evaluations, Most Significant Change (MSC) and Outcome Mapping/Outcome Harvesting.[96] MSC is an iterative process using interviews and focus groups or community meetings to discuss what the MSC was that took place in a community. The most significant of the stories are then selected through a group process of review and selection, which sometimes includes community members, but not always. Outcome harvesting works with "change agents" or intervention staff to identify changes in behaviors and relationships.[97]

---

[88] Chigas et al. 2014.
[89] Scharbatke-Church 2011: 466.
[90] Chigas et al. 2014: 27.
[91] Scharbatke-Church 2011: 465.
[92] Catley et al. 2013: 4; Carruth 2018: 19.
[93] Autessere 2014: 93.
[94] Catley et al. 2013.
[95] Chigas et al. 2014: 38.
[96] Chigas et al. 2014: 39.
[97] Chigas et al. 2014: 40.

Participatory approaches to evaluation usually do not stand on their own and most typically complement more standard forms of experimental or nonexperimental monitoring and evaluation such as logframes, theories of change and indicators where beneficiaries and communities are rarely included in the establishment of the terms and standards of evaluation and measurement. In fact, evaluators often conflate qualitative approaches with participatory ones, and see both as less rigorous or robust than quantitative approaches. As one evaluator told me, indicating that they are already conducting "participatory or qualitative" evaluations, that these don't "actually test" the effectiveness of peacebuilding: "But the more participatory, qualitative aspects of evaluation are actually a better strength for us than impact evaluation and *really* testing out the effectiveness of peacebuilding."[98] This perspective, that quantitative and positivist approaches to measurement are more accurate at evaluating impact in peacebuilding, is one that that I have encountered repeatedly in INGOs and IOs working in the peacebuilding sector.

Small-p peacebuilding evaluations also rarely take into account other interventions in communities.[99] In fact, it is rare that organizations share information about what projects they are conducting or have conducted in a community.[100] In part, this is because organizations often do not keep extensive records themselves and the institutional memory of past interventions is quickly lost once a project ends or staff leave.[101] The lack of coordination and organization makes it difficult to effectively design or evaluate projects because key information is missing and a mapping of other interventions in aggregate is impossible. For example, two large international peacebuilding organizations in Nigeria funded by the same donor and currently operating in the same region do not have any official mandate to coordinate in the field. Although they informally work together on the ground, each will also conduct a separate evaluation of their programming.[102] Coordination between organizations such as these would be cost effective and give a more comprehensive picture of the impact of interventions in the communities affected *Big-P*. Peacebuilding evaluations are extremely rare at the community level. In fact, apart from this study, I am unaware of any other studies looking at all the interventions implemented in a community after a violent event. In part this is because it is extraordinarily difficult to establish what occurred in any given community during a time period extending more than a

---

[98] Interview, Search for Common Ground, Washington, DC, July 27, 2016. Impact evaluations are based on quantitative analysis and typically take a positivist stance.

[99] Interview, April 19, 2016 in Washington, DC.

[100] This reasoning provides the basis for dmeforpeace.org and its establishment by a consortium of NGOs and IOs including Search For Common Ground, USAID and the Alliance for Peacebuilding. "We are a global community of practitioners, evaluators and academics that share best and emerging practices on how to design, monitor and evaluate peacebuilding programs. Through greater collaboration and transparency we hope to increase the effectiveness of the peacebuilding field."

[101] Heideman 2016; this has also been my experience in collecting information on past interventions, especially in Uganda.

[102] Interview, Search for Common Ground, Washington, DC, July 27, 2016.

few years. This is particularly challenging when peacebuilding organizations do try to take a comprehensive look at interventions in a community when doing a conflict analysis and mapping in a context in which they have worked for a long time.[103]

Small-p evaluations and measurement ideally provide a possibility for organizations to substantiate or invalidate their theories of change in any given intervention. When evaluations confirm or refute theories of change, it is argued that the design of interventions can become more effective and robust. However, many obstacles stand in the way of this actually happening. Among them are the politics behind interventions among organizations and between organizations and donors that hinder the evaluation process and lead to inconclusive or vague results. As Andy Blum puts it, "often the main concern with evaluation results is not negative evaluations that find problems with peacebuilding programs; it is that evaluations do not reach any strong conclusions, positive or negative."[104]

It is important to keep in mind that the evaluation challenges enumerated here are not unique to peacebuilding. The development and humanitarian sectors also suffer from questionable or problematic evaluations that report predominantly positive results.[105] However, peacebuilding and peace do have underlying conceptual challenges that require a more integrated and participatory approach in order to assess effectiveness.

In sum, the challenges for *small-p* peacebuilding evaluation have been well documented. Its tendency for myopic, project-level analysis that is often less participatory than expected leaves little room for comparison or a more general ability to make claims about peacebuilding effectiveness at the regional, national or global level.

CONCLUSION

As we have seen in this chapter, the process of developing and tracking indicators at all levels is rarely participatory and inclusive of beneficiaries – outsiders (researchers, donors, NGO or UN staff) typically develop indicators at both levels. Local vernacular knowledge or "experience near" concepts are rarely considered or included as indicators.[106] A comparison of the everyday peace indicator lists presented in this study with those used to measure SDG 16 demonstrates a striking difference. Clearly, there is a danger of obscuring local level realities when aggregating measurement at the country or macro-level. Most countries affected by violent conflict do not experience armed violence ubiquitously. Instead only certain areas of a country may be affected, and data from those areas is obscured by national level statistics.

---

[103] Ibid.
[104] Blum 2011: 4.
[105] Catley et al. 2013: 3–4.
[106] Merry 2016: 7.

For these reasons, there is growing recognition in the policy and practitioner communities that the existing suite of peace and stability indicators is limited in its ability to measure peace. The limitations of existing indicators are methodological in that they tend to measure proxies of peace rather than peace itself and many existing peace indicators are unable to see the differences, often subtle, within and between communities. In addition, many techniques are limited to project evaluation, which may tell us little about the wider dynamics of the society in transition. Current peace-related indicator exercises are often top-down and originate from the Global North, with exogenous actors initiating, organizing and designing surveys and indicators, and therefore, the marginalized position of the subjects of research may be reinforced by the ways indicators are represented and disseminated. For example, the statistical rendering of data may not be the lens through which communities see themselves. Tobias Denskus' observation that this approach has, "served to erase the particularity of places and experiences through its inevitable generalisation"[107] applies to a great many studies.

The significant increase in demand for the quantification of peace comes from the desire of international organizations and governments to compare and make claims about the levels of peacefulness in countries around the world. Policymakers and practitioners require universal measures to be able to demonstrate progress and impact for global efforts. Generally little concern is paid to interrogating whether the results from top-down, technocratic measurement and evaluation systems are measuring outcomes based on the values and needs of donors, governments and other elite interests, or whether they reflect those of the people the interventions are actually intended to assist. Neither *small-p* nor *big-P* Peacebuilding actors adequately deal with the challenging conceptual questions surrounding what they are measuring. This has detrimental consequences for the long-term effectiveness of interventions implemented after war. As Fred Schaffer warns at the end of his book on social science concepts: "The words we social scientists use are swords. We had best learn to handle them with courage and humility."[108]

---

[107] Denskus 2007: 657.
[108] Schaffer 2016: 98.

2

Who Counts in the Measurement of Peace?

INTRODUCTION

This chapter discusses the dynamic relationship between international interveners and the beneficiaries they hope to serve. It presents the tensions between elites and local actors and illustrates how these groups interact in a push-and-pull, hybrid relationship to negotiate a local and contextualized peace. This different epistemological perspective allows us to more effectively address some of the flaws raised in the previous chapter regarding current efforts to measure peace. The chapter discusses in greater depth the conceptual challenges in measuring difficult concepts such as peace, and demonstrates why it is necessary to include beneficiaries in the design of measurement and evaluation tools in more meaningful ways. The chapter provides the theoretical grounding for the everyday indicators approach and gives background on what is known in the social sciences as participatory numbers – quantitative data collection in collaboration with researched populations.[1] It concludes by presenting the everyday indicators framework as a technology of Indigenous Technical Knowledge (ITK).

MOVING FROM A LIBERAL TO A HYBRID PEACEBUILDING MODEL

As we have seen, many of the causes of flawed local interventions after war are well documented. Analyses by practitioners and academics within the liberal peace paradigm itself have demonstrated the difficulties of integrating *small-p* peacebuilding into *big-P* Peacebuilding systems, standards, and evaluation.[2] To address these well-known problems, liberal peace practitioners tend to argue that the constituent

---

[1] Holland 2013.
[2] Autesserre 2014; Call and Cousens 2008; McCandless 2013; Doyle and Sambanis 2006; Fortna 2008.

programs and sequencing of peacebuilding projects at the community level should be integrated and coordinated among agencies and tied together in a systematic way to achieve sustainable peace. Many of the solutions proposed by organizations and governments working within the liberal peace framework only address the symptoms rather than the roots of the problems at hand. Addressing coordination, sequencing and implementation of interventions is important, but not helpful if the interventions themselves are not relevant for communities or if unequal power dynamics have not been addressed.

The problems and proposed solutions identified by supporters of the liberal peace model, however, are generally seen by scholars critical of the liberal peace as "problem-solving" approaches that do not attend to fundamental core problems at the heart of the liberal peace model. Many critical scholars argue the model is culturally inappropriate (at best) and neocolonial (at worst) in its practices.[3] The debate between problem-solving and critical approaches in peacebuilding is one that centers around the "coordination challenge."[4] Critics argue that problem-solving approaches address the symptoms of peacebuilding ineffectiveness, such as issues of coordination and sequencing, rather than dealing with the root problems of the neo-liberal peacebuilding agenda, such as the economic marginalization of affected communities by the Western societies purportedly trying to help them. Problem-solving scholarship and practice is seen as problematic by critical scholars because it does not address the underlying policy assumptions and decisions – often economic and strategic on the part of Western governments, based on universally applied liberal ideals – that go far deeper than any superficial "problem-solving" might fix. For example, critical scholars argue that you cannot build a state without first building a nation.[5] The Western liberal assumption that a state can be built technocratically ignores the fact that an underlying unity and social fabric is required to actually ground and stabilize the institutions and mechanisms necessary for a state to function. Additionally, critical scholars contend that a problem-solving approach, by aiming to "fix" the problem from the outside, overlooks and discounts the agency of marginalized populations and denies them the space to exercise power in contributing to a solution.[6] Liberalism, they contend, is not inherently a bad idea, but its imposition and implementation from the top-down is shortsighted and ineffective.

---

[3] Edington and Hughes 2016: 109; Mac Ginty 2015: 3; Jackson 2015: 23–25.
[4] Newman 2013: 315.
[5] Lemay-Hébert 2009.
[6] Jackson 2015: 32.

In practice, it is argued by critical scholars, local actors actually have some agency and impact when it comes to the implementation of top-down liberal peace efforts. Instead of passively standing by to allow international actors to implement programs, locals interact and enmesh themselves into interventions, making each one a unique political project. A kind of hybridity emerges in post-war dynamics between the international community, local elites and marginalized populations.[7] Hybridity challenges notions that offer static accounts of categories of interaction between actors. It demonstrates that there is more of a dynamic, interactive push-and-pull relationship between international and local actors, even when interventions arrive in a top-down fashion in a community. It is "the composite forms of social thinking and practice that emerge as the result of the interaction of different groups, practices and worldviews."[8] Liberalism is just one set of norms and practices that form part of a hybrid approach to building peace. It should not be excluded, but nor should it be the only perspective in the conversation.

The challenge lies in finding effective forms of communication, exchange and implementation that are representative of all parties involved in the hybrid architecture, without forgetting the inherent power relationships present in such a structure. As Christine Sylvester demonstrates when discussing "empathetic cooperation," which encapsulates the kinds of hybrid relationships that can emerge: "[it is] where soldiers and mothers blend stories and assignments in ways that jostle our sense of statecraft, and where local cooperatives teach international donors about the need to aid families that produce."[9] Sylvester eschews the rigid structures of traditional international relations approaches to human relationships and encourages scholars to aspire to a certain "homelessness," as she calls it, to understand multiple perspectives in the international arena – from the mother to the soldier or from the everyday to the United Nations. Therefore, hybridity means challenging existing ontological perspectives and approaches to become more comfortable with uncertainty, ambiguity and ambivalence. As Mac Ginty and Richmond explain,

> Much of the liberal internationalism of the 1990s and the early (neocon) years of this century were attended by certainty: in the righteousness of liberalism as an idea and as operationalized in institutions covering the realms of politics, law and the economy, in the fitness of the Weberian state, the opportunities come in and trickle down from foreign direct investment (FDI) and the global economy, and in the ability of the rapid use of military force to achieve desired outcomes. This certainty has been punctured and replaced, to a certain extent, by a policy willingness to investigate and even tolerate ambivalence, ambiguity and uncertainty. It is in this

---

[7] Mac Ginty 2011b; Richmond 2012; Roberts 2011b.
[8] Mac Ginty 2011b: 8.
[9] Sylvester 2002: 264.

context that we can best explain the "hybrid turn" or the rediscovery of hybridity as a conceptual lens.[10]

Hybridity shows us why a template, universal approach to interventions after war is ineffective and fundamentally impossible. When interventions are found to be successful, it is not necessarily that the intervention can work in any context, but that it worked in a specific context, with a certain set of actors – local, national and international – that combined to ensure its success. In other words, the ingredients for success cannot be attributed universally because those ingredients cannot be found everywhere and are unique to each context. The push and pull of a hybridity cannot be standardized. An intervention in one context may be hugely successful, whereas in another it might not work at all. Therefore, while you can draw upon universal frameworks to help understand and decipher individual situations and challenges, you cannot approach peacebuilding or post-war interventions with a universal solution.

ADDRESSING CONCEPTUAL CHALLENGES TO ASSESSING PEACEBUILDING EFFECTIVENESS

A hybrid approach to peacebuilding effectiveness must similarly incorporate multiple perspectives of what constitutes "success" for an intervention. Peacebuilding scholars such as Séverine Autesserre define peacebuilding effectiveness thus: "A peacebuilding project, program or intervention is effective when a large majority of the people involved in it – including both implementers (international interveners and local peacebuilders) and intended beneficiaries (including local elite and ordinary citizens) – view it as having promoted peace in the area of intervention."[11] However, translating this principle into practice immediately becomes problematic for both practical and conceptual reasons. What happens when there are differences and disagreements in a community over priorities or ideas of what constitutes peace? Perhaps more importantly, what happens when there is disagreement among ordinary citizens and local elites, or international interveners and local peacebuilders?

Due to the many parties involved, peacebuilding and peace have underlying conceptual challenges that require a more integrated and participatory approach in assessing effectiveness. Establishing *whose* peace we are talking about when measuring success requires sustained attention to on-going conceptual challenges and skepticism toward the tools we use to measure peace. We should be asking more critical questions about what programs should be implemented (and when) in a community, how to fill data gaps, and how to establish common standards that

---

[10] Mac Ginty and Richmond 2016: 232.
[11] Autesserre 2014: 8.

fulfil the agendas of local and international actors. More effort should be put toward incorporating the measures of ordinary citizens in the standards and indicators used to measure effectiveness. There is still very little discussion and debate about how to include beneficiaries in these decisions in real and sustained ways.

Involving the people being measured in the creation of their own indicators of peace can give us much-needed insights into understanding what to measure when we are aiming for successful peacebuilding interventions. Otherwise, measurement will embody the concepts and categories of outsiders rather than those of everyday people, and impose external meanings on their social reality.[12]

Of course, there have also been accusations of a tendency to "romanticize" the local and to ascribe overly benign interpretations to the actions and motives of local groups.[13] It seems that, all too often, we have conceptualized indigenous knowledge in unproblematic and even naïve ways, and therefore it has turned out to be less helpful as a peacebuilding and development tool than has been supposed or hoped for.[14] There has also been skepticism toward the extent to which participatory approaches to research can ever hope to truly understand the experiences of individuals and groups who have undergone the fear, violence and dislocation associated with conflict.[15] Scholars critical of participatory approaches argue that participation is usually constrained by implementing agencies and is thus perfunctory,[16] or that it is too naïve to understand the dynamics of political power plays and realpolitik at play in most contexts.[17] Criticism has also been made that some anthropological studies amount to the crass instrumentalization of local voices, especially when those voices align with Western progressive politics and are strategically useful. Anja Nygren notes how selected local communities in the global south were variously identified by environmental research patrons as "paragons of ecological virtue" and possessors of "primordial environmental wisdom." Of course "local knowledge was legitimized only if it conformed to experts' principles of sustainability."[18] Similarly, Mohan and Stokke demonstrate that too much of a focus on the value of the "local" and "local participation" underplays local inequalities and power relations, as well as national and transnational economic and political forces.[19] Most of these criticisms, however, admit that these issues arise mostly with poor implementation and exceedingly high expectations of participatory approaches. Therefore, caution is

---

[12] Chambers 2007b: 51.
[13] Richmond 2009.
[14] Howes and Chambers 1979.
[15] Mac Ginty 2014.
[16] Branch 2011a: 150; Cooke and Kothari 2001.
[17] Ferguson 1990: 241.
[18] Nygren 1999: 274 and 273.
[19] Mohan and Stokke 2000.

necessary when claiming to represent local voices without taking into account local inequalities and dynamics and the limitations of participatory approaches.

If the aim is to understand peace through the eyes of communities experiencing conflict, we should be measuring peace according to the everyday use of words in the practices of daily life or language "in gear" – as suggested by Wittgenstein.[20] Wittgenstein demonstrates through language games "the fact that the 'speaking' of language is part of an activity, or form of life."[21] For Wittgenstein, concepts can be "blurred" and do not need to be clearly defined to be meaningful. Wittgenstein does not accept the foundational premise of measurement, which is that concepts can be concretely defined. He believes sharp linguistic boundaries and definitions create concepts that are no longer specific enough because the contextual relativity of a concept is lost when isolating it in an attempt at definition. This leads to a place where "anything – and nothing – is right."[22] Therefore, ethnographic and qualitative approaches to concept formation based on empirical observations, that give more nuance and contextual detail, are often best placed to formulate a more holistic understanding of a concept for a given community. What's more, participatory approaches are arguably significantly more effective in defining concepts than *a priori* approaches based on theoretical deduction. When seeking to understand or predict conflict events in any given community, sometimes understanding the perceptions of its residents is much more helpful than understanding their actual reality.

Similar to "emic" and "etic" distinctions, Clifford Geertz used Heinz Kohut's distinction between "experience-near" and "experience-distant" concepts. Experience-near concepts are those that are effortlessly used by an individual "to define what he or his fellows see, feel, think, imagine, and so on, and which he would readily understand when similarly applied to others." This is in contrast to experience-distant concepts, which "various types of specialists … employ to forward their scientific, philosophical, or practical aims."[23] Looking at indicators in measurement in the same way, "experience-near" indicators would be those tangible things that people use in their daily lives to make decisions or determinations about a certain concept. They are relative and context-specific. "Experience-distant" indicators are those developed by outside experts to analyze people's decisions or determinations about a certain concept. For the purposes of measurement, experience-near indicators give us the kind of information that helps us to eventually define and organize experience-distant concepts. However, starting with experience-distant indicators does not allow us to accurately reflect the experience-near.

---

[20] Schaffer 2016: 32.
[21] Wittgenstein 2010: §23.
[22] Wittgenstein 2010: §§76 and 77.
[23] Geertz 1975: 47–8.

For example, if we take the SDG 16 indicators listed in the previous chapter, we can see that they differ quite significantly from the everyday indicators listed in Chapter 5, and are perhaps more reflective of the broader categories that have been created for the factor or category analysis of the everyday indicators.

To give this example more context, take SDG 16 indicator 16.3.1 – "Proportion of victims of violence in the previous 12 months who report their victimization to competent authorities or other officially recognized conflict resolution mechanisms." We can see here that this is a sufficiently general indicator to allow for several different contextual situations to arise. The indicator captures what it intends to measure in a very practical and pragmatic way that amplifies the possibilities of what might be included in different contexts. It would be a good general description of an EPI category – or the category analysis presented in Chapter 5 of similar classes of experience-near indicators – and specifically would align with the EPI category of Conflict Resolution. However, it lacks the necessary context, detail and proximity to be easily translated to a specific locality and to be adequately used as a measurement tool without significant additional contextual interpretation. This brings up questions such as what it means to measure these things at the local level, and who decides how to interpret this indicator in each context it is measuring?

In addition, overarching indicators such as the SDG 16 indicator 16.3.1 can be measured differently in different contexts and yet still have meaning for the indicator. Using "two-level theories," for example, allows for the formation of secondary-level dimensions to form concepts.[24] Taking this example further, we could say that in one village reporting a violent event to a religious leader would constitute "reporting their victimization to competent authorities," whereas in another, villagers may only consider a local government leader a "competent authority." Therefore, indicators may vary from place to place, but they all measure the same thing: "reporting victimization to competent authorities." But those making decisions about indicators need to be experiencing the context to make these important decisions.

Furthermore, the everyday peace indicators tell a very different story from already established top-down indicators such as SDG 16 indicator 16.3.1. In Colombia, for example, we see that people are primarily preoccupied with the response of authorities to their victimization along the following lines of inquiry: Does the authority know the truth about victimizing events? Has justice been sought for victimizing events? Or, are there conditions that guarantee that victimizing events will not be repeated? In terms of reporting, people are more concerned with participation than with reporting. They choose indicators such as: Do victims participate in the design of interventions for reconciliation? Do we invite the police to participate in town meetings? Is there any dialogue between community members? Or, do politicians work for everyone, not just those who voted for them? Questions such as these reflect

---

[24] Goertz 2006b: 237. See Chapter 5 for more discussion on two-level theory and concepts.

Addressing Conceptual Challenges to Assessing Peacebuilding Effectiveness   61

the current situation in Colombia as Colombians navigate the peace process, and shows how the priorities of outsiders can differ completely from those of insiders, since these communities do not demonstrate any interest in "reporting victimization to competent authorities."[25]

When policymakers and scholars concerned with measurement discuss its shortcomings, they typically focus on data gaps or indicators that have not yet been adequately measured by existing data collection mechanisms, such as the Tier III indicators in the SDGs. Generally, the formulation of indicators themselves is less of a concern. The selection of indicators is seen to be the superintendency of experts who decide what indicators are most relevant to measurement of a given concept. In the creation of indicators, experts use "experience-distant" concepts that are constructed based on theoretical debates, with the goal being the reconstruction of those concepts for scientific use.[26] Experts fashion precise conceptual tools – indicators – to be able to effectively measure the scientific concepts they have created. These "experience-distant" concepts then allow data collection for precise indicators that specify the composition of each concept.

However, the reconstructed concepts may be far from the meaning and use of the concepts in lived practice, or "in-gear" and "experience-near" usage. Yet, they provide a kind of "constructed objectivity" that claims to represent the reality it aims to describe with concrete numbers and benchmarks.[27] Take, for example, the indicator of "police presence" for peace and security. Experts often use this indicator to represent improved security or peacefulness in a society, with the reasoning that people feel more secure and therefore more at peace when guarded by a large police presence.[28] However, in pilot studies of the EPI approach in South Africa, that indicator only partially reflected community realities. For example, if you look at the "experience-near" indicators in the pilot community of Hanover Park, "the presence of colored police" was chosen as an indicator of peace. An increased police presence would not necessarily mean much to the community if the police were white, but an increase in colored police officers would indicate more stability. Similarly, we can imagine that in some communities in the United States an increase in police presence would not be considered an indicator of peace, considering the mounting tensions between African Americans and law enforcement in the last few years.

Adcock and Collier define measurement validity as being concerned with the relation among scores (numerical and qualitative classification), indicators, and the systematized concept (the specific formulation of a concept adopted by a particular

---

[25] Indicators of peace and reconciliation were collected in Colombia. The analysis in this book presented in Chapters 5 and 6 is based solely on the indicators of peace.
[26] Schaffer 2016: 7.
[27] Broome and Quirk 2015: 821.
[28] See, for example, the indicator of police presence used in the Global Peace Index.

researcher).[29] In other words, "[m]easurement validity is achieved when indicators meaningfully reflect the concept a researcher seeks to measure."[30] If indicators are unable to ensure measurement validity, then the data, and therefore the results of a study, will be inaccurate or irrelevant.[31] In the example above, the indicator of police presence does not have measurement validity because it does not accurately reflect the concept it seeks to measure – peace. A universal study using the indicator of "police presence" to track and analyze levels of peace in a community would arrive at erroneous conclusions.

Often a "paradox of measurement" occurs when it is easier to measure what has already been identified as measureable, even if it misses the mark. What has not been measured, because of a lack of contextual knowledge or acknowledgement of the relativity of concepts, is harder to translate into numbers or make commensurable with other things.[32] It is hard to measure what you don't know is there and consequently it is difficult to establish measurement equivalence or "the comparability of measured attributes across different populations."[33] Only communities have the local knowledge needed to ensure alignment of concepts and the indicators that seek to measure them.

The Everyday Indicators as a Technology of Indigenous Technical Knowledge

The term indigenous technical knowledge (ITK) emerged in the development literature in the late 1970s, primarily associated with two scholars based in the United Kingdom (UK), Michael Howes and Robert Chambers.[34] They presented ITK as a methodological approach in reference to agricultural development and the knowledge cultivated by local farmers over years of farming their lands. Indigenous technical knowledge is seen as a body of knowledge generated or acquired by local people through the accumulation of everyday experiences, community interactions and trial and error.[35] Indigenous technical knowledge has been traditionally discussed in the anthropologically rooted fields of ethnoscience and human ecology and in the development-focused areas of farming systems and participatory development.[36] Scholars have distinguished indigenous technical knowledge from anthropology, arguing that ITK is more of an applied pursuit than an intellectual one and that

---

[29] Adcock et al. 2001: 533.
[30] Cyr 2015: 14.
[31] Davidov et al. 2014: 56.
[32] Merry 2016; Merry and Wood 2015.
[33] Davidov et al. 2014: 58.
[34] Howes and Chambers 1979.
[35] Mercer et al. 2009: 217.
[36] Sillitoe 1998: 224.

"its objective [is] to introduce a locally informed perspective into development – to promote an appreciation of indigenous power structures and know-how."[37] For example, Sillitoe demonstrates that scholars interested in indigenous technical knowledge make connections between local people's understandings and practices from those of outside researchers and development workers,[38] therefore finding ways of integrating Western and indigenous approaches. He refers to indigenous technical knowledge interchangeably as "indigenous knowledge," "local knowledge," "popular knowledge," and "folk knowledge."[39]

The relevant academic debates on indigenous knowledge are primarily focused on the tensions between indigenous approaches and Western science. Howes and Chambers presented a strict binary between scientific (and Western) knowledge and indigenous technical knowledge, arguing that the latter was inferior in its ability to explain and predict and to speedily accumulate knowledge.[40] Western science is seen to be universal and global, rigorous, objective and dependable, whereas indigenous technical knowledge is seen to be provincial and limited, subjective, primitive and untrustworthy.[41] These artificial distinctions were later criticized by development scholars, who called for more integrated frameworks using participatory approaches in which relevant indigenous and scientific knowledge could be used.[42] Although indigenous and Western approaches may use different epistemological and ontological frames, they often overlap and feed off one another. Dichotomizing began to be seen as unhelpful because indigenous and scientific knowledge are not always distinguishable, and knowledge is dynamic, fluid and adaptable.[43] Indeed, Agrawal goes as far as calling ridiculous the distinction of forms of knowledge as "Western" and "indigenous."[44] He advocates a more integrated approach to discussing multiple domains and types of knowledge rather than creating fixed categories. Briggs points out that Western science is as much a social construction as indigenous knowledge. He goes on to say that Western science has not proven itself as a universal standard in development since it has failed significantly in transforming poor people's lives and therefore should not be overly valued.[45] His argument might be in line with the extreme empowerment view, which comes close to advocating that the disadvantaged may be better off left to their own devices.[46]

---

[37] Ibid.
[38] Ibid.
[39] Sillitoe 1998: 223 (footnote 2).
[40] Howes and Chambers 1979: 2.
[41] Briggs 2005; Mercer et al. 2009; Agrawal 1995.
[42] Agrawal 1995; Briggs 2005; Mercer et al. 2009.
[43] Mercer et al. 2009: 218; Agrawal 1995.
[44] Agrawal 1995: 30.
[45] Briggs 2005: 104.
[46] Sillitoe 1998: 225.

However, if we indeed agree that science does have something to offer, perhaps in combination with indigenous technical knowledge, then there are several considerations that must be acknowledged if we want to more effectively improve development and peacebuilding programming and therefore address people's needs. Issues of power and positionality emerge when discussing indigenous knowledge as a technology for development or peacebuilding. The fear is that indigenous technical knowledge will be co-opted, or worse, hidden and dismissed if it is integrated into scientific approaches.[47] Conversely, others see the integration of indigenous technical knowledge into Western scientific study as a form of empowerment and progress for the world's poor.[48] Indeed, the use of indigenous knowledge may involve both, which is why its use as a form of technical knowledge must be so very carefully carried out, with significant understanding of context and application, in order to avoid ethical concerns such as those encountered by the United States Army Human Terrain Systems.[49] Clearly, there are ethical and political challenges in the distillation of peace into short, measurable units of indicators and measurement tools to quickly assess the impact of interventions.

The use of indigenous technical knowledge as a tool for development and peacebuilding requires a step beyond traditional anthropological approaches, which require significant time and effort and in-depth study of a specific area. Instead, "it requires the formulation of research strategies that meet the demands of development and peacebuilding – cost-effective, time-effective, generating appropriate insights, readily intelligible to non-experts, etc. – while not compromising anthropological expectations."[50] Creating systems that combine anthropological skills with technical and scientific knowledge has been recognized by anthropologists as a necessary future application of anthropology.[51] Interdisciplinary approaches have also been seen as central to this effort.[52] Recent debates on appropriate methodologies in conflict-affected communities have been influenced by sociology and anthropology.[53] There is a strong emphasis on conflict-sensitive methods and reflective practice by the researcher.[54] In many cases, conflict-sensitive research depends on face-to-face encounters that allow the researcher to use emotional intelligence and

---

[47] Mercer et al. 2009: 218.
[48] Briggs 2005: 99.
[49] The Human Terrain Systems (HTS) program embedded anthropologists and other social scientists in military teams in Iraq and Afghanistan in order to provide military commanders and staff with an understanding of the local population. The program was launched in 2007 and ended its operations in 2014. See American Association of Anthropologists for its statement opposing HTS, www.americananthro.org/ConnectWithAAA/Content.aspx?ItemNumber=1626 (accessed September 27, 2017).
[50] Sillitoe 1998: 225.
[51] Sillitoe 1998: 230.
[52] Sillitoe 1998: 231.
[53] Nordstrom and Robben 1995; Mazurana et al. 2013.
[54] Gullette and Rosenberg 2015.

make professional judgments about risk to the research subjects and their ability to exercise informed consent.

USING PARTICIPATORY NUMBERS TO MEASURE PEACE

In 2007, Chambers advocated for the operationalization of approaches that quantitatively capture ITK in a working paper for the Institute of Development Studies entitled "Who Counts? The Quiet Revolution of Participation and Numbers." In this paper he presents the idea of participatory approaches and methods that generate numbers using rapid rural appraisal techniques, or what he calls "participatory numbers."[55] He argues, and presents evidence, that these participatory numbers are not only alternatives to conventional methods, but are superior since they are able to address some of the conceptual challenges of top-down measurement in inclusive ways.[56] The participatory numbers approach demonstrates an attempt to bridge the gap between positivist methods of quantitative experts and interpretivist methods of qualitative scholars. It offers the rigor and replicability of quantitative approaches with the nuance, context, and local concept development of qualitative participatory approaches.

The Everyday Indicators framework collects and works with ITK in the context of participatory numbers and the re-evaluation of indicators.[57] It is particularly influenced by scholarship and practice from the sustainable development field that seeks to include the researched in measurement and observation.[58] The Everyday Indicator system offers several advantages over current attempts to re-evaluate peace-related indicators. First, the indicators respect the autonomy and status of local residents as they are chosen by local respondents rather than invented in the Global North and "imposed" on local communities. Secondly, the indicators are in an idiom or language that is meaningful to local communities. Context-specific meaning is deployed when using these indicators, in contrast to more top-down indicators that often reflect the priorities of outsiders. It centers around what Fred Schaffer calls "grounding," or figuring out how actors themselves understand a concept.[59] Thirdly, the indicators are flexible and change during the lifetime of the project. Project participants choose different indicators as circumstances change. For example, as conditions improve after war, respondents may notice more tourists or a more regular mail service and identify these as indicators of peace. Fourthly, participatory

---

[55] Chambers 2007b: 7.
[56] Chambers 2007b: 10.
[57] Another similar effort called "Participatory Tracking" is being led by the World Bank's Social Observatory with a pilot in India. Women participate in focus groups to develop indicators that constitute a "good life," www.worldbank.org/en/programs/social-observatory/brief/participatory-tracking-data-collection (accessed July 18, 2017).
[58] Parkins et al. 2001; Reed et al. 2008; Chambers 2007b.
[59] Schaffer 2016: 52.

statistics that result from the indicators can influence policy and change the perspective and approach from which policy issues are approached. These participatory statistics can both empower local people and provide valuable information for implementing agencies and donors, as well as governments.[60]

Finally, as opposed to NGOs extracting or harvesting data without reporting back to the communities from which the data is gathered, the project findings can be reported horizontally in the local community, in other communities in the same country, and upward to NGOs and INGOs, the national government, bilateral donors and international organizations. Although communities already have an informal network of indicators that they use in their daily lives, their formalization allows community members to systematically monitor, measure and record indicators over time and communicate these to decision makers at the regional and national levels.

The Everyday Peace Indicator framework emerges from a long history of critical scholarship in international relations and peace and conflict studies. It is sympathetic with bottom-up, participatory approaches. In particular, it concerns itself with finding effective ways to include the local perspective into international discourse and policy. The underlying aim is to serve as a megaphone by which to amplify the concerns of the locals to their governments and the international community. Therefore, it is an effort to interrogate and challenge current top-down approaches, many of which have been proven to be ineffective. It is a tool that seeks to assist policymakers in questioning the assumptions that lie behind the existing peacebuilding measurement systems and move beyond traditional "hegemonic orthodoxies."[61]

CONCLUSION

As we have seen, top-down approaches rarely take into account ITK in the design of measurement and evaluation tools. For peacebuilding, the result is that the expertise, priorities and ontologies on matters regarding peace are imposed upon communities. The measurement of peace embodies the concepts and categories of outsiders rather than those of everyday people. By introducing more hybrid approaches to the measurement and evaluation of peace and peacebuilding, we can achieve a more effective, negotiated peace between local and international actors. The everyday indicator approach outlined in this book is an example of an effort to bring together indigenous technical knowledge and scientific approaches to create a system that is participatory, draws on local knowledge and is useful to development

---

[60] Holland 2013.
[61] Pugh 2013: 11.

and peacebuilding practitioners for both program design *and* measurement and evaluation purposes. It is an example of a hybrid approach that attempts to integrate the knowledge and needs of local communities with the priorities of policymakers and practitioners.

The next chapter explains the EPI methodology, which attempts to resolve many of the existing conceptual challenges of measuring peacebuilding effectiveness by including beneficiaries in defining their own peace.

3

A New Approach to Measuring Peace

INTRODUCTION

It is important to give a thorough overview of the EPI methodology and approaches in this book that are used to make claims about peacebuilding effectiveness at the local level, since these are new and relatively unchartered territory for many social scientists and practitioners working in war-affected contexts.[1] This chapter outlines the everyday indicator approach as it was conducted for this study and gives a detailed explanation of the indicator collection and development process and subsequent longitudinal survey-based data collection. It showcases this new approach to measuring peace, and demonstrates ways in which communities can be more involved not only in the evaluation, but also in the design of external interventions.[2] The chapter also discusses why such an approach is necessary and important, and offers some reflections on its place along the Participatory Action Research (PAR) spectrum.[3]

The Process: Indicator Collection

Focus groups are a ubiquitous feature of qualitative studies and are also used to verify quantitative studies, as explained later in more detail. The approach presented in this book takes the use of focus groups in survey questionnaire development a few steps beyond their traditional role in order to bridge the divide between conceptual

---

[1] The research conducted for this book was approved by the George Mason University Institutional Review Board (project #653459-3).
[2] The everyday peace indicator approach can be used for other big concepts that are difficult to measure. It has also been piloted for indicators on reconciliation, justice, inclusion and violent extremism. We are developing further other initiatives related to the measurement of difficult to define concepts or Everyday X Indicators (EXI).
[3] Parts of the this chapter were previously published in Firchow and Mac Ginty 2017a.

richness and the need for quantifiable data.[4] It heeds concerns of measurement bias, particularly in light of existing considerations regarding inclusion and participation of communities in survey question design and the imposition of concepts and categories by outsiders.[5] Instead of merely using focus groups to inform the survey generation process, these groups become the forum in which community members themselves create and select the indicators that provide the basis for survey questionnaires. Instead of "experts" and "scholars" developing indicators of success, communities themselves are asked to establish their own everyday indicators of peace, which are then categorized, analyzed and measured longitudinally. Unlike other participatory impact assessment approaches that use community generated indicators specific to a particular development project,[6] this process captures indigenous technical knowledge in the form of indicators that is already being used by individuals to navigate their own daily lives and is unrelated to any specific intervention. This approach addresses further calls by scholars to include those who are the targets of measurement in the construction of indicators.[7] Focus group researchers have found that this method is valuable for researchers who are more actively engaged with participant concerns and pursue goals such as empowerment, or use approaches such as PAR.[8] The everyday indicators generated by the focus groups, and complemented by discussions with local civil society partners, form the basis of the longitudinal survey questions and the category analysis of the indicators.

In each community, the EPI research team conducted three focus groups with individual groups of women, men and youth (ages 18 to 30) and asked questions about their definitions, understandings and signs of peace.[9] In order to determine the composition of focus groups participating in the indicator collection process, segmentation was used to create groups that consisted of particular categories of participants.[10] Participants were selected using consistent criteria based on community demographics such as ethnicity, socio-economic status, leadership roles and relationship to the partner organization. Eight to twelve participants were selected for each focus group (female, male, youth) and every effort was made to select community members from different sectors of the community. In most cases, focus

---

[4] I use the definition for focus groups provided by Morgan 1996: 130. "Focus groups [are defined] as a research technique that collects data through group interaction on a topic determined by the researcher."
[5] Chambers 2013 (first published 1983): 51; Merry and Wood 2015.
[6] Catley et al. 2013.
[7] Merry 2016: 217.
[8] Morgan 1996: 149.
[9] The research teams included myself, staff members of the Everyday Peace Indicators project and staff from our civil society partners. In Uganda, our civil society partner also served as translator.
[10] Morgan 1996: 143. Segmentation is a widely used focus group sampling strategy that intentionally varies the composition of groups.

group participants either did not know one another or were from different groups or geographical areas of the village(s). This was done in order to be as representative as possible of the community. I was well aware of the possible biases involved with drawing only from one group of the community, since perceptions and knowledge of peace indicators might vary significantly depending on the composition of the groups.[11] Groups were composed of the unemployed and employed, community leaders, direct and indirect victims of the war,[12] vulnerable groups (ethnic and religious minorities, migrants), and different ages including youth and the elderly. The recruitment for the focus groups was done through local partner organizations that worked with local leaders to convene groups with the desired characteristics.

We started with general questions such as, "What does peace mean to you?" in order to open a conversation about peace and how participants perceived peace in their communities.[13] Once the group was warmed up and engaged, we began to lead them by asking questions about how they measure peace, questions such as, "How do you recognize the signs that there is peace in your own community and everyday life?" or, "What factors do you use in your daily life to determine whether you are more or less at peace?" In the instances when this line of questioning did not produce valuable indicators of peace, I would probe the group even further to ask questions about how they determined whether it was safe to send their children to school or how they determined whether they could attend festivals. Intensive probing is fundamental in this process. When I asked respondents about the tangible signs they used to determine whether things were improving for them in their everyday lives, these often needed to be narrowed down to concrete observations. Participants often did not understand that we wanted this kind of local, anecdotal, almost banal information and therefore tried to summarize it or put it into a context that was not their own. Overcoming this hurdle was particularly challenging. It was also important for us, at this stage, not to give any examples of indicators or to lead the groups into certain directions. Therefore, we encouraged participants to generate as many indicators as possible and even probed for more detailed indicators to generate lists (sometimes up to forty indicators in each group) from these initial discussions.

After the initial focus groups were conducted and recorded by a voice recorder, they were transcribed and (in the Ugandan case) translated. The research team then used the transcriptions and cross-checked notes in order to validate the indicators and create long lists from the discussions. I generated indicators by reading through

---

[11] See Briggs 2005: 105 for more discussion on the uneven, mediated and fragmented nature of indigenous knowledge.

[12] Since these communities were so ravaged by the wars in their respective countries, most everyone was displaced and therefore an indirect victim of the war. However, some lost close family members or were themselves harmed by the conflict and are therefore considered direct victims of the war.

[13] Peter Uvin asked this question in Burundi and classified the answers according to positive and negative peace responses. For more about his findings, see Uvin 2013: 43–51.

the transcripts and my notes and by listing the indicators or signs that people mentioned they used to determine their peace and safety in their surroundings. The civil society partners were instrumental in this process because they were able to help clarify questionable indicators and help to interpret them. It was necessary to test and carefully interpret the language used by the communities before selecting indicators in order to avoid potential misunderstandings and repetitions. For example, in one community in Colombia receiving reparations was chosen as an indicator of peace, but so was compensation for harms caused. Although our understanding was that these were one and the same, after consultation with community members, it was clear that they saw them as being two distinct and different indicators, which was why I ultimately kept both.

Once the lists were developed, we were ready for our Verification Focus Groups (VFGs). The purpose of the VFGs was to rigorously vet the final list of indicators that would be included in the community-wide surveys. The VFGs also allow for the verification of the indicators gleaned from the focus group transcripts. Participants often had a much clearer idea of what we were trying to collect once they saw these lists and were able to add more relevant indicators. In addition, some of the original indicators had little or no value and were merely anecdotal. Therefore, the VFGs offered an opportunity to discuss the lists with the groups again and ensure that the final selected indicators were the most representative of a particular community. In the VFGs, representatives from each of the original groups met with each other in order to discuss and determine the final integrated list of indicators. This was because it was unfeasible to include all participants in a second focus group due to time constraints and conflicting schedules. During these discussions, the participants were reminded of the goals and intentions of the indicator generation process. I felt comfortable at this juncture giving participants the lists since they had been generated by earlier community conversations, rather than being examples or indicators written by the research team and imposed on them

Through two group exercises, the participants in the VFGs narrowed down their lists in order to decide which indicators or questions were to be included in the final survey. First the representatives discussed their group's indicator lists and decided what their finalist indicators would be. These groups were facilitated and supported by moderators, especially in areas with high illiteracy. Representatives were encouraged to add or amend the lists generated by the original focus group discussions. These lists were then written on large sheets of easel paper and posted visibly on a tree or wall (Figure 3.1).

Once group members had determined their lists, additional participants were invited from the community to join the VFG. All of the areas where the research was conducted suffered from high unemployment so the pool of potential participants was considerable. Participation was voluntary and so it was probable that focus group participation was skewed in favor of those who were particularly interested in local issues – certainly focus group discussions were often passionate. Participants

FIGURE 3.1. Verification Focus Group participants and lists in Odek, Uganda
Photo credit: Lindsay McClain Opiyo

voted with stickers or pieces of paper for their favorite ten indicators.[14] When deciding which indicators to include in their finalized lists, the premise of the community generated indicator process was explained again to participants and they were asked to consider the following question: Which indicators do you use most often in your daily life when determining whether there is peace in your community?

The final list was discussed in order to conclude the process before being included in surveys conducted in the communities, as described below. Active facilitation by a skilled moderator was key in the second stage of the VFG because individuals were sometimes pressured by their groups to choose certain indicators. Moderators ensured that people were free to choose whichever indicators most reflected their perceptions and also encouraged participants to select from different lists. Depending on context, moderators worked with community members to create a safe space to

[14] I arbitrarily chose ten votes, but kept this constant throughout all of the pilots. In another (more recent) project based on this methodology in the Nangarhar and Kunar Provinces of Afghanistan, I decided to allow community members twenty votes and also kept this number consistent throughout all the villages in that study. Obviously, the more votes that are given to community members, the more indicators that are produced.

allow them to select indicators that most applied for them. In many cases, this meant creating a context where everyone was on their feet voting at once so there was less peer pressure to select a particular indicator.

One of the main challenges of the indicator collection is not unique to this kind of participatory process. Knowledge is constantly evolving and therefore indicators do not remain stagnant. The relevance of indicators is constantly in flux and in question. When and how often communities need to be revisited to determine new indicators is a complex process, one that is dependent on multiple factors. In the survey collection for the cases covered in this book, I did not revisit communities to reconfirm indicators because no significant events had occurred during the timeline of this study.[15] However, I recognize the importance of returning and reconfirming indicators in situations where a community has experienced a significant event, such as a large influx of interventions or another violent event.

USING FOCUS GROUPS FOR MEASUREMENT VALIDITY IN SURVEYS

One of the ways in which social scientists ensure that survey questions are relevant to and understood by respondents is through testing questions or results with focus groups. It is widely recognized in the social sciences that using focus groups is appropriate as a pretest for assessing measurement validity in surveys and other types of instruments.[16] Focus groups can help guide researchers with the kind of nuance necessary to test whether the questions we use in surveys mean what we want them to mean. Therefore, researchers in the social sciences concerned with measurement validity often use focus groups as a strategy to inform questionnaire design, from the formulation of whole question categories to the fine-tuning of wording on particular questions.[17] In order to avoid systematic biases and the data distortions surveys can produce, researchers use focus groups to confirm that survey questions indeed measure what they seek to measure. They can also use focus groups to help interpret results, assess respondent reactions to surveys or simply to triangulate results.[18]

Focus groups have also been used before surveys to anticipate survey nonresponse or refusal problems in hard-to-reach populations and to explore ways to minimize these potential sources of sampling bias.[19] Jennifer Cyr gives examples of recent research in political science and sociology journals that uses focus groups to strengthen survey results. She finds that out of the twelve articles that used this approach, five used focus groups as a pretest to test the validity of their survey instruments. Other studies

---

[15] In November 2016, I returned to the Ugandan communities to revisit the indicators that were chosen three years prior.
[16] Cyr 2015; Wolff et al. 1993; Fuller et al. 1993; O'Brien 1993.
[17] Wolff et al. 1993: 120; Morgan 1996: 134.
[18] Wolff et al. 1993: 120; Cyr 2015: 11.
[19] Desvousges and Frey 1989.

used focus groups to help code dependent variables, to pretest a video used in an experiment and to pretest interview questions, for example.[20]

In addition, proponents of focus groups argue in survey design that focus groups help to reveal or establish consensus and that they can help to relieve the high-effort cognitive thought that is necessary when dealing with complex questions. Therefore, survey participants display less of an inclination to "satisfice" or provide inaccurate answers because the questions require too much cognitive burden and complexity to respond appropriately.[21] Other survey researchers have addressed concerns about shortcomings in open-ended surveys by creating "anchoring vignettes" that elicit responses to hypothetical examples as a way to correct for the "incomparability of responses to survey questions."[22]

Using focus groups and other strategies can help survey researchers develop questions that are easily understood in colloquial language and terminology in order to ensure that better quality data is collected. Specific values of this approach aside, most scholars agree on the value of combining focus groups and surveys in multiple ways and find that this mixed methods approach is one of the most practical ways of bringing together qualitative and quantitative methods.[23]

The Process: Mobile Phone Surveys

The second phase of this study gathers data using mobile phone handset surveys to track change over time in a longitudinal survey based on the everyday indicators.[24] During the survey process, the same survey is repeated several times over a certain time period to track whether or not people's perceptions of peace in their communities have changed. Surveys were conducted on a yearly basis to allow for an adequate amount of time to measure change. The EPIs were surveyed in the community at large through a series of mobile phone handset surveys. Data were collected using mobile phones using an application with the supporting software platform, Mobenzi Researcher.[25]

---

[20] Cyr 2015: 9.
[21] Cyr 2015: 15.
[22] King et al. 2004: 192.
[23] Morgan 1996: 136; Cyr 2015; Wolff et al. 1993.
[24] Panel surveys consisting of repeat households (not respondents) were conducted in both countries; however, the panel surveys were only limited to a small sample of respondents in Uganda since it was difficult to find repeat respondents due to a high level of movement of respondents. On the second and third iterations of the survey, respondents were asked if they had responded to the first survey. In the cases where survey respondents were different, we provided them with the opportunity to find the original respondent or to do the survey themselves, in which case all demographic details were collected. There were thirty-seven repeat respondents in Odek and forty-seven in Atiak on the second round of surveys. However, we ultimately did not use the data in panel survey format since our interest was in tracking change over time for the community as a whole rather than tracking individuals.
[25] www.mobenzi.com/researcher/home

This relatively new data collection process goes by multiple names: mobile phone–assisted personal interviewing (MPAPI),[26] mobile phone handset surveys,[27] mobile researchers[28] or mobile application development platforms. All of these approaches involve face-to-face interviews using an application on a mobile phone or tablet to enter data from responses. Few academic studies exist about mobile phone data collection in conflict-affected contexts, but this kind of survey data collection is becoming more prevalent in studies across the social sciences, and especially in civil society and government sectors. In addition to studies conducted by international organizations,[29] previous "population-based" surveys have been conducted on issues of peace, safety, security and transitional justice.[30]

Various companies offer applications that can be downloaded to mobile phones or tablets, and open source applications are now available.[31] Such applications offer researchers the possibility to upload a survey, which is then distributed to multiple handsets and can be amended in real-time, depending on need, by pressing a button. Fieldworkers use mobile phones to administer the surveys in the field, and once submitted the data is sent directly to the computer interface and can be accessed by the researcher. Mobile application surveys are also appropriate for contexts with little mobile phone reception or access to mobile phones, since they allow for data storage and automatically upload surveys when linked to a network. They can allow for respondents to be randomly selected through a random operator and for fieldworkers to collect data via face-to-face interviews.

Mobile application surveys and personal digital assistant (PDA) surveys are the closest of the mobile phone-based surveys to traditional, clipboard and paper-based surveys. The use of mobile phones and PDAs has been found to be an effective tool for data collection, preferable to a paper-based approach and, in low-income countries, has been used primarily in large-scale public health and agricultural studies.[32] Mobile phone-based systems offer advantages over paper-based surveys by ensuring less margin of error in data entry (due to paper survey loss, destruction or enumerator error), automatic uploading and real-time data analysis. It also allows random selection of respondents through a random operator, GPS and photo integration into surveys, encrypted access to a web-based interface that provides data security and respondent confidentiality, and multi-lingual survey options (versus carrying multiple paper surveys to remote locations). Mobile phone handset surveys can also be more cost effective than paper-based surveys, especially when using open source solutions

---

[26] van Heerden et al. 2014.
[27] Firchow and Mac Ginty 2017b.
[28] Tomlinson et al. 2009.
[29] Demombynes et al. 2013.
[30] See www.peacebuildingdata.org/
[31] http://opendatakit.org/ or www.kobotoolbox.org/
[32] Tomlinson et al. 2009; Yu et al. 2009; van Heerden et al. 2014.

such as opendatakit.org or kobotoolbox.org.[33] Disadvantages can be associated with the risk of the enumerator carrying an item of relative value in areas with high rates of crime, battery life issues, the need to connect to a network in order to update surveys and possible increased training times for enumerators.[34] Van Heerden et al. also found that the advantages of survey mode depend on the context in which the survey is being undertaken. Handset surveys may be more amenable to large, complex studies lasting several years across multiple sites with poor infrastructure (such as this one), whereas paper surveys may be more useful when start-up time is limited.

EPI Survey Data Collection

Survey participants in the communities were asked to answer questions on a 1 to 5 Likert-type Scale: 1. Never; 2. Rarely; 3. Sometimes; 4. Often; or 5. Always. Wherever possible, all participants, regardless of survey mode, were provided with a printed Likert-type Scale card, which provided visual representation and local language translation of the possible answers. In the event that the card was unavailable, enumerators were trained to repeat Likert-type Scale answers after every question. A Likert-type Scale response was chosen because it provided the most detailed account of people's perceptions while still providing the researchers with a quantifiable response. This was the most effective way to control for *differential item functioning* (DIF), a term for interpersonal incomparability or the incomparability of responses to survey questions in cross-cultural surveys.[35] In addition, survey participants were asked demographic questions about levels of education, location (within the villages), gender, ethnic identity and age. Respondents were also asked questions about interventions in the communities and their perceptions of whether or not they had been beneficiaries of these interventions and who provided them. Response fields were set to different options, such as skipping questions or rerouting questions depending on previous answers. The survey started with an introduction and the following statement to comply with ethical requirements:

> Welcome to the Everyday Peace Indicators survey. The purpose of this survey is to understand everyday experiences of peace and safety in Atiak. It contains two sections and will require 20 to 25 minutes to complete. Your participation in this survey is voluntary and your responses are anonymous. You may stop participating at any time. Do I have your permission to begin the survey?

A total of 2,038 surveys were conducted for this study. The research teams conducted 1,230 surveys in El Salado and Don Gabriel, Colombia, and 808 surveys in Atiak

---

[33] van Heerden 2014: 318.
[34] van Heerden 2014: 319.
[35] King et al. 2004: 192.

and Odek, Uganda.[36] The response rate in the villages was extremely high because local enumerators were working with the mobile phone applications.[37] Sampling of individual village residents varied by country.[38] In Colombia, the entire villages were surveyed and therefore did not require a sampling procedure.[39] In Uganda, Odek and Atiak are sub-counties, which are then further divided into parishes and then villages. Atiak has eight parishes and sixteen villages, and Odek has four parishes, which are further divided into twenty-four villages. I used cluster sampling to select parishes over villages because of population sparsity and the long distances needed to travel. We selected three parishes in Odek – Palaro, Lamola and Binya – and four parishes in Atiak – Kal, Okidi, Pacilo and Parwaca – by pulling names out of a hat.[40] The responses in Atiak were relatively evenly distributed among parishes (except in the first round where the majority of responses came from Kal). In Odek, the majority of respondents came from Palaro.[41]

Every second home in each parish was then selected to respond to the surveys. When enumerators arrived in the villages, they were instructed to spin a bottle and start counting in the direction of the bottle. Randomization was a complex process and required significant training of enumerators and partner staff to ensure the process was done as thoroughly as possible.[42] Because I was unable to obtain lists of

[36] A total of 606 surveys were conducted in the first round of surveys in March of 2016 in Colombia (306 in El Salado and 300 in Don Gabriel). 624 more surveys were conducted between February and June of 2017 (308 in Don Gabriel and 315 in El Salado). A total of 202 surveys were conducted in the first round in August of 2014 (101 Atiak and 101 in Odek) and a total of 302 surveys were conducted in July of 2015 (152 in Atiak and 150 in Odek). Another 304 surveys were conducted in Uganda in July 2016 for a total of 808 surveys.

[37] In the first round, only four households in El Salado were not surveyed, because of refusals or because the inhabitants were away. In Don Gabriel, fifteen households refused to be surveyed or were away for the duration of the survey time. Of the surveys completed, all questions were answered.

[38] This was mainly due to the difficulty of access and expansiveness of terrain in Uganda and the different kind of organization of villages and parishes at the local level than in Colombia. Villages in Uganda are often more like Veredas (the surrounding areas to villages) in Colombia and households are at significant distances from each other. This complicates the survey process significantly, which was why there was a lower number of surveys in Uganda as well.

[39] Both communities are approximately at 20 kilometers from the municipality (Carmen de Bolivar in the case of El Salado and Ovejas in the case of Don Gabriel) and have a population size of approximately 1,500 to 2,000. Both villages depend mainly on agricultural-generated livelihoods and the villages have electricity (although the surrounding areas do not). Inhabitants are of mestizo origin and both communities have Catholic and protestant/evangelical communities and churches. See Chapter 4 for more information on the community selection process.

[40] I had the local authorities and sub-county commissioners do this in our presence so that they felt comfortable with our selection of respondents.

[41] As of 2014, Atiak sub-county had a population of 38,300 and Odek sub-county had a population of 32,218. Inhabitants of both communities primarily identify as Acholi. Average daily income in both communities is under one dollar and inhabitants are mainly peasant farmers and traders. Atiak is on the highway and border between Uganda and South Sudan with an active border market at Elegu. Odek has a trading center with surrounding villages and is not located on a main road. See Chapter 4 for more information on the community selection process.

[42] Kapiszewski et al. 2015: 322.

residents, our selection of participants was as random as possible given the operating circumstances. Whenever possible, we tried to work during times in which families were in their homes, although it was sometimes difficult to include those working or traveling in the random selection process. In order to ensure a representative sample of household members, a random operator was set into the application survey design that ensured random selection of respondents within each household:

> A randomly selected member of your household will be asked to complete this survey. We will begin with some basic details. Including you, how many people live in your household? Please give me the names of the people who are currently at home and are above the age of 18. We would like to speak with XX who has been randomly selected to complete this survey.

Necessary Connections

By now it must be clear to the reader how important it was to secure a trusted civil society partner in order to carry out the fieldwork required for both the qualitative and quantitative data presented in this book. The work was carried out effectively because of the strong community connections of the two civil society partners I worked with, and because of their knowledge of the issues and challenges confronting the communities selected for the study. Such partnerships are fundamental for the everyday indicator generation to be successful and produce quality indicators for both research and evaluation purposes. Also, questions of access and trust were made simpler because of our work through our partners, who had long-standing connections and relationships with people in the regions (if not in the communities) in which we worked. Kapiszewski, Maclean and Read stress the importance of partnering with local organizations when conducting field research and experiments, since they can legitimize an experimental study and encourage participation.[43]

Yet, working with NGO partners does not come without its challenges. Civil society actors can be very political – the idea that civil society is an unbiased, autonomous and representative counter-weight to the state is often misplaced. As discussed in Chapter 1, in many countries civil society elites are much closer to political elites than the people they purportedly represent. They are thus susceptible to elite capture or may shape or manipulate decision-making processes in ways that serve their own interests.[44] Civil society also varies enormously between and within contexts. The label has a meaning which those in the peacebuilding or development community might all share, but the reality of civil society on the ground is often different and far more complex. When we use it as a conceptual label to refer to a shared ideal it risks becoming a limiting if not meaningless term. Therefore, it is important

---

[43] Kapiszewski et al. 2015.
[44] Platteau 2004; Fritzen 2007; Labonte 2011: 91.

to choose wisely when working with a partner to ensure that they see the value in using everyday indicators to monitor their own work in communities. A combination of local acumen, incentive and common interests and goals are necessary when choosing an adequate partner to implement the EPI framework.

Kapiszewski, Maclean and Read also point to Judith Gueron's essay, in which she deals at length with the tensions that can arise between researchers and partner organizations. Such tensions, she writes, often stem from partners' commitment to a randomized study before fully understanding its implications and challenges. Therefore, the onus is placed on the researcher to ensure that selection criteria, research goals, research guidelines and training guides are thoroughly communicated through research protocols; however, research expectations should always be confirmed and discussed in personal communications through phone and in person with NGO staff since, there may be insufficient reading of these documents within the busy rhythms of NGO workdays. Whether using the Everyday Indicators for research or monitoring and evaluation purposes, it is of extreme importance to have personnel responsible for consistently working with partners across the various contexts to maintain consistency and quality of indicator collection and monitoring. In addition, in projects such as this one that function over a multiple-year timeframe, staff turnover can be a serious impediment to a fluid execution of the research design. Therefore, it is imperative to remain flexible and to visit project sites often and keep in touch with project personnel.

Fundación Semana (Colombia) and the Justice and Reconciliation Project (Uganda)

The civil society partners that formed a part of the research team for this study were the *Fundación Semana* in Colombia and the Justice and Reconciliation Project in Uganda. Both organizations have well-established connections to the communities participating in this study, especially to those that have received large amounts of interventions. Fundación Semana was created in 2009 by *Semana*, a leading weekly news and analysis magazine in Colombia. They recount their mission as addressing

> the most important topics for Colombia in the next decades: post-conflict and reconciliation.[45]

Fundación Semana was led until recently since its establishment by Ms. Claudia García, a former journalist and the wife of Mr. Daniel Samper Ospina, the nephew of former President Ernesto Samper Pizano. Fundación Semana started out primarily by publicizing El Salado and gaining national attention through a campaign selling

---

[45] www.fundacionsemana.com/seccion/quienes-somos/6 (translation by author; accessed September 26, 2017).

bracelets to support reconstruction programming in the village. Quickly, the organization also established an office and base in the village with a young and energetic staff primarily from Bogota. They worked with the community to establish community development plans in seven fundamental areas: infrastructure, economic development, community development, education, culture & sports, health and security. Based on these plans Fundación Semana developed workplans in coordination with national and local government entities as well as other nongovernmental organizations. For example, the village had gone for years without a health center or funding for any kind of medical assistance. Fundación Semana helped redirect government health funding that was already earmarked for El Salado, but had been stopped because of corruption, violence and displacement, in order to furnish the health center with a nurse and rotating doctor. Breakdowns that had occurred because of the war and displacement were relatively easy for the Fundación to disentangle through a few phone calls, due to its connections in Bogota.

However, Fundación Semana also depends largely on soft money or money funded for specific programs, and is therefore largely donor-driven. Grants are often given in an *ad hoc* manner when García is approached by other Colombian elites to fund projects or initiatives in the village. There is little proactive pursuit of funding for the participatory development plans established at the beginning of Fundación Semana's tenure in El Salado.[46] Understanding Fundación Semana's role in El Salado is fundamental to comprehending the results of this study and the interventions and dynamics that have developed in the village over the last decade.

The Justice and Reconciliation Project (JRP) is a Gulu-based organization in northern Uganda. The organization began with a study on the meanings and relevance of spiritual dimensions of justice for the Acholi people, including traditional justice mechanisms such as *mato oput*. The report from their study, "Roco Wat I Acoli – Restoring Relationships in Acholi-land: Traditional Approaches to Justice and Reintegration," was published in 2005. JRP began working around the Juba Peace Talks, documenting and publishing field notes on northern Ugandans' experiences with the war that had ravaged the region up until that time.[47] Co-founded by Professor Erin Baines and Mr. Michael Otim in 2005, JRP conducts community-based and victim-centered peacebuilding research and advocacy. JRP works mainly in the area of what they call "local level transitional justice" and focuses on community documentation, community mobilization and gender justice. Their work was mainly funded by the Norwegian government and other international donors, including USAID (until recently). JRP documented the Atiak massacre and

---

[46] Interviews with Fundación Semana staff (March 2016); interviews with community leaders in El Salado (March 2016).
[47] Voices, Issue 10, November 2015. http://justiceandreconciliation.com/publications/newsletters-magazines/2015/voices10/ (accessed September 26, 2017).

widely disseminated its report,[48] supported memorialization efforts, conducted victim exchanges between survivors from Atiak and from other communities, as well as conducting capacity building on advocacy and transitional justice-related issues. In 2013, when I began working with JRP, they had not yet conducted any work in Odek. However, JRP's experiences in Odek conducting focus groups for the EPI project precipitated documentary work once they saw how neglected the community was, due to the stigma surrounding its identity as Joseph Kony's birthplace.[49] As JRP is one of the few organizations in the region dedicated entirely to *small-p* related peacebuilding activities, understanding their role in the community is also fundamental to understanding the analysis of the survey results and indicators collected for this study.

Participatory Research in Action

Significant experimentation was necessary in order to capture participatory, bottom-up indicators of peace. While participatory methods have been widely developed, especially in development studies, this methodology remains underutilized, particularly to source quantitative data. Our approach has been to combine qualitative and quantitative methods to produce participatory numbers and participatory statistics.[50] The research design for this project is driven by the premise that communities affected by war know best what peace means to them and, therefore, should be the primary and first source of information on peacebuilding effectiveness. However, unlike pure participatory approaches, the everyday indicator process had already been conceptualized prior to contact with the communities, and we only needed community input and participation to create the indicators.[51] Therefore, this approach is not a straightforward form of PAR, since we enter communities with a formulated plan developed by researchers. As Rajesh Tandon explains, there are three determinants of the basis of participatory approaches: 1) people's role in setting the agenda of inquiry; 2) people's participation in data collection and analysis; and 3) people's control over the outcome and the whole process.[52] Robin McTaggart distinguishes PAR from other kinds of research by its unit of analysis. He argues that other methodologies typically make people the objects of their research (therefore doing research *on* people), whereas PAR's unit of analysis includes the researcher and therefore does research *with* people.[53]

---

[48] The Justice and Reconciliation Project Field Notes, No. 4, April 2007. http://justiceandreconciliation.com/wp-content/uploads/2007/04/JRP_FN4_Atiak.pdf (accessed September 26, 2017).
[49] The Justice and Reconciliation Project Field Notes, No. 21, November 2014. http://justiceandreconciliation.com/wp-content/uploads/2014/12/Forgotten-Victims-Recounting-Atrocities-Committed-in-OdekSub-County-by-the-LRA-and-NRA.pdf (accessed September 26, 2017).
[50] Chambers 2007b; Holland 2013.
[51] Firchow and Mac Ginty (2017); Mac Ginty 2013a.
[52] Tandon 1988: 213.
[53] McTaggart 1991: 171.

Participatory research typically requires the respondents in a research project to serve as co-researchers, therefore changing the traditional dichotomy of the researcher and the researched. Those who are usually considered the subjects of a research project must actively participate in the process of creating that research project. PAR proponents also distinguish actively between involvement and participation and warn that merely involving people can risk their cooptation and exploitation in the realization of the plans of others.[54]

The everyday indicator approach requires communities to develop indicators themselves (with guidance and facilitation) as well as participate in the experimental phases of their development. This is in keeping with participatory impact assessment techniques in human development approaches.[55] However, it does not allow them to set the agenda of inquiry. It does provide them a vessel through which their input can influence potential research or interventions. It offers a strategy to communicate community needs and problems to third parties in a systematic way. The everyday indicator approach does not give people control over the outcome and the whole process as Tandon recommends. However, it does indirectly include the communities in the development of both applied and academic research and intervention projects.

Some PAR researchers might take issue and contend that the everyday indicators approach does not constitute PAR because it is only participatory insofar as it uses participatory processes to influence policymakers, and does not impact communities directly. It is true that there is no inherent direct benefit to the community members participating in the project, apart from the dialogue created in the focus groups, especially if the project in question is strictly research-related and not tied to the design and implementation of intervention. Yet, the process and systematization of the indicators creates a direct feedback loop that is very participatory and accessible both to elites as well as community members and local peacebuilders, in a language and context that everyone can understand.

In 1983, Robert Chambers published one of the cardinal texts on PAR, *Rural Development: Putting the Last First*. In it he argues exactly what the title implies – that academics and practitioners should focus on the rural, impoverished areas of the world when doing research and address poverty rather than participate in the more elite-focused, urban-centered work driven by outsiders. Chambers uses the term Participatory Rural Appraisal (PRA) when he discusses the approach he uses for participatory research in villages. For Chambers, the many different kinds of PRA-related efforts share a space and come from the same family, but differ in decisive ways. In fact, there are myriad different kinds of participatory research models, including activist participatory research, agro-ecosystem analysis, applied

---

[54] McTaggart 1991: 171.
[55] Catley et al. 2013: 18–25.

anthropology, field research on farming systems and rapid rural appraisal.[56] I will focus on two of these here – activist participatory research and rapid rural appraisal – since these are the most applicable to the everyday indicator system.

Activist participatory research uses dialogue and participatory research to empower communities and individuals to work toward change. It is influenced by the work of Paulo Freire and his book *Pedagogy of the Oppressed* (1968), in which he argues that the poor and exploited should reflect on their own situations and participate in the analysis of their own realities.[57] This *conscientization* or critical consciousness-building process is a cornerstone of activist participatory research that enables people to reflect on their own situations as an outcome of historical and political processes. Chambers classifies activist participatory research as the home for both participatory research and PAR, in which outsiders have roles as conveners, catalysts and facilitators and the marginalized can be empowered through doing much of their own investigation, analysis and planning.[58] An activist participatory research ethos meshes well with the development of the everyday indicators approach as an advocacy tool to use indigenous knowledge to affect policy decisions.

Rapid Rural Appraisal (RRA) was developed in the late 1970s as a fast, cost-effective and persuasive tool for planning and evaluation in development. There are many different forms of RRAs, and they do not all necessarily have to be conducted in rural settings. But all RRAs have a few things in common: they are typically faster-paced than more conventional methods of participatory assessment and evaluation; they involve fieldwork in the studied setting; they emphasize learning directly from local inhabitants; they leave room for flexibility and are typically semi-structured and multidisciplinary or multi-method; and, finally, they emphasize producing timely insights or hypotheses rather than final truths or fixed recommendations to inform program development and evaluation. RRA is essentially a faster and more cost-effective way to gain insight from local people and is a set of tools for gathering their indigenous technical knowledge. RRA is typically more concerned with methodological rigor than most PAR approaches and also focuses on communicating results to the outside world rather than the community itself, very much like the EPI process.

Some may consider the Everyday Peace Indicators project as being another form of RRA. Although EPI exhibits some of the characteristics of PAR, they are predominantly extractive and elicitive since the information collected is taken to policymakers, this is unlike more participatory-oriented research that focuses on empowering local people directly through research. Therefore, it is more akin to RRA forms of PAR. For example, we purposefully did not want to reveal from the outset that we were gathering indicators of peace for fear of inadvertently influencing the participants. It was more important for us to create a comfortable environment

[56] Chambers 2013 (first published 1983): 954.
[57] Freire 2000 (originally published in 1968).
[58] Chambers 2013: 954.

in which participants could speak about their perceptions of peace and how they went about identifying it, than to explain our intentions to create lists of indicators. This approach is, of course, in contrast to traditional PAR processes, where objectivity and distance from the researched are sacrificed for reflective subjectivity.[59] Yet the EPIs can be seen as a tool that promotes learning for both outsiders and locals and that can promote sustainable local action if used by the community members and local peacebuilders. It also promotes discussion and organization around matters concerning peace in a community and can be seen as a peacebuilding tool in and of itself. It is a matter of how that tool is used which influences its impact on communities. It may be that the EPIs lie somewhere on the participatory spectrum and, depending on how they are used and the consequences of that action, are more extractive or more empowering. Regardless of the form of participation, qualitative and quantitative rapid rural appraisal forms and approaches to measuring and planning development and peacebuilding programming form a part of action research that involves communities and takes an inductive approach.

It is my view that there are several approaches to PAR and all are part of a family of research methodologies that pursue action and research at the same time through participatory channels. The EPIs are an attempt to systematize such processes in order to directly influence program development and evaluation with community input and form part of a quantitative subset of PAR.[60] Of course, Robin McTaggart's warnings should be heeded and the cooptive potential of the everyday indicators acknowledged, since they can be highly vulnerable to cooptation if they are taken out of context and used without solid contextual knowledge of the communities within which they are collected.

The next chapter describes the community selection process for the implementation of the everyday peace indicator process as part of the larger study to empirically investigate the impact of local level interventions on community-defined peacefulness. It gives an overview of the communities selected as well as a justification for their selection.

---

[59] McTaggart 1994.
[60] Chambers 2010.

PART II

Evaluating Everyday Peace

4

Everyday Peace in Uganda and Colombia

INTRODUCTION

Even with a commitment to inclusion in design and evaluation, how do we go about adequately assessing the effectiveness of peacebuilding interventions in communities after conflict? There are often a significant number of programs and projects undertaken after war, implemented by a plethora of actors. And, as we assess what is effective, and what is needed, how can we identify which local experiences are highly contextual and unique to a certain community, and in contrast, those post-conflict needs that might be shared by other, very different communities emerging from conflict?

To answer these questions, this cross-national study was designed to compare and contrast levels and definitions of peace between and among four post-conflict communities in Uganda and Colombia. A cross-national study offers a dependent variable – levels of community-defined peace – to give insight into two independent variables: levels of post-conflict intervention and cultural particularism (or conversely, universality). The first order comparison, across communities in the same country, examines levels of postwar intervention while controlling for historical, demographic and geographic similarity. The study pairs two communities in each country that share demographic, and geographic traits and have similar histories of violence, but experience very different levels of postwar intervention. The second order of comparison, across countries, allows for the study of a second independent variable – that of cultural particularism – to determine what postwar community perceptions or needs may either be universal or unique to that community or country. It enables us to draw more global conclusions about the role of intervention in determining levels of community peace and the universality or uniqueness of community perceptions of peace and recovery. Case studies from two significantly different contexts allow for comparison and increased understanding of which community experiences in postwar recovery are culturally dependent and which may be universal.

This chapter gives background to and justification for the selected case studies. The study uses a rigorous matched case research design in these four communities, supplemented by interviews with community members, local elites and national elites in both countries. The conclusions of this study are based on 2,038 surveys in Uganda and Colombia in addition to an analysis of the selected everyday indicators. Data from the study demonstrates the utility of the everyday peace indicators in measuring peace in a range of post-conflict contexts, both within and between countries.

CROSS-NATIONAL CASE SELECTION

Few comparative studies exist of communities involved in peacebuilding processes after experiencing mass violence.[1] Cross-regional studies are even more rare at the sub-national level.[2] A notable exception is the Listening Project's work in twenty-one countries, gathering experiences of more than 6,000 people who have received international aid.[3] An academic preoccupation with institutional design and system-level effects has resulted in too little concern for how peacebuilding processes affect the recipients of community-based programs. The current study is part of a recent effort to fill this gap in scholarship.[4] There have been ample individual case studies and ethnographies that have shed light on the way societies experience and deal with the aftermath of mass violence in Peru,[5] Cambodia,[6] Indonesia,[7] Northern Uganda,[8] Guatemala,[9] South Africa,[10] Rwanda,[11] and Burundi,[12] among others. These studies are strong resources for evaluating the consequences of local, post-conflict interventions, but, because they each focus on different specific conflicts and case studies, they are not as effective as a comparative cross-national analysis in establishing links and general patterns that contribute to the study of local-level interventions after war. Nor do they offer strong insight into which post-conflict recovery dimensions are culturally unique and which ones may be universal across contexts.

The selected cross-continental case studies are designed to illustrate the utility of the everyday indicator framework in two very different contexts. Variance is found

---

[1] Overall, there are few cross-regionally comparative studies of conflict analysis and resolution. Another exception is: Christia 2012.
[2] Backer 2009.
[3] Anderson et al. 2012.
[4] Skaar, Malca et al. 2015; Christia 2012; Riaño-Alcalá and Baines 2011.
[5] Theidon 2012.
[6] Hinton 2004b.
[7] Dwyer 2012; Dwyer and Santikarma 2018.
[8] Baines 2007; Finnström 2008.
[9] Arriaza and Roht-Arriaza 2008.
[10] Minow 1998.
[11] Clark 2010; Thomson 2013.
[12] Nee and Uvin 2010.

in most dimensions – language, culture, ethnicity, location, etc. However, countries that share two core similarities were selected. The first is key factors of interest: selected communities had similar experiences with mass violence and displacement and were targets of rebel groups during the same time periods. The second is the outcome of violence: communities had uneven experiences with third party interventions in the aftermath. Such an approach allows an investigation of the relationship between levels of postwar intervention and levels of community-reported peace across contexts that experienced similar levels and types of violence around the same time periods.

The selection of two conflict-affected contexts such as Uganda and Colombia allows us to see if interventions work similarly across continents and cultures. It gives third parties an idea of the effectiveness of the Everyday Peace Indicators approach in different cultural contexts, therefore broadening the scope of the project.[13] Cases are selected where civilians and, more specifically, collectives (e.g. villages) have been the victims of mass violence and displacement, since these experiences are especially important for measuring their perceptions of peace after varying levels of third party interventions.[14]

A cross-national study of community perceptions of peace and justice across cultures and contexts is useful for many reasons. By reflecting the different experiences of communities affected by mass violence, the study can help identify trends and comparisons of the multiple dimensions of peace that give us insights into differing community-level perceptions of and interactions with violent conflict. It helps us understand what mechanisms and interventions may be more effective for addressing the aftermath of violent conflict and allows us to investigate which are more or less useful in different contexts. It also gives us the opportunity to follow the stories and experiences of communities in different contexts in order to understand more fully how they are accompanied by outside actors working in communities affected by war. Whether or not experiences in different contexts are similar for communities is interesting to scholars, practitioners, and community members themselves, who are working to most effectively build sustainable peace after war.

The cross-national and cross-continental comparison presented in the study is important for evaluating cultural and geographical variance and to confirm findings. We can have a greater level of confidence in conclusions about the efficacy of postwar intervention if they are reached in two different contexts. I now turn to the comparisons between Uganda and Colombia, in experiences of violent conflict that provide the basis for an effective cross-national comparison.

---

[13] Walker and Cohen 1985.
[14] For more on generating lists of potential case studies for case selection, see Goertz 2016.

Violent Conflict and Its Legacy in Uganda and Colombia

Uganda and Colombia share long legacies of violence, which can be traced back through decades if not centuries of their colonial histories. Both have been challenged by non-state armed actors and have experienced significant human rights abuses, as well as internally displaced populations. Communities and civilians were targeted in both countries and many villages were displaced after experiencing gruesome massacres because their allegiances with armed actors from both sides were questioned.

Not only did communities suffer at the hands of armed actors in both countries, but they were also targeted precisely because of their relationships with opposing groups. In what Carolyn Nordstrom calls a dirty war, in which "both states and guerrilla forces use the construction of terror and the absurd as a mechanism for gaining or maintaining socio-political control over a population,"[15] civilians were used as pawns to escalate conflict and create an environment of fear. Many scholars have argued over the years that since the end of the Cold War, civilians have become more entangled in war, often as direct targets of armed combatants.[16] Uganda and Colombia are examples of this kind of warfare, both prior to and after the end of the Cold War. Communities were torn apart, civilians targeted by both government and insurgent groups, families destroyed – all before 1990. However, violence intensified by the end of the decade and into the early 2000s in both countries, and in particular in those areas included in this study, until attempts at cessation of hostility were made in both countries around 2005. All of the participating communities in this study in Colombia and Uganda were affected by massacres and displacement during a similar time frame – from 1995 to 2005.

Although efforts were made around 2005 to halt the political violence between armed actors and against civilians in Uganda and Colombia, criminal activities surrounding the conflicts expanded in both countries. The demobilization of the paramilitary groups in Colombia and the cessation of political violence in Uganda did not end the war and, most definitely, did not create peace for Colombians and Ugandans. In Uganda, criminal groups are frequently connected with the Ugandan army and are linked to post-conflict networks. The *Boo-Kec* and *Pit Kumi* in Acholi or *Cel Ibong* in Lango carry guns and grenades sometimes given to them by Ugandan army commanders in order to capitalize on the chaos of conflict to harass, loot and kill. These groups aim to take advantage of the spoils of war.

Ugandan criminal groups are less organized and certainly less financially powerful than those in Colombia. Colombia's drug trade has fueled the conflict there for at least forty years and paramilitary and other armed groups were actively involved in the smuggling, processing and taxing of cocaine production throughout the conflict

---

[15] Nordstrom 1992: 261.
[16] Kaldor 1999; Duffield 2001.

period. When a political peace process disbanded the paramilitaries in 2005, eliminating them as official actors in the war, criminal gangs stepped into the vacuum and grew more powerful as they created a network of post-conflict criminal activities. Many paramilitary members continued their activity in the drug trade under another name. They took advantage of the opportunities provided by the ceasefire, including the weapons no longer needed for political violence. The name *Bacrim* – an abbreviation of the Spanish for criminal gangs: "BAndas CRIMinales" – was created by President Uribe to distinguish between the United Self Defense Forces (AUC) and the criminal gangs. All of the Bacrim organizations originated from military or paramilitary groups and continue to have some ties to the military.

Sustained criminal and political violence also created a large number of Internally Displaced Persons (IDPs), often living in IDP camps, in both countries. In Uganda, villagers were forced by government forces, often at gunpoint, to move into IDP camps near their villages for their alleged safety, but effectively to remain under the control of the government. In both cases, all of the most affected communities were uprooted and entirely displaced because of the violence they experienced, and have only been resettled in the last five years, if at all. All of the communities in this study experienced extreme displacement and in all cases the villages were left empty for a time period due to fear and forced displacement. All the villages have now been resettled by many of their former inhabitants. Colombia continues to have a significant IDP problem, whereas in Uganda most IDPs have been resettled and communities now deal with a critical refugee problem from neighboring South Sudan. In 2006, UNHCR estimated that Uganda had at least 1.4 million IDPs.[17] The same report ranked Colombia as the second largest displaced population in the world after Sudan with 2 to 3 million displaced persons.[18]

Human Rights, Development and Peacebuilding Interventions

Both Uganda and Colombia experienced the peculiarity of having transitional justice mechanisms implemented before the armed conflicts were officially terminated, and in the absence of signed peace accords.[19] Unlike most countries where transitional justice has been used as a tool for transitions to democracy, the Ugandan

---

[17] UNHCR 2007.
[18] In addition to some shared war experiences, the countries are both majority Christian, although there is an important Muslim minority in Uganda. Religious syncretism is practiced widely in Uganda and Colombia and the Christian majorities are often influenced by indigenous religions. Officially, in Uganda, Catholics made up 42 percent of the population according to Uganda's 2002 census (the last census that asked this question), followed by 36 percent Anglicans and 12 percent Muslims. In Colombia, located in a traditionally Catholic region, 79 percent of people identify as Catholics, 13 percent as Protestant and 25 percent as other. As in the rest of Latin America, Colombian membership in the Catholic Church has decreased as more people report finding protestant churches more attractive and attentive to their needs.
[19] Reparations in the case of Colombia and ICC indictments in the case of Uganda.

and Colombian governments have stayed intact during implementation and discussion of transitional justice efforts.

Uganda

Yoweri Museveni has been the president of Uganda since 1986, and although his tenure was significantly challenged in the 2006 elections by Kizze Besigye, he continues to hold power. It was Museveni who had referred the rebel Lord's Resistance Army (LRA) to the International Criminal Court (ICC) in December of 2003, which caused significant upheaval and contributed to the foundering of the peace agreement. In October 2005, the ICC issued its first arrest warrants since its establishment. Five LRA commanders were targeted: Joseph Kony, Vincent Otti, Raska Lukwiya, Okot Odhiambo and Dominic Ongwen. The ICC's alignment with Museveni was evident and was a sign that politics would be influential in the decisions of the fledgling criminal court since there was little discussion of indicting government officials for their part in the war. In 2000 an Amnesty Act was implemented that allowed thousands of combatants from all rebel groups operating in Uganda to return to their homes and access reintegration packages. The Act was withdrawn in May 2012 on the grounds that the war was over, but reinstated again in 2013 after significant outcry from civil society organizations that were concerned it would disincentivize combatants still fighting in the bush.

In addition, the government of Uganda established a war crimes division in the Ugandan High Court, named the International Crimes Division (ICD), in 2011. The ICD purports to have the ability to conduct fair trials for serious crimes against humanity. However, a report by the International Center of Transitional Justice refutes this claim.[20] The report demonstrates the weaknesses of the court as evidenced by the trial of Thomas Kwoyelo, an LRA commander charged with kidnapping and intent to murder. Although the ICD was in existence at the time of Dominic Ongwen's arrest, he continues to be on trial at the ICC and has not been transferred back to Uganda to be tried by the ICD.

The Government of Uganda created a development program for Northern Uganda in 2007 covering fifty-five districts and nine municipalities. Implemented from 2009 to 2015, the Peace Recovery and Development Plan (PRDP) attempted to provide a framework for recovery of the region for all development actors (non-governmental and governmental) along four strategic objectives:

1. Consolidation of state authority
2. Rebuilding and empowering communities
3. Revitalization of the economy
4. Peacebuilding and reconciliation

---

[20] Kihika and Regué 2015.

Initially funding for the PRDP was only available until 2012, but it was extended until 2015 in order to "consolidate peace and strengthen the foundations for development in Northern Uganda."[21] Examples of interventions under this plan encompass everything from: the provision of equipment and logistics to ensure the functionality of existing local government facilities; human rights training for all police personnel; support to traditional and transitional justice processes; constructing new prisoner wards; training and equipping Village Health Teams; classroom construction and rehabilitation; the provision of safe water through construction of water points; constructing and rehabilitating valley tanks, valley dams, canals, drainage, ponds, constructing market facilities; sensitization on the Amnesty Law process to enhance community unity.[22] The current PRDP plan mainly deals with livelihoods, job creation and placements. Although the PRDP includes some *small-p* peacebuilding initiatives, overall it is clearly a *big-P* Peacebuilding initiative with a pronounced emphasis on economic development and reconstruction.[23]

In addition to these government-led initiatives, there have also been smaller scale interventions led by local and international civil society actors.[24] At the community level, a range of local rituals have been used to reintegrate former LRA combatants and reconcile them with victims and affected communities. These practices, including the Acholi rituals *mato oput* and *gomo tong*, focus on perpetrator confession, cleansing, reparation and reintegration.[25]

Colombia

Every sixth Colombian is now officially classified as a victim of the war.[26] Victim categorization includes anyone who was killed, forcibly disappeared or displaced since the war began in 1956. Colombia has been groundbreaking in its approach to post-conflict recovery by placing a premium on victim involvement and participation in the peace process and also including victims in peace agreement discussions in Havana.[27] Colombia's so-called Victim's Law of 2011 (Law 1448) – the most ambitious reparations law of its kind according to legal scholars – is an example of a fervent effort to integrate reparations into a post-conflict transition.[28] It, along with

---

[21] PRDP 2.
[22] See PRDP 2 for more details.
[23] For a commissioned evaluation report of the impact of the PRDP on peace and conflict on the region, see International Alert's 2014 report "Monitoring the impact of the Peace, Recovery and Development Plan on Peace and Conflict in Northern Uganda." http://international-alert.org/publications/monitoring-impact-prdp-2014 (accessed March 15, 2018).
[24] See list of interventions in Appendix 1.
[25] Harlacher et al. 2006.
[26] This is according to my own calculations taking into account the number of victims in the National Victims registrar divided by the current population of Colombia. Parts of this section were published previously in Firchow 2017.
[27] Bouvier 2015.
[28] Summers 2012.

several other laws, decrees and judicial rulings, forms part of Colombia's policies regarding direct and indirect (displaced) victims of different armed actors since the internal war began in 1956. Law 1448 explicitly lists reconciliation and peace as its central aims and declares itself to be founded on the principles of transitional justice. It also specifically lists the goals of reparations as national and local reconciliation and establishes a Victims Unit as the agency responsible for oversight.[29]

In addition, transitional justice committees, which included civil society and government actors, were established to oversee the war to peace transition. Civil society actors have also been active in many communities to implement projects mandated at the national and international levels.[30]

In both cases, the state has discussed repairing victims of the conflict. However, the Colombian state has actually begun the reparations process, whereas the Ugandan state has only gotten as far as establishing a governmental inter-ministerial working group dedicated to transitional justice matters.[31] Colombia passed Law 975, also known as the Justice and Peace Law, in 2005. This law provided the legal framework for the demobilization of the AUC and the official dissolution of the paramilitary groups as a political armed actor. Unsurprisingly, there was widespread criticism of the process and many human rights groups decried it as incomplete and unfair because many AUC members were granted amnesty as a part of the agreement. There were some small efforts at supporting victims of the conflict after Law 975 was passed, including reparations, but it was not until 2011, when President Santos passed the Victim's Law, that greater recognition and reparation was paid to victims of the armed conflict. More recently since July of 2016, the signing of the Peace Accords between the Government and FARC portends further changes, as

---

[29] Law 1448 clearly stresses goals of reconciliation and peace. Article 8 states that transitional justice should "have the final goal of achieving national reconciliation and durable and sustainable peace." Article 9 states: "In terms of transitional justice, judicial and administrative authorities should *overridingly adjust their actions in order to obtain reconciliation and a durable and stable peace* (emphasis my own)." Article 11 states, "the law seeks to complement and harmonize the different efforts of the state to guarantee the rights to truth, justice and reparation of victims and smooth out the path to national peace and reconciliation." Article 12 "seeks to complement and harmonize the measures of restitution, compensation, rehabilitation, satisfaction and guarantees of non-repetition, with a view to smooth out the path to peace and national reconciliation." Article 33 recognizes that the state, civil society and the private sector should be included, especially in terms of reparations, in order to work for national reconciliation and victim rights. Article 139 discusses measures of satisfaction and mentions the construction of public monuments as a form of reparation and reconciliation. Article 145 discusses education as a form of reconciliation. Article 149 discusses guarantees of nonrepetition and a social pedagogy of reconciliation, as well as the implementation of strategies, projects and policies of reconciliation in line with law 975, both at the social and individual levels. All of the quotes in this paragraph have been translated by the author directly from the original Spanish. Law 1448, www.alcaldiabogota.gov.co/sisjur/normas/Norma1.jsp?i=43043 (accessed March 15, 2018).
[30] See Appendix 1 for more information on community-level interventions.
[31] Sarkin 2014.

the Government has said it will use the official end of the conflict to "strengthen and energize" the existing programs for victims.

In Uganda, the government signed a truce with the LRA in 2006, essentially moving the war permanently into neighboring South Sudan and the DRC. Since there was no official peace agreement and demobilization, the Ugandan government has done little to support peacebuilding and reconciliation efforts and any formal transitional justice efforts have been spearheaded by the ICC (apart from the amnesty). This key difference sets the two apart and allows for interesting comparative insights into the effects of post-conflict state support after mass violence.

To conclude, Colombia and Uganda share some similar legacies of violent conflict and postwar responses, including transitional justice efforts, at the macro-level and during a similar time period. By controlling for conflict and post-conflict experiences, which include targeting of civilians, internal displacement, and transitional justice efforts, we can focus on the relationship between levels of postwar intervention and levels of community peace at the micro level across cultural contexts. The results of the cross-national comparison are grounded in a comparative community-level analysis within each country, to which I now turn.

COMMUNITY-LEVEL CASE SELECTION

Correlational inferences in this study are only made at the community level, which, in contrast to the cross-national analysis, employs a *most-similar,* matched case research design.[32] Experimental research designs have become increasingly popular in the evaluation of peacebuilding and development projects. In order to draw valid and concrete conclusions about the effectiveness of an intervention, practitioners and scholars alike see some value in creating controlled experiments, such as randomized control trials, that measure the impact of a certain treatment (e.g. postwar intervention) on a population and compare results to a control population that does not experience the same treatment.

However, creating experiments out of lived experiences is often fraught with uncertainty and the possibilities for error and misjudgment are enormous. Therefore, the restrictions placed on many impact evaluations and experimental designs limit the participatory aspects of including beneficiaries and communities in the design process. The result – these experimental approaches designed by outsiders – often lead to questionable results when taking into consideration the priorities and perspectives of the researched. Integrating the everyday indicator approach into a quasi-experimental design is an attempt to begin to look for more participatory ways to conduct impact evaluations, such as participatory impact assessments.[33]

---

[32] For another matched case research design at the village level, see Maclean 2010.
[33] Catley et al. 2013.

The matched case research design includes a case selection of two demographically similar communities in each country that experienced similar incidents of severe violence and displacement with varying levels of postwar interventions. The research design contributes to the literature on peacebuilding effectiveness in that it can draw some conclusions from the control community about the independent variable of third party intervention, since the matched case communities are otherwise relatively similar. Observing the outcomes and trends over time of the EPIs in these communities, as tracked through longitudinal surveys, lends itself to an experimental research design that can make some inferences about the impacts and consequences as well as the potential of third party interventions. Assuming that the experimental design is valid, it is possible to make conclusions and identify correlational factors associated with the interventions.[34]

The selected communities in each country are as similar as possible, with common demographic backgrounds, histories of violence and displacement, ethnic and colonial histories and geographic locations. Collecting the relevant information about each community was not without its challenges. Institutional memory in the peacebuilding and development world is often very short-lived and community recordkeeping is not consistent. No repository of data on previous interventions and actors exists, so I spoke with religious leaders, local government officials, local NGOs, our civil society partners and schools, and cross-checked this information with third party international interveners wherever possible. Developing a composite picture of post-war intervention required maintaining charts and figures of information gleaned from interviews, taking photographs of community documents and recording any additional information obtained from the interviews. The information that I obtained on interventions in each community since their first massacre can be found in Appendix 1. Demographic details were also sometimes difficult to come by. Some were easily obtained by a recent census, but oftentimes the data were not specific enough to obtain information for a particular village or sub-county. Therefore, I spent time going through archives of the local community government office in order to try to piece together exact demographic details in addition to doing interviews with local leaders and organizations. I supplemented archival research and interviews with data from the EPI surveys in which we asked demographic questions as well as questions about interventions.

---

[34] See Appendix 1 for accounting of interventions in each community. A word of caution is necessary. I cannot fully account for preexisting differences between the communities, and that those differences might explain why they received the treatment in the first place, therefore we must exercise some caution when drawing conclusions from this study.

A SNAPSHOT OF THE FOUR VILLAGES

A brief profile follows of selected community pairs in Uganda and Colombia. As explained above, community pairs were similar demographically and historically, but experienced radically different levels of post-conflict intervention.

Northern Uganda

In Northern Uganda, the Acholi-majority villages of Atiak and Odek were the birthplaces of two of the four ICC-indicted LRA commanders – Vincent Otti and Joseph Kony, respectively. Atiak is a sub-county in the Amuru district near the border of South Sudan. It has eight parishes and sixteen villages and includes a trading center. The inhabitants of Atiak are scattered in the various villages surrounding the trading center and at significant distances from one another. In 1995, more than 250 villagers in Atiak were murdered by LRA soldiers over the course of one day on April 20. What is perhaps most shocking is that the alleged LRA commander in charge was Atiak's own Vincent Otti, who returned home to murder his neighbors. Prior to the 1995 massacre, Atiak was a small trading center on the only (dirt) road to South Sudan with most of the people living in homesteads in the outskirts of the village. After the massacre, most of Atiak's residents moved to the IDP camp placed in Atiak by government forces. Currently, there is significant displacement from the border areas with South Sudan due to the conflict in that country. Local people leave border areas for fear of violence spreading into Uganda and because, according to them, some South Sudanese come into the area and raid their livestock.

Odek is a small trading center named after the stream that runs across its territory. Until recently it was an outward-lying sub-county of Gulu district, but in 2016 Odek was integrated into the newly created Omoro district. Seventy-eight men and women lost their lives as a result of a massacre committed by the government's National Resistance Army (NRA) on November 1, 1988.[35] Following the massacre, villagers continued to be persecuted and accused by the government of harboring Joseph Kony and supporting the LRA. In the early 1990s, the government ordered all civilians in villages in northern Uganda to leave their homes and relocate to IDP camps as a strategy to prevent them from helping the rebels.[36] Sixteen years later, the community suffered another massacre, this time at the hands of the LRA that had taken control of the area. On April 29, 2004, Dominic Ongwen led a massacre in which Ninety-three men, women, and school children were murdered in the Odek IDP camp.

---

[35] The National Resistance Army (NRA) was renamed The Uganda Peoples' Defence Forces (UPDF) in the 1995 constitution.
[36] JRP Fieldnote 2014; Atiak population 38,300; Odek population 32,218 (Uganda National Population and Housing Census 2014, November 2014).

Villagers in Atiak and Odek were perceived and accused by both armed actors as supporting their opponent, a dynamic found in the Colombian villages as well. Doubts from armed groups of civilian neutrality contributed significantly to local persecution and entanglement in the conflict, and were one of the main reasons for the massacres in all four villages. In Atiak and Odek, in particular, the government feared village sympathy for the LRA since they were home to key leaders in the armed group. Community members attempted to dissuade the government of their alleged LRA affiliation by spying on LRA activities. When the LRA came onto the scene in Atiak in the late eighties and early nineties, its relationship with locals was good. The LRA did not engage in forceful abduction, nor did it kill civilians. Instead, LRA soldiers asked local people for food and recruited youth from willing families. When the LRA discovered that some people were collaborating with government soldiers by revealing rebel hideouts and the locations of weapons caches, the rebels' approach toward the civilian population changed dramatically.[37] The LRA leaders became furious with villagers they perceived as pandering to NRA requests. Armed groups' lack of certainty regarding civilian allegiances and loyalties meant the 1988 massacre committed by the NRA in Odek was followed by a 2004 LRA massacre, with civilians victimized twice.

Both Otti and Ongwen are now indicted by the ICC, along with Joseph Kony. Ongwen has been on trial by the ICC in The Hague since December 6, 2016, and villagers from Odek and surrounding areas have testified. LRA leaders such as Ongwen not only led massacres of innocent civilians, but they also forced children and young men and women to join their armed group, creating a large group of forcibly displaced and formerly abducted individuals. However, only Ongwen was indicted by the ICC for war crimes associated with the Odek massacre. The massacre in Atiak was not within the statute of limitations for an ICC indictment of Otti. Therefore, only Odek has been directly involved in ongoing ICC proceedings, although both Atiak and Odek were victims of the same actors.

Community Interventions in Atiak and Odek

Immediately after the massacre occurred in Atiak, the government delivered 2,000 iron sheets for victims, presumably to help shelter those who had lost their homes, although most were immediately sold by the recipients. In addition, only 1,500 sheets were distributed to these surviving relatives of the victims and the rest are suspected to have been misappropriated. Otherwise, survivors were given blankets and maize (corn) by the government and other organizations.[38] Before 2010, most of the assistance given to communities was in the form of humanitarian assistance – food,

---

[37] JRP Fieldnote 2007.
[38] JRP Fieldnote 2007.

A Snapshot of the Four Villages

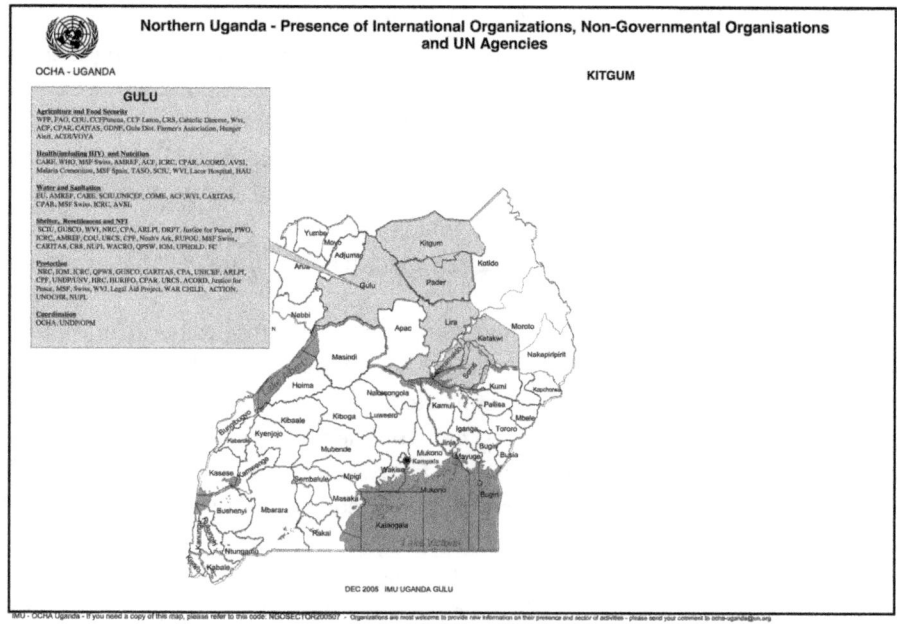

FIGURE 4.1. Map of 2005 presence of INGOs, NGOs, IOs and UN agencies

shelter and basic needs. This assistance was coordinated by UNOCHA, although multiple agencies (NGOs, government and international organizations) functioned in the area (see Figure 4.1). Humanitarian assistance was designed to satisfy immediate needs and did not have any ambitions for longer-term sustainability. Although many prominent organizations had some contact with all the different sub-districts of northern Uganda, their work was not evenly distributed, for reasons of security, access and stigma. As one of my respondents explained, "What is important is not to ask who is working there, but what are they doing. Impact should go beyond the names of the interveners, it should be about what they are accomplishing."[39]

Since that time, several organizations have continued to do work in Atiak with differing mandates related to reconstruction, infrastructural development, agricultural development, livelihood training and, to a much lesser extent, *small-p* peacebuilding and traditional justice initiatives. Examples of the many civil society organizations that have worked or are currently working in the area are: UNICEF, World Vision, Chafford, War Child, AVSI, Acord, NRC and Save the Children. UNICEF supported schools and health centers, Chafford promoted food security, and War Child supported informal and vocational training. AVSI offered counselling and economic

---

[39] Interview, Staff, World Vision, December 1, 2016.

support and did case management for children and vulnerable people. Save the Children conducted voluntary counselling and gave support to struggling schools. In addition, extensive development work has been done. Livestock has been provided, schools and roads constructed, and oxen and grinding machines have been given to some parishes for farming. Twenty boreholes were drilled in 2012/2013. Business has also come to Atiak with a $70 million sugar factory covering 25,000 acres currently in development. Finally, and perhaps most importantly in terms of economic development initiatives, the Juba road that runs through Atiak was completed in 2015/2016.

The Justice and Reconciliation Project (JRP) has been one of the main *small-p* peacebuilding-related organizations working in Atiak. In Atiak, JRP supported memorialization efforts, conducted victim exchanges between survivors of the Atiak massacre and survivors of other places, and conducted capacity building on advocacy and transitional justice-related issues. They worked with survivors, sub-county officials, local leaders, victims and formerly abducted persons. JRP also documented the Atiak massacre and widely disseminated a report in 2007.

JRP only released a report on the Odek massacre in 2014, after the Everyday Peace Indicators Project began collecting data in Odek. In contrast to Atiak, Odek has had little postwar intervention and, for the most part, has been isolated and ostracized for its association as the birthplace of Joseph Kony. Many in the community feel that their needs for truth, justice and reconciliation have been disregarded because of their unfortunate history. "Memorial prayers are held in places like Lukodi and Atiak whereas in Odek no one has bothered," a respondent stated in an interview conducted by the JRP.[40] Villagers would like to come to terms with their past, and believe that Kony (and the spirits) should atone for their deeds in Odek. JRP began some reconciliation work, in particular the documentation of the events of the massacre, after the EPI project chose Odek as a case study. It became quickly clear to JRP staff that much violence had occurred in Odek, but little had been written or done in the years after the end of the war. Compared with Atiak, Odek is also relatively geographically isolated and far from Gulu, which may also have contributed to its neglect. As the LCIII village chief told me during my last visit: "When you come to Odek you are already tired."[41]

Many of the actors working in Atiak have also had contact with Odek. However, the extent and reach of these actors and programs were not nearly as significant in Odek as they were in Atiak. In addition, many of these actors have only recently come to Odek, whereas they have been in Atiak since the war ended. Appendix 1 gives an overview of the organizations that have conducted some limited work in Odek, primarily in development, education and public health. There was some limited *small-p* peacebuilding work, for example, Gusco worked to resettle and

---

[40] JRP Fieldnote 2014.
[41] Interview LCIII village chief, Odek, November 25, 2016.

reunite some of the formerly abducted persons and implement income-generating activities. They facilitated a traditional cleansing ceremony at Te Olam, as well as a dialogue meeting between the community and the formerly abducted in 2012. World Vision also worked with formerly abducted persons and offered psychosocial and reintegration support through its Children of War Rehabilitation Center. In addition, a Christian initiative by the government conducted a prayer intervention in 2005 called "Operation Gideon," in which three area pastors prayed over Odek to rid it from witchcraft at the high places where Kony performed ritual sacrifices. After several weeks of fasting and prayer, the team gathered at the high place on the Awere Hill of Odek, where Joseph Kony used to gather with his army, to bless the area and perform a kind of exorcism of its evil past.

Although many organizations have worked in both places, all of the people I interviewed in Gulu, Atiak and Odek agreed that Odek had received far less intervention than Atiak. Many stated that although multiple actors had operated around Odek, they had not implemented as substantial and sustainable of initiatives as they had in Atiak. Interventions were delayed in Odek, whereas in Atiak there was more immediate and sustained assistance after the war. Even though many of the same organizations that worked in Atiak also eventually came to Odek, especially the economic development investments in Atiak were much more significant than they were in Odek. Everyone I interviewed in Gulu, Odek and Atiak agreed that Odek was far behind the rest of Acholiland and definitely much further behind Atiak in receiving interventions. For example, a staff member from the ICC Outreach Section told us that:

> I would say Atiak seems to have gotten more interventions by different stakeholders. Many NGOs went to Atiak, including government. People in Odek seem to have gotten less of that. They started getting attention much later. I don't think they (Odek) have specifically gotten anything, whereas there's an Atiak survivors association and technical school in Atiak, which is not the case in Odek. All you see in Odek is the normal sub-county which is everywhere.[42]

And another staff from the Refugee Law Project explained:

> I first of all see a lot of differences. One: Atiak is more empowered than Odek. Even in terms of services, in terms of the way people conduct themselves they are more empowered than Odek. I think it's just because they created the alarm so early and many people responded to their problems, they've always been reached and people picked a lot of interest in them, so they are more empowered. And Odek was very difficult. I think also that history of Kony coming from Odek made some people shy down.[43]

---

[42] Interview, ICC Outreach Section Staff, Gulu, January 20, 2016.
[43] Interview, Refugee Law Project Staff, Gulu, August 23, 2016.

The difference between the two sub-counties is also quite striking when you visit them. Odek is clearly less developed and residents have no modern amenities. They are also less exposed to external actors than Atiak, which is demonstrated by their lack of familiarity with external actors. For example, many areas of Odek do not have electricity (electricity only came to the village during the time period we were conducting surveys), and there is not much cell phone coverage in the area and no internet access. Most areas of Atiak, on the other hand, have all of these resources due to the large influx of external actors and the construction of the Juba road. Finally, World Vision told me that they will be most likely starting an Area Development Program (ADP), one of World Vision's signature initiatives, in the Omoro district, with Odek being included as one of the recipients because there is such a high level of need there. They "decided that an ADP was not necessary in Atiak because there were already so many actors working there."[44] Demonstrating a continued need in Odek as identified by a major INGO.

Montes de Maria, Colombia

Both of the communities of El Salado and Don Gabriel are located in the Montes de Maria region in the departments of Bolivar and Sucre, an area that was highly affected by paramilitary violence in the early 2000s and also had significant guerilla activity previous and concurrent to the paramilitary violence.[45] As a consequence, both communities were entirely displaced between 2000 and 2002 due to paramilitary violence. The region was one of the most violent until after the paramilitary demobilization in 2005. It is now considered to be in a post-war period.[46]

A strategic location for drug trafficking, El Salado was the target of armed violence, for the most part, at the hands of the paramilitaries. Before the arrival of armed actors, El Salado was a very wealthy town for the region, which primarily cultivated tobacco. There was low unemployment and a wide range of commercial activity. One community member explained: "Before the violence, local development existed because of our own efforts and not because of the government."[47] Community members felt that their families had been fundamental in acquiring resources for the town and that the government had a very limited presence from the

---

[44] Interview, Staff, World Vision Gulu, December 1, 2016.
[45] The Montes de Maria is a mountainous region that covers the departments of Sucre and Bolivar and forms part of the Western mountains of San Jeronimo. This was a principal area under the control of the FARC and other guerrilla groups during the 1980s and into the 1990s. In the 1990s and 2000s there was widespread fighting with the arrival of paramilitary groups in the region.
[46] See statistics for the region from 1984–2012 (its most violent period) at verdadabierta.com: (www.verdadabierta.com/cifras/3829-estadisticas-de-desplazamiento) (displacement) and here: (www.verdadabierta.com/cifras/3828-estadisticas-masacres) (massacres).
[47] Focus group in El Salado, July 7, 2012.

beginning. The community did not have a history of expectations or trust regarding resources from the state in terms of security, education, health or infrastructure.

In 1997 and 2000 there were two major massacres that affected El Salado, and individual lynchings and disappearances occurred between 1997 and 2003. Five people were publicly murdered in 1997 by members of the AUC and another sixty-six were killed in the massacre of 2000. In both cases, paramilitary soldiers entered the town and gathered people from the village in the central square and there began to kill various community members. The massacre of 2000 was particularly gruesome and apparently arbitrary with paramilitaries drinking and accompanying the killings with music played on village instruments, while Colombian military just a few miles away did nothing to stop the violence.[48] Villagers speculate that the two massacres were connected and viewed them as retaliation by the paramilitaries, although they were not committed by the same individual members of the AUC. After each massacre, the village inhabitants left El Salado and lived in a state of displacement for varying amounts of time. Approximately 4,000 people out of 7,000 returned after the 1997 massacre and approximately 1,000 returned in 2002 (since then the number has grown).

In the nearby village of Don Gabriel, community members were displaced in January of 2001 because of a paramilitary massacre that occurred in its neighboring village of Chengue. Prior to the displacement, Don Gabriel experienced selected killings, committed mainly over a three-year period, by FARC and other guerrilla groups. It was also the scene of a demobilization of an armed group, the Workers Revolutionary Party of Colombia (PRT), in 1991.

Don Gabriel and El Salado have similar histories of violence, but similar to Atiak and Odek, there are some differences to keep in mind. A high profile massacre was committed by the paramilitaries in El Salado, whereas Don Gabriel experienced selected killings committed mainly over a three-year period by FARC guerrillas, and Don Gabriel's displacement was due to a massacre in the neighboring community of Chengue rather than a direct experience of massacre. In El Salado sixty-six people were massacred and another fourty individuals were victims of selected killings by FARC and paramilitaries, whereas an estimated fifty people were victims in Don Gabriel, primarily by the FARC.[49] As a result, the two communities also have very different political identities, since the community of El Salado sees itself mainly as a victim of the paramilitaries, whereas the community of Don Gabriel felt more persecuted by guerrilla groups.

---

[48] Rohter 2000.
[49] The information here is based information collected from my fieldwork, including conversations with community members and information collected by Fundación Semana staff. In addition, data were taken from a report published in 2014 by the Fundación Semana (with the support of USAID) entitled "Resultados consolidados de la priorizacion de acciones a nivel de los corregimientos" that gives information on each village in the Montes de Maria region.

External interventions in El Salado and Don Gabriel

As for the communities in Uganda, the two communities in Colombia were selected because they are demographically similar, have similar histories of violence, are situated in the same geographical area, but have vastly varying levels of intervention.[50] What distinguishes the two rural communities is the extraordinary difference in external interventions, including reparations schemes. Since 2009, El Salado has seen more than 120 external, private and public actors enter the community with post-conflict programs.[51] El Salado has had significant and widespread intervention from civil society, international NGOs, national NGOs and government actors. They have implemented projects in education, infrastructure, health, community development and security. The village has been called a Laboratory for Peace in Colombia and is perceived as a model for the region and the rest of the rural areas of the country that have suffered from the conflict.[52] In addition, the Colombian military maintains oversight over the village from a military post nearby and the police have recently brought a police post staffed with ten officers to the community.

El Salado has become a household name in Colombia because of widespread campaigns by non-governmental actors, in particular the Fundación Semana. Most of the external actors have been facilitated or accompanied by the Fundación Semana, which has a significant presence in the village. Fundación Semana began working in El Salado around 2009 when it started a campaign raising awareness of the needs of El Salado as emblematic of the region as a consequence of the brutality of the paramilitaries in the early 2000s. It saw its role in El Salado as a post-conflict innovator, to demonstrate how external organizations can help in the reconstruction of the village in a participatory and sustainable way over time. Fundación Semana had a permanent presence and office in El Salado for about eight years and coordinated external public, private, national and international efforts in El Salado.[53]

---

[50] Both communities are approximately 20 kilometers from the municipality (Carmen de Bolivar in the case of El Salado and Ovejas in the case of Don Gabriel) and have a population size of approximately 1,500–2,000. Both villages depend mainly on agricultural livelihoods and the villages have electricity (although the surrounding areas do not). Inhabitants are of mestizo origin and both communities have Catholic and protestant/evangelical communities and churches.

[51] Please see pages 36–8 of Fundación Semana. December 2014. *Tiempo de Sequia*. El Salado: Boletin #5, https://issuu.com/fundacionsemana/docs/salado_2014 (accessed September 27, 2017) for a listing of 96 actors. This estimate is according to calculations by Fundación Semana staff using spreadsheets accounting for all the programs and actors with whom they have been affiliated. Since not everyone working in El Salado is affiliated with the Fundación Semana, the actual number of actors and entities exceeds 120.

[52] Linde 2014; Guillermoprieto 2018.

[53] November 16, 2013. El posconflicto de los Montes de María. Revista Semana, www.semana.com/nacion/articulo/posconflicto-montes-de-maria/364734-3 (accessed September 27, 2017).

A Snapshot of the Four Villages

In 2017, Fundación Semana closed its office in El Salado, but maintains a small office in the nearby municipality of El Carmen de Bolívar.

Fundación Semana most likely selected El Salado from a group of 143 villages and sixteen municipalities in the Montes de Maria region because it had the highest number of victims in one day – sixty-six people died as a consequence of the paramilitary massacre from February 16 to 21, 2000. But peasant activism on the part of the residents of El Salado, and the length of time that the village was abandoned (almost two years), likely contributed to the selection by Fundación Semana. This has given El Salado the unique experience of having not only a strong sense of community organization, but also a permanent outside presence to help strengthen their claims and guarantee their demands. Unlike Don Gabriel, El Salado has had continuous support to publicize its plight and to help it achieve peace and stability.

El Salado was also one of the original pilots of the government's first collective reparations program (PIRC) implemented by the Organization for International Migration and financed by USAID.[54] Although the collective reparations project in El Salado is still ongoing, it has completed many projects, including a paved road, a community center and library, cell phone coverage for the village, one-hundred new houses in December of 2015, agricultural and other income generating activities. Most of these collective reparations were implemented with the participation of community members through a five-step process designed by the CNRR and the Unidad that has now become the basis of the collective reparations process throughout Colombia.

The massacre of El Salado is very publicly mourned every February with participation of the local government, national government agencies such as the Unidad para las Víctimas, security forces, non-government organizations (Fundación Semana, among others) and the media. Inhabitants of El Salado have also received individual reparations in the form of compensation, although approximately fifty-five families are yet to be compensated as of July 2017. One important point to keep in mind is that, much like in Atiak, the great majority of interventions that El Salado has received have been focused on development, health and education. Of the large amount of intervention El Salado has seen, only a small percentage would be classified as *small-p* peacebuilding work. In fact, there have only been three main interventions that would be categorized as such: the documentation and publication of the massacre in El Salado,[55] the psychosocial support given through a court

---

[54] Firchow 2013b.
[55] Grupo de Memoria Histórica (2009). La Masacre de El Salado: Esa Guerra no era nuestra (The El Salado Massacre: That war was not ours): www.centrodememoriahistorica.gov.co/descargas/informes2009/informe_la_masacre_de_el_salado.pdf (accessed September 27, 2017).

order to the community by the Fundación Mi Sangre[56] and, most recently, a process of dialogue, mourning and reconstruction of the community's social fabric called Entrelazando, conducted by the Unidad para las Víctimas.[57] These projects have been complemented by some public memorialization activities in the community.

In contrast, Don Gabriel has not seen many external actors since the violent events and subsequent displacement. Of the handful of external entities they have seen, these have mostly been state entities. The only private entity that has worked in Don Gabriel is the *Fundación Red de Desarrollo y Paz de los Montes de Maria*, which conducted some activities with youth in the village. Otherwise, there has been some inconsistent contact with the Unidad de Victimas, the Mayor's office, INCODER, the Unidad de Restitucion de Tierras and Colombia Responde (all government programs). The only assistance they have received is through the Programa Familias en Su Tierra to help them re-establish their homes after being displaced, and some humanitarian assistance in the form of individual payments from the DPS. There are plans to build houses for direct victims, but only one house has been built to date (the preschool). Inhabitants routinely confuse government agencies and projects that they have encountered, attributing projects to different agencies. Don Gabriel has not yet received any reparations from Law 975 or 1448 – neither collective nor individual. However, some villagers who lost family members in the 1990s did receive humanitarian assistance or compensation according to Law 418. Therefore, there is also significant confusion surrounding reparations and what reparations mean.

CONCLUSION

As we can see, the similarities in demographics, geography and conflict history and displacement between Atiak and Odek in Uganda, and El Salado and Don Gabriel in Colombia, combined with highly uneven postwar intervention treatment, allow us to investigate the impact of intervention on levels of peace and reconciliation in each community. The community-level comparison allows us to have confidence that findings on the impact of interventions after war on community-generated indicators of peace are strong. Community-level findings are then extended by the cross-national comparison, which allows us to demonstrate findings and observations across contexts and cultures.

---

[56] For the judgment in Spanish: www.corteconstitucional.gov.co/relatoria/2010/t-045-10.htm (accessed September 27, 2017).

[57] This process was only started in 2016. For more about Entrelazando in Spanish, visit: www.unidadvictimas.gov.co/sites/procesos_caracterizados/38.%20PROCEDIMIENTO%20ENTRELAZANDO%20v3.pdf (accessed September 27, 2017).

As a result of this research design, we can now ask questions about the impact of external interventions as tracked by community-generated indicators of peace. A basic assumption of community peacebuilding work is that most intervention works. By using everyday indicators we can now more effectively glean the impact of external interventions on community perceptions of peace to determine their effectiveness as well as to understand where there is a need for further focus and attention. I now turn to an analysis of the everyday peace indicators to discover what indicators the selected communities use to determine their daily peace.

5

The Multidimensionality of Everyday Peace

INTRODUCTION

Community-identified indicators can be dismissed as idiosyncratic, anecdotal and hyper-localized. Some of the micro-narratives they reveal raise issues that are discussed only at the margins of policy and academic debates on post-conflict societies: the social impact of alcohol, religious faith, and superstitions. Yet serious efforts to assist communities emerging from violence must understand local priorities and dynamics in order to succeed and therefore must take seriously these issues at hand.

The everyday indicators differ from existing measurement systems in that they not only measure impact, but also articulate detailed context and meaning regarding communities' perceptions and experiences of peace and conflict. The indicators tell a story of priorities and issues within communities and allow us to understand better what factors are most important to community members when measuring and defining peace. One of the main strengths of the everyday indicator approach is that, beyond generating quantitative data through survey results, it creates a process in which the everyday acumen of communities can be systematically collected and analyzed to make conclusions about people's everyday priorities and needs that can also help with planning and design of interventions.

This chapter presents and analyzes the everyday indicators generated by local communities to offer a new conceptualization of local peace in communities in Uganda and Colombia. The chapter demonstrates the ability of everyday indicators to accurately capture the factors, dimensions and characteristics of peace and to measure the effectiveness of peacebuilding projects from a community perspective, rather than relying on outsiders to determine what constitutes success.

The chapter also presents characteristics of locally-defined peace across different contexts to contribute to attempts to conceptualize difficult, normative concepts such as peace. The cross-national comparison finds three main characteristics of local conceptions of peace. First, everyday peace is a multidimensional, integrated concept that reflects characteristics of both negative and positive peace. When analyzing indicators by category, it was evident that people everywhere looked toward indicators related to security, but also to development, education or to routine social activities such as parties or festivals. Second, people often look toward very localized, contextual indicators around them, in their communities and homes, in order to determine whether they are more or less at peace in their daily lives. This finding demonstrates that universal indicators are insufficient to ascertain the impact of external interventions on communities. Indicators must be in tune with community acumen in order to appropriately measure what they intend. Finally, this chapter demonstrates that everyday peace is dynamic and evolving, changing as communities experience different phases of conflict. Nowhere did we find only one static category of indicators that represented peace for a community, nor did we find any communities with completely identical indicators, although some were very similar.

The finding that everyday peace is multidimensional, contextualized, and dynamic has significant implications for peacebuilding design and implementation. It helps us to see *how* interveners can often be disconnected from community needs. The indicators also help us to see what is required at a local level to effectively implement programming that addresses post-war needs and sustains peace. It illustrates and stresses the importance of tailoring interventions to context and not relying on top-down, template approaches unfamiliar with the local context.

The next section explains the everyday indicator categorization process. The coding and categorization of indicators allow us to compare and contrast the ways communities define peace and whether they look mostly toward security, development, human rights, etc. to determine if they are more or less peaceful. The chapter provides the background and justification for the factor classification of everyday indicators in order to identify trends and associations. It also outlines the coding process of the indicators into categories. The chapter next discusses what the indicators tell us about the case study communities in Uganda and Colombia. The following section discusses findings from the cross-national comparison about the nature of local conceptions of peace. It concludes with a discussion about how the findings demonstrate trends similar to those of Maslow's hierarchy of needs. The final section demonstrates the importance of the indicators themselves for program development and contextual knowledge, and further discusses how they differ from existing indicators.

THE CODING AND CATEGORIZATION OF EVERYDAY INDICATORS

Because of the inevitably distinct nature of the EPIs – each indicator is uniquely chosen by a community to reflect its particular measurement of peace and safety – the potential for direct comparison is limited. A pressing issue in one community may be the violence associated with gang feuds, while in another area it might be a poor harvest or the influx of a large number of internally displaced people. These issues may not resonate in other communities. In addition, the way various issues are measured may be quite different depending on the circumstances of a particular community. For example, in one community a certain kind of music may be an indicator of gang activity, whereas in another it is a specific way people are dressed, etc. The diversity of contextually-specific indicators poses additional challenges to scholars and practitioners attempting to identify commonalities across different contexts.

Yet, indicators do fall into general categories that can be found in most communities. Ensuring the timely removal of bodies off the street after a gang feud is one type of public health concern. Not having access to a traditional food staple because of a bad harvest is a type of food insecurity. Scholars analyzing social phenomena from social revolutions to common pool resource institutions use generalized categories to enable analysis of contextualized data. These so-called "two-level theories" use categories to prove a relationship between an independent and dependent variable, that some factor X is a necessary condition for outcome Y.[1] X and Y, however, are populated by different phenomena that are categorized into the same concept. For example, in Eleanor Ostrom's work on common pool resource institutions, she sets monitoring as a requirement for successful local common pool resource management.[2] However, monitoring can take many different forms, depending on the context and the common pool resource being managed. For example, managing a river for fishing may require different kinds of monitoring resources than managing a field for sheep. Therefore, although the overarching categorical requirement set by Ostrom is monitoring (by monitors that are accountable to appropriators), the form of monitoring usually varies from case to case. Similarly, in Theda Skocpol's work on social revolutions, she sets state crisis as a condition for social revolution. However, the form that a state crisis takes depends on the context and situation of each case study.[3]

As in the prominent studies conducted by Skocpol and Ostrom, the everyday indicator categorization process uses secondary-level dimensions to form concepts. By categorizing everyday indicators, I create factors necessary for the analysis of a particular concept (peace in this case) and populate these factors with individualized, context-specific indicators.[4] Doing so allows us to measure a particular factor or issue differently from case to case, but still gives us the necessary common ground to be able to establish comparisons and conclusions. Similar to processes undertaken in two-level theory analysis, I use content analysis and process tracing of the indicators in order to categorize the everyday indicators and to inductively create factors.[5]

---

[1] Goertz 2006b: 237.
[2] Ostrom 2015.
[3] Skocpol 1979.
[4] I use the terms factors and categories interchangeably.
[5] To make results comparable, I created macro-indicators – namely categories and dimensions – that grouped several indicators into shared concepts such as health, education, security forces.

With the categories identified I then created a coding tool to assign each indicator to one or more categories to facilitate a higher-level analysis (see Tables 5.1 and 5.2).[6] In addition, the categories themselves were subsequently coded into larger dimensions: security, human rights, development, and social, to enable identification of macro themes and trends across communities.

Categories allow us to adjust for the fact that certain indicators may be fundamental in some contexts but irrelevant in others. Take, for example, the indicator of "urinating outside at night," which was selected in EPI research conducted in South Africa. In some communities where toilets are communal or separated from the home, people have to feel safe enough to leave their homes to urinate at night. But if people feel insecure they will use a container indoors and empty it in the morning. Therefore, for some, this is an important indicator that tells us whether there is a large uptick in political or criminal violence. However, not every community may choose the same indicator and it may not be applicable in all communities. Some may have toilets in their homes.

Creating secondary level dimensions and categories enables us to have a means of comparing otherwise incompatible indicators across communities. Such categories can be populated with community-specific, experience-near indicators that accurately measure each category. In this case, urinating at night was categorized in the daily security category. This categorization allows us to compare and analyze indicators from diverse communities, avoiding the irrelevance of some indicators in different contexts.

While experience-near indicators can help scholars build categories from the bottom up, they can also complement and enrich top-down indicator systems, such as the SDG 16 indicators, by giving more detailed ways to measure generalized indicators and giving local context to particular issue areas to ensure internal validity. Since the everyday indicators demonstrate that people experience insecurity and peace in different ways depending on circumstances, this should be taken into consideration in measurement, because measuring something in one community may not mean the same thing for the community next door. Experience-near indicators can help us to count and populate experience-distant categories and dimensions more effectively.

Yet, it is important to remember that by coding indicators into experience-distant categories we also lose the experience-near, or more localized, understanding of people's indicators of peace. In doing so, we also lose some of their value in providing detailed context for the design of interventions, although we gain a

---

The establishment of macro-indicators or categories makes it possible to establish more accurate comparison between communities who share similar, albeit not identical, indicators. Finally, I created a broader categorization comprised of four dimensions, to compare categories related to security, human rights, development, and social traits among communities.

[6] The codebook for the indicator coding is available at everydaypeaceindicators.org.

TABLE 5.1. Everyday peace indicators in Uganda by community and category

Atiak		Odek	
Everyday peace indicator	Categories	Everyday peace indicator	Categories
Local businesses booming	Economics	Sleeping safely at home at night	Security/Daily
Development of roads	Infrastructure	Access to clean water	Food & Agriculture, Health
Availability of medical care for families	Health	Access to medical care for families	Health
Children attend school when it is in session	Education	People dig in their gardens	Food & Agriculture
People dig in their gardens	Food & Agriculture	No discrimination – people are not treated differently because of their tribe or how much money they have	Cohesion & Interdependence, Discrimination
Walk freely at night	Daily Security, Freedom	Police are available at the sub-county police post	Security/Forces
People sleep safely in their homes at night	Daily Security	Children attend school when it is in session	Education
People don't hear gunshots	Daily Security	Freedom of speech – people feel safe to speak freely	Freedom, Transitional Justice & Human Rights
Formerly abducted and non-formerly abducted people live together peacefully	Cohesion & Interdependence, Conflict Resolution	Freedom to practice whatever religion	Freedom
Leaders listen to the community views	Cohesion & Interdependence, Leadership	Electric power – there are few power outages; the family has access to working electric power	Infrastructure
Presence of NGOs	Leadership	Development of roads	Infrastructure
Victims of crimes lay charges	Security/Crime, Transitional Justice & Human Rights	People are free to do what they want – people are not forced to do things against their will	Freedom, Routine Social Activities
Internet is available	Infrastructure	People are not superstitious	Routine Social Activities
		People are able to participate in traditional festivals, rituals and cultural practices	Cohesion & Interdependence, Routine Social Activities

Peace indicators – Atiak and Odek, Uganda

TABLE 5.2. Everyday peace indicators in Colombia by community and category

	Don Gabriel		El Salado	
Everyday peace indicator	Categories	Everyday peace indicator	Categories
Reparations by the armed groups	Conflict Resolution, Transitional Justice & Human Rights	Traditional Festivals are routinely celebrated	Cohesion & Interdependence, Routine Social Activities
Jail time for the armed groups participating in the violence	Transitional Justice & Human Rights	People work for the benefit of the community without expecting anything in exchange	Cohesion & Interdependence, Leadership
Permanent presence of the police and/or military (fuerza publica)	Security/Forces	Access to higher education	Education
Effective attention to victims	Conflict Resolution, Transitional Justice & Human Rights	Comprehensive healthcare	Health
Health center staffed with professionals	Health	Comprehensive reparations	Conflict Resolution, Transitional Justice & Human Rights
Ability to study	Education	Knowing the truth about the victimizing events	Conflict Resolution, Transitional Justice & Human Rights
Development of infrastructure	Infrastructure	Justice about victimizing events	Conflict Resolution, Transitional Justice & Human Rights
Taking care of the environment	Health, Routine Social Activities	Non-repetition of victimizing events	Conflict Resolution, Daily Security, Transitional Justice & Human Rights
Freedom of expression	Daily Security, Freedom	There is a pedagogy of peace available to the community	Conflict Resolution, Education, Transitional Justice & Human Rights
Participation in community organizations without stigmatization	Cohesion & Interdependence, Daily Security, Discrimination, Freedom, Routine Social Activities	Equality in benefits for families	Cohesion & Interdependence, Discrimination, Economics

(*continued*)

TABLE 5.2 (Continued)

Don Gabriel		El Salado	
Everyday peace indicator	Categories	Everyday peace indicator	Categories
Activities with neighboring communities	Cohesion & Interdependence, Leadership, Routine Social Activities	Leadership is transparent in its dealings	Cohesion & Interdependence, Leadership
Access to potable water	Food & Agriculture, Infrastructure	New leaders emerge	Cohesion & Interdependence, Leadership
The military asks forgiveness for the victimizing events	Conflict Resolution, Transitional Justice & Human Rights	Income opportunities for women	Cohesion & Interdependence, Discrimination, Economics, Transitional Justice & Human Rights
A good attitude from the local government	Conflict Resolution, Leadership	No Drug consumption	Security/Crime
Social investment	Cohesion & Interdependence, Routine Social Activities	Integration with neighboring communities	Cohesion & Interdependence, Routine Social Activities
Families are being strengthened	Cohesion & Interdependence, Routine Social Activities	Land ownership	Food & Agriculture
Compensation for victims	Economic, Transitional Justice & Human Rights	The community is united	Cohesion & Interdependence, Leadership
No delay in the payment of humanitarian aid	Discrimination, Economic, Leadership	The social fabric is being reconstructed	Cohesion & Interdependence, Leadership, Routine Social Activities
Dialogue within the community	Cohesion & Interdependence, Conflict Resolution, Education, Transitional Justice & Human Rights	Respect among members of the community	Cohesion & Interdependence, Routine Social Activities
Good relationships with other communities	Cohesion & Interdependence, Conflict Resolution, Routine Social Activities	Trust in the public sector	Cohesion & Interdependence, Leadership, Security/Forces
People forgive the victimizing events	Conflict Resolution, Transitional Justice & Human Rights		
The armed groups ask for forgiveness for the victimizing events	Conflict Resolution, Security Forces, Transitional Justice & Human Rights		

Peace indicators – El Salado and Don Gabriel, Colombia

broader understanding of the policy priorities identified by a given community. In other words, experience-near indicators give us the granularity of people's localized understanding of peace, but are difficult to compare. Whereas experience-distant categories allow comparisons, but are unable to pick-up on the local detail. While cross-community comparisons are possible through experience-distant categories, experience-near indicators remain particularly valuable as a diagnostic tool for programming and interventions in a specific community, an issue to which I return at the end of the chapter.

INDICATOR ANALYSIS IN UGANDA AND COLOMBIA

I now turn to an analysis of the categorized indicators, which allows us to identify which areas are of most concern to individual communities in Uganda and Colombia, as well as how they compare to one another.[7] It allows for a more accessible and overarching snapshot of the highly localized indicators that were chosen by community members. Categorization also gives a clearer understanding of the extent to which external interventions match community needs and priorities. From the case studies presented here, we can see that communities with high levels of intervention – Atiak in Uganda and El Salado in Colombia – prioritize indicators related to social issues such as conflict resolution and reconciliation. In addition, Atiak prioritized development-related indicators while human rights-related indicators came to the fore in El Salado. In both contexts, social issues related to peacebuilding and reconciliation are of priority to people in communities that have received high levels of intervention. Possibly, communities with high levels of intervention are more aware of a need to rebuild more than just the physical buildings and resources they have lost since many of these have already been restored.

Odek and Atiak, Uganda

Sverker Finnström, a well-known Swedish ethnographer of the Acholi, discusses the multidimensionality of peace in northern Uganda in his book *Living with Bad Surroundings*. He explains how the Acholi identify negative peace as their "bad surroundings" (*piny marac*) and positive peace as their "good surroundings" (*piny maber*).[8] The "bad surroundings" exist for the Acholi when "armed fighting is intense, but it is also true in periods of lull, when the war, at least on the surface, seems far away." In contrast, "good surroundings" exist when there is a balance for people "with the greater scheme of things, persons, relatives, ancestors, and God."[9]

---

[7] Indicators of peace and reconciliation were collected in Colombia. The analysis in this book is based solely on the indicators of peace.
[8] Finnström 2008.
[9] Ibid.,10.

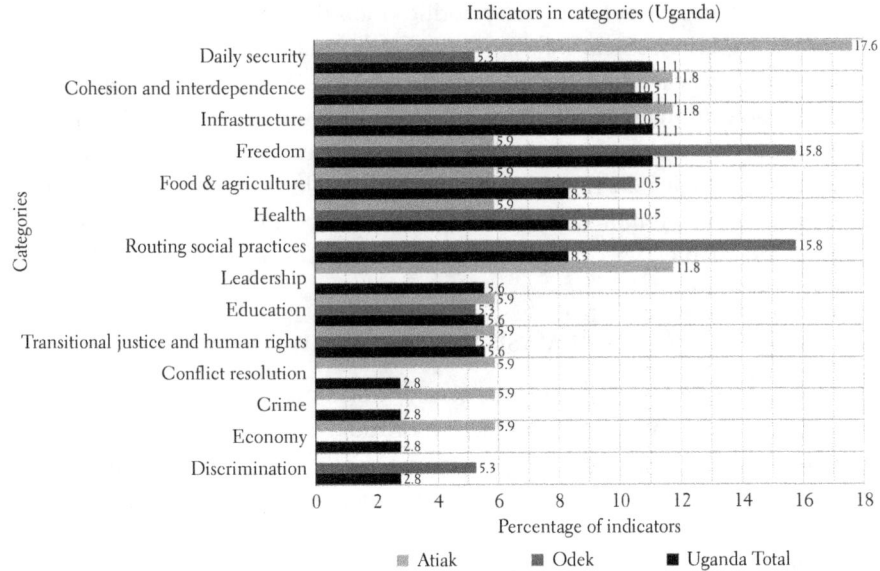

FIGURE 5.1. Percentage of peace indicators by category in Odek and Atiak

These, as Finnström points out, are not absolute categories that are frozen in time, but represent a process of categorization for the Acholi between war and peace. The indicators collected in Uganda reinforce Finnström's findings and demonstrate that people in northern Uganda continue to define peace in multidimensional ways that fall into both "bad surroundings" and "good surroundings" categories. The analysis of the indicators chosen demonstrates that the communities in our study are currently more focused on issues to do with good surroundings (Figures 5.1 and 5.2). A list of the indicators chosen in both communities follows below:

Overall, both communities primarily used indicators of positive peace to identify whether they felt more or less peaceful. People predominantly selected indicators to do with freedom of movement, economic progress and community ties. Freedom and routine social practices were clear priorities for inhabitants of Odek, with each category accounting for 15.8 percent of indicators selected. Freedom included indicators such as freedom of speech and freedom of movement. Second tier categories included cohesion and interdependence, infrastructure, food and agriculture, and health, with each accounting for 10.5 percent of indicators chosen.

In Atiak, the top category was daily security, which represented 17.6 percent of all the indicators. Leadership (11.8 percent), infrastructure (11.8 percent) and cohesion and interdependence (11.8 percent) were of next greatest concern. It is difficult to attribute correlations for the differences in categories between Atiak and Odek, but the variety of categories chosen demonstrates that both communities

Indicator Analysis in Uganda and Colombia

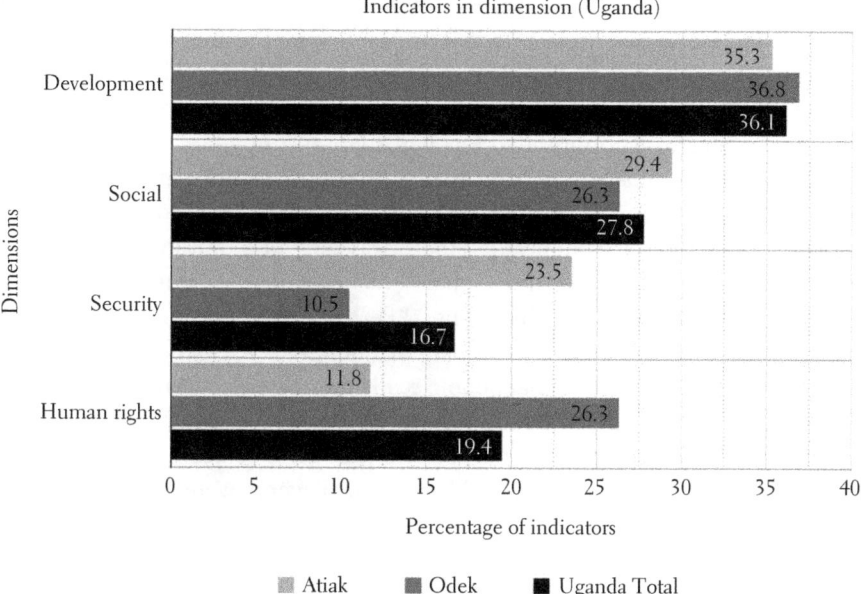

FIGURE 5.2. Percentage of indicators by dimension in Odek and Atiak[a]

[a] For a full description of the categorization, see everydaypeaceindicators.org for the indicator codebook. The dimensions are comprised of the following categories. *Security*: crime, daily security, security forces; *Development*: infrastructure, education, economy, health, food and agriculture; *Social*: cohesion and interdependence, conflict resolution, leadership, routine social practices; *Human Rights*: discrimination, freedom, transitional justice and human rights.

chose many different kinds of indicators to measure everyday peace, indicating the multidimensionality of local peace. Atiak also chose "presence of NGOs who visit us more often to support and train us" as an indicator of peace. This sort of indicator came up in many of the communities across the wider EPI pilots, but rarely made it into the short lists. Usually, these were more general as well, such as "foreigners or outsiders coming and visiting our community," indicating freedom of movement. General indicators that could be applicable to any context, such as sending children to school or accessing hospitals and treatment, were chosen. But we can also see more specific indicators dealing with community-relevant issues such as having a police post at the sub-county in Odek and more frequent visits by NGOs to Atiak.

Although both communities had relatively low levels of indicators in security-related categories, Odek struggles less with security issues than Atiak. Community members in Odek chose only 10.5 percent of indicators in security-related categories – crime, security forces, and daily security – whereas those in Atiak chose 23.5 percent. Of the three security-related categories, both communities chose indicators that fell into the daily security category. Odek did not choose any indicators in the crime category, but did choose indicators in the security forces category, while the opposite was true for Atiak. The difference could perhaps be attributed to Atiak's location near a recently paved main road that brings more traffic and outsiders to the village, therefore exposing the village to more crime than Odek, which is more remote.

Few indicators fell into political and civil rights and transitional justice categories. Strikingly, for a country that has had such an important impact on transitional justice and human rights scholarship, transitional justice and human rights indicators were not among the top categories in any of the communities.[10] In contrast to the Colombian indicators, there was only one transitional justice and human rights related indicator in the short lists for either community in Uganda – "formerly abducted now live with victims."[11] Perhaps this is not surprising considering the low level of enthusiasm for formal transitional justice mechanisms in northern Uganda.[12] It demonstrates that people really do not look toward legal redress as a primary indicator of peace, reinforcing the claims made by civil society actors in northern Uganda that the Acholi do not prioritize legal redress over reintegration and reconciliation with former LRA soldiers, some of whom were formerly abducted from their villages.[13]

El Salado and Don Gabriel, Colombia

In Colombia, the most prevalent everyday peace indicator category for El Salado was cohesion and interdependence (24.4 percent). Transitional justice and human rights (15.6 percent), and leadership (13.3 percent) came in second and third as the most prevalent indicators people looked to in order to determine their everyday peace. In Don Gabriel, in contrast, three categories were almost equally important: transitional justice and human rights (16 percent), conflict resolution (16 percent) and routine social practices (12 percent). In the Colombian communities, people primarily make decisions about their peacefulness based on social relationships rather than looking to more tangible and outcome-oriented indicators in the areas of security or development. This means that these communities prioritize social relationships, conflict resolution and transitional justice issues and primarily look to these factors when determining their overall peacefulness (Figures 5.3 and 5.4).

Interestingly, neither community had representative indicators in all categories. For example, Don Gabriel did not choose indicators in categories to do with

---

[10] Indicators were collected in these communities before the trial of Dominic Ongwen began in the International Criminal Court in 2016. However, I returned to the communities in 2016 to reconfirm indicators selected in 2013 and found that people continued to select indicators outside of human rights categories when determining their everyday peace.

[11] See codebook for definition and coding of the Transitional Justice & Human Rights category. This indicator was definitely at the margins of an already contested category and label. For more on this see Bell 2009: 27.

[12] Firchow and Mac Ginty 2018

[13] Baines 2010.

Indicator Analysis in Uganda and Colombia

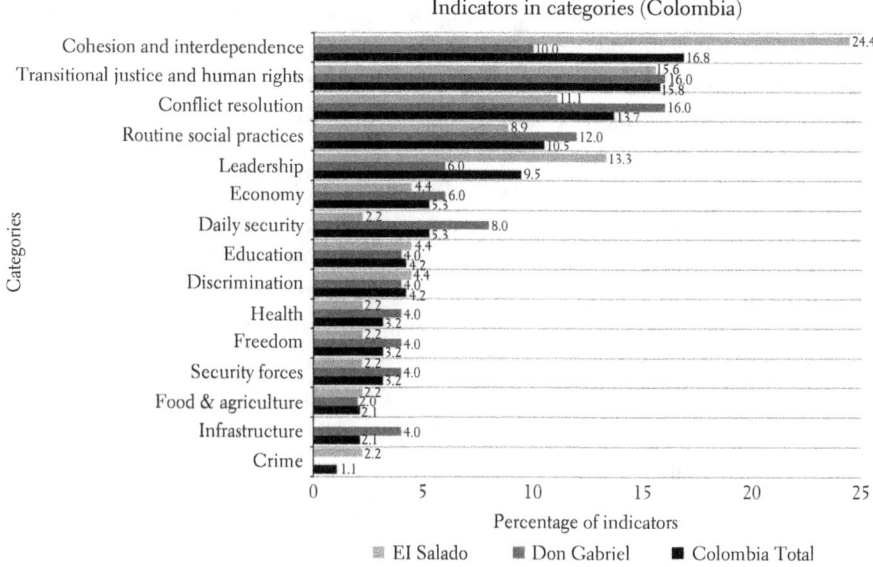

FIGURE 5.3. Percentage of peace indicators by category in El Salado and Don Gabriel

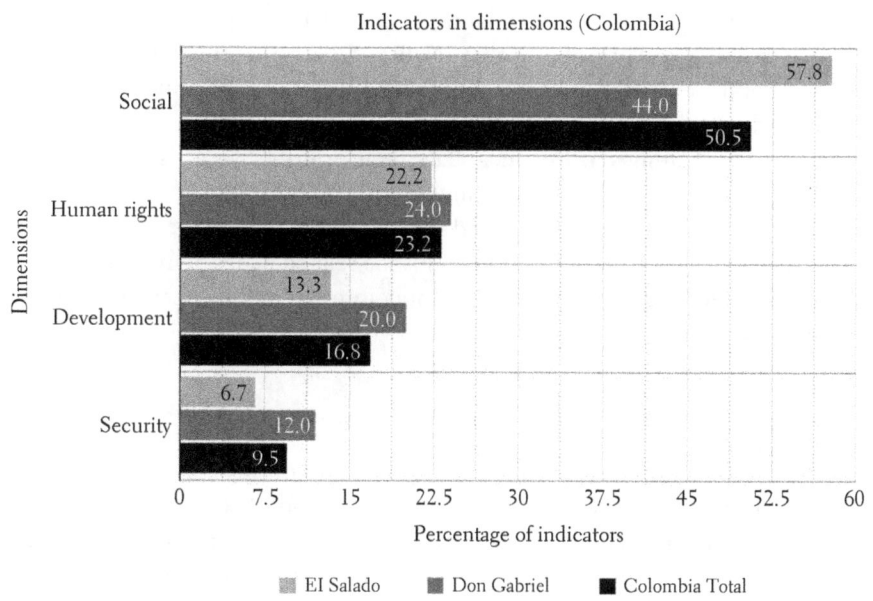

FIGURE 5.4. Percentage of indicators by dimension in El Salado and Don Gabriel

food and agriculture or crime, indicating that these were not as much of concern when determining daily peacefulness in their community (Table 5.2). This may be because they are not acute problems that community members in this particular remote village were concerned about. For example, in Don Gabriel farming may have been relatively unaffected by the war except during the time period when villagers were displaced over ten years ago. In turn, in El Salado community members did not choose indicators surrounding infrastructure. Again, this may be because these were issues that did not cause problems for them since they have received a large influx of development and reconstruction assistance.

In terms of social indicators, community members in El Salado and Don Gabriel chose indicators such as the ability to celebrate traditional festivals or activities with neighboring communities. The fact that villagers were able to participate in their traditional activities and show pride in their villages, through festivals and regional activities, was an important indicator of peace to people. Concern about leadership was expressed through indicators conveying expectations that people should work for the community without expecting anything in exchange or that a good attitude from the local government is important to villagers' everyday peace.

In contrast to Uganda, many issues associated with transitional justice and conflict resolution were highlighted by the everyday indicators in Colombia. Community members chose reparations, truth, justice, non-repetition, jail time, forgiveness and apology, as well as effective attention to victims as indicators of peace in their communities. Clearly, people are negotiating issues related to peace and justice and making decisions about priorities as they relate to these sometimes conflicting issues. The results of the everyday indicator process make sense considering the enormous amount of discussion surrounding the peace agreement and the potential consequences for communities as they negotiate their priorities vis-à-vis retributive and restorative justice for past harms done to them. In contrast, discussions surrounding transitional justice in Uganda happened right after the war (in the early 2000s) and the lack of engagement about transitional justice related issues demonstrated by the Ugandan indicators may be a result of a disappointment in the effectiveness of these processes or a belief in more traditional means of justice.

CROSS-NATIONAL ANALYSIS

From an analysis of local communities across different country contexts, several qualities of locally defined peace emerge. Everyday indicators of peace are directly correlated with everyday aspirations and needs of communities. For example, community members in Don Gabriel highlighted potable water as an indicator of peace. There was much discussion in the focus groups surrounding this indicator since community members were concerned that their water source was being contaminated by local cattle grazing and bathing in their water well, and they clearly wanted the issue resolved since it was a source of conflict among neighbors. Other indicators, such as the lack of presence of the public sector (civilian, police or military) in the village and a lack of medical attention, were also factors that affected life on a daily basis. In Uganda, many indicators reflected daily needs such as farming, education, freedom of movement and roads.

The everyday indicators are revealing about the immediacy of people's security context. People use indicators that are close at hand. In the community-sourced short and long lists of indicators, we found localized indicators such as the prevalence of barking dogs (a sign of prowlers), the ability for boda-boda cyclists to move about freely and the possibility to urinate outside at night (signs that there is freedom of movement and security). Indicators were locally contextualized and vernacular. When looking at security-related indicators, most are conceptualized as personal and related to the neighborhood or family. Such indicators, and the transcripts of the discussions around them, tended not to invoke overtly political narratives that saw security in terms of party politics or ethnic groups – ideas that might be used by ethnic or political entrepreneurs, or others who would want to exploit inter-group tensions. Moreover, and as further illustrated previously in Chapter 1, it is notable that most everyday indicators are not to be found in official indicators of (in)security, whether created by states, international organizations or donors.

Oliver Richmond has demonstrated that peace (and thus peacebuilding success) means different things to different people and organizations at different places and times. My own empirical research confirms Richmond's insights.[14] The indicators chosen revealed that community members used myriad factors to determine their peace and safety and did not focus exclusively on negative peace indicators. The categories created reflect those of positive peace, including education, employment, health, and human rights, as well as those of negative peace: crime, daily security and security forces. Everyday peace is a multidimensional and integrated concept. Community members had ontological notions of peace and security that considered multiple aspects of life and they struggled to compartmentalize different aspects of security. Indicators and discussions of peacefulness included issues of security and war and economic development, but also focused on freedom, social cohesion, gender violence, human rights and traditional practices. In addition, the indicators selected tell stories of the precariousness of life in conflict-related contexts and the fuzzy boundaries between criminal and political violence at the community level.

By coding indicators into categories, a picture of the multidimensionality and variability of peace begins to emerge. Reflecting the malleable nature of what peace means to individuals, there was significant variance in different communities' definition of peace and the environmental indicators they used in order to recognize it. Disaggregating by gender revealed that indicators sometimes reflected priorities relevant to traditional gender roles.[15] Yet the majority of indicators chosen across the

[14] Richmond 2005.
[15] Mac Ginty and Firchow 2016.

different research sites could be associated with basic needs and aspirations such as safety from violence or access to public services and human rights.

MASLOW'S HIERARCHY OF NEEDS AND THE EVERYDAY INDICATORS

Analysis of the indicators also revealed the dynamic and evolving nature of local conceptions of peace. Locally defined peace is a moving target. A cross-national comparison demonstrates that communities facing immediate threats of violence are more likely to look toward security-related indicators to determine peace than those that have had relative stability in recent years.[16] This finding reinforces those from previous studies that also use local level data. For example, Patrick Vinck and Phuong Pham compare data from the Eastern Democratic Republic of the Congo (DRC) and northern Uganda to demonstrate that the further a country is from conflict, the more development-related needs will take priority, while security takes precedence in places where conflict is ongoing.[17] The findings resonate with Maslow's basic needs conceptualization – a framework that has played a significant role in the development of peace and conflict theory.[18] As people become temporally removed from conflict and preoccupations with imminent security threats subside, they can turn their attention to more social and material issues.[19]

A shift from security-focused to development-focused concerns over time is even more apparent when analyzing all of the indicators collected by the Everyday Peace Indicators project in fourteen communities in five countries (South Africa, South Sudan, Uganda, Zimbabwe and Colombia). An analysis of everyday indicators coded into categories and then dimensions across these fourteen communities demonstrated that communities that were further away in time from violent conflict tended to choose more positive peace indicators than those closer to violent political conflict and crime (see Figure 5.5).[20]

The same finding was also mirrored at a country level. Urban communities experiencing higher levels of crime used predominantly security-related indicators to measure peace in their everyday lives. In Uganda, for example, the urban community of Kanyagoga was highly concerned with issues of security (42 percent).[21] This reflects the reality of an urban post-conflict context of economic and war-related

---

[16] This is based on a factor analysis of the different categories. The more everyday indicators that were chosen in a particular category meant that this category was weighted more heavily than the others. Since individuals choose their own top indicators through a voting process, we can assume that overall averages represent priorities for the different localities.
[17] Vinck and Pham 2008.
[18] Burton 1993.
[19] Maslow 1943.
[20] See Uvin 2013: 46 for more about the link between crime and war for local communities in war torn societies.
[21] Kanyagoga neighborhoods (wards A, B and C) have a total population of around 19,000 inhabitants (Gulu District Local Government Statistical Abstract 2012/2013).

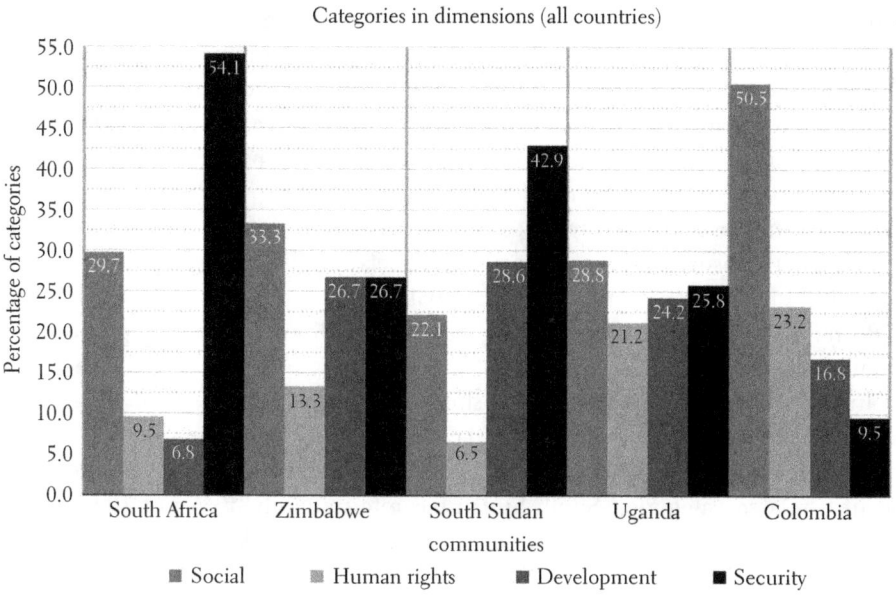

FIGURE 5.5. Dimensions of everyday indicators in five countries

IDPs living in a densely populated space that has had a recent influx of Dinka refugees from South Sudan. However, overall in Uganda, the security categories contained only 26 percent of indicators, similar to Zimbabwe at 27 percent. Routine social practices was the most selected category for Zimbabwe and Uganda. These countries were both several years post-conflict when this study was conducted and rural communities were experiencing relative calm. Therefore, it makes sense that the rest of the indicator categories were related to positive peace issues such as infrastructure, economic development, education, freedom, leadership, cohesion/interdependence and food/agriculture.

Communities and countries experiencing higher levels of violent conflict chose higher levels of negative peace indicators. For example, South Africa's top category was daily security (28 percent) and all three security categories constituted 54 percent of the indicators chosen in all three South African pilots. The pilot communities we worked in have deeply entrenched and powerful gangs that began to gain power in the 1980s, nurtured by the instability created by social dislocation and related organized crime, drug trade and other illicit activities.[22] The EPI indicators from South Africa tell a story of concerns about daily security and crime, and a disappointment with peacebuilding efforts in their communities. They demonstrate unease among residents with the categorization of gang violence simply as criminal

[22] Pinnock 1984.

violence, rather than a representation of a legacy of Apartheid, and accentuate the racial dimensions still prevalent in people's perceptions of their peace and safety.[23] For example, an indicator from the community-sourced short list in Hanover Park demonstrates that people do not only feel safer when there is a police presence in the community, but they feel even more at ease when that police presence includes *coloured* police officers – something which is clearly important to a community that identifies itself primarily as coloured (94 percent of inhabitants according to the 2011 census), and something that reflects the historical dimensions of the relationship these communities have had with the South African police. Thus, the EPIs reflect a concern with the lasting legacies of political violence in post-conflict contexts.[24]

Insecurity was slightly less though still prevalent in South Sudan, where daily security represented 23 percent of indicators, security/crime represented 10 percent, and security/forces 9 percent, for a total of 42 percent of indicators falling into security-related categories. South Sudan has intermittently been in a state of civil war since December 2013 (the same year we began our pilot there). Hundreds of thousands have been killed and many more displaced since then. The indicators selected in South Sudan show once again that security is of premium importance when defining everyday peace by those who are under violent threat.

It is important to note, however, that research was done with everyday civilians and not with armed actors or militants and activists. Studies have shown that certain groups are willing to forego their basic needs, such as safety and physiological needs, in order to fight for a common cause.[25] This was not the case among the communities we worked with, although this may be because of the snapshot in time in which we collected indicators. It may also be that groups willing to forego security and shelter or food as priorities have reached a certain threshold where they no longer have certainty that they will have those things in the future. Another possibility is that those groups have not recently experienced violent conflict and are therefore more willing to risk losing their basic needs or prioritizing issues like justice, dignity or identity over security and wellbeing. These groups also may not make up the majority of communities and tend to stand at the sidelines until there are enough grievances to constitute a critical mass prepared to fight for human needs higher up the pyramid. Whatever the case may be, we saw a clear trend across our pilot studies that indicated to us a strong priority for security in communities directly affected by violent conflict, whereas those further away from violence prioritized development and issues surrounding social cohesion and conflict resolution. Local concepts of peace evolve over time and through phases of conflict and recovery.

---

[23] Jensen 2010; Lemanski 2004.
[24] Gibson 2003.
[25] Burton 1990.

APPLYING EPI TO BETTER INTERVENTION DESIGN

The everyday indicators were designed to better understand what communities prioritize and look to in order to define their peace. This, in turn, can help those working for peace or change in a community design and plan their projects in more applicable ways that are in tune with community needs. For example, many indicators in Uganda dealt with issues of infrastructure and development, such as internet access or the construction of roads and electrical power. Programs that address and prioritize these specific issues would strengthen community perceptions that not only are their concerns being addressed, but that their everyday peace is a priority for their government and external interveners. Thus, the everyday indicators can be used to help guide policy and to design more effective intervention strategies of importance to beneficiary communities.

Indicators can help to identify specific areas for program design that may not otherwise be known to third party interveners. For example, in El Salado, Colombia, an indicator that was selected was "people working for the benefit of the community without expecting anything in exchange." Clearly, there are issues of the legitimacy of leaders and the motivations behind their actions. Reconsidering how interveners and governments incentivize local leaders would be a specific issue that could be addressed to deal with potential conflicts in the community. Indicators can also identify groups of people in specific locations that are of concern. For example, in South Africa people often identified groups of men hanging around certain stores as a cause for alarm or the coroner not picking up dead bodies in a timely fashion. These are all examples of ways that these experience-near indicators can help direct programs to address community grievances.

CONCLUSION

This chapter has given a brief illustration of bottom-up worldviews as captured by community-generated indicators of peace. From the analysis of the indicators, it is clear that international and local indicators and narratives of peace should be aligned when conducting external interventions with normative goals of peace and reconciliation. In addition, the chapter demonstrates how local indicators can inform external interventions by giving nuance to program design as well as demonstrating needs and priorities in broad areas of intervention. A lack of coordination between communities and external interveners can have serious political and social consequences if international peacebuilding interventions fail to deal with the needs and expectations of local populations.[26]

The categorization of indicators allows us to compare and contrast the ways communities define peace and determine whether or not they look more toward

---

[26] Roberts 2011b.

security, development, human rights, etc. in evaluating their levels of peacefulness. The everyday indicators themselves give us more localized, contextual detail that is accessible to policy-makers and is easy to understand. Together, the everyday indicators and categories give more information about what people prioritize in their daily lives, which issues should be most addressed and how. The everyday indicators are representative of the community as a whole and are not the individual opinions of community elites or local NGO staff, thereby mitigating some of the elite capture that often comes with program implementation.

In Colombia and Uganda, we can see that communities in both countries with high levels of intervention prioritize indicators related to social issues such as conflict resolution and reconciliation. In other words, social issues related to peacebuilding and reconciliation are of priority to people in communities that have received high levels of interventions. This finding indicates that *small-p* peacebuilding and reconciliation programming are indeed prioritized by communities with high levels of intervention after war, perhaps because they have the ability and space to see the need for non-material forms of reconstruction. It also finds that the communities in this matched case study did not prioritize security-related indicators when determining their everyday peace. This is consistent with our findings from the analysis of the pilots, which demonstrate that communities currently or recently experiencing violence are more likely to choose security-related indicators to measure peace than those further away from violent events. The latter are more likely to use social cohesion or development-related indicators.

Everyday indicators of peace are highly variable and dependent on context, which has significant implications for peacebuilding design and implementation. This clearly demonstrates that template approaches to peacebuilding are not sufficient to address localized concerns and that much more attention must be paid to finding ways of contextualizing interventions to circumstances. I now turn to an analysis of the EPI survey data collected in the communities in order to reflect further why local level interventions in these communities failed and why they succeeded.

6

Why Do Local Level Interventions Fail and Why Do They Succeed?

INTRODUCTION

If communities have a voice, how does our definition of successful interventions change? By using community-generated indicators of peace to formulate survey questions, we can track levels of peace – as defined by communities – over time. When we do so, a picture of community perceptions of peacebuilding success – or lack thereof – emerges, with significant implications for peacebuilding practice and intervention design.

This chapter presents a statistical analysis of survey data from the matched case research design and offers insights into why local level interventions fail or succeed in achieving peace in communities.[1] It suggests that external interventions after conflict have not contributed to significantly higher perceptions of overall community-level peace as defined by community-generated indicators of peace. The study finds that the communities in the matched case research design within each country display similar levels of peace according to community-defined indicators, and that there is only some difference between the villages in average levels of community-defined peace in each community according to the survey results. From the comparative case studies in Colombia and Uganda, results indicate that more intervention in communities does not necessarily result in significantly better overall

---

[1] For this analysis, survey results were analyzed as follows. Descriptive statistics were first calculated on demographics and on each response to the EPI questions in order to get a general overview of peace perception within communities. Then, each question was separately analyzed, and responses were looked at based on demographic variables like age, sex, gender, length of stay in the community, level of education, occupation, and by benefit collection, if applicable. Each of these analyses allowed me to look for underlying differences in peace perception. A test on difference of means for all communities was run to achieve statistical certainty of my claims, as well as box and whiskers graphs to identify major trends in responses. The STATA statistical package was used for this analysis.

outcomes.[2] As discussed earlier, this result suggests that more focus is needed on the constituents and distribution of interventions, as well as the level of investment and local participation of communities in interventions.

KEY FINDINGS

When looking at the results of community-wide surveys that measure levels of peace as defined by community-generated indicators, the results in Colombia and Uganda both indicate low substantive average difference between the two communities chosen in each country in the matched case research design, despite significant differences in external intervention received. The cross-country comparison shows that overall levels of community-defined peacefulness are significantly higher in both communities in Uganda than they are in Colombia.[3] Although I find a statistical difference between the two communities in each country, the difference is not substantive for the overall average.[4] In other words, there is a statistical difference between the communities, but this difference is not big enough to support claims about a substantive difference in average levels of peacefulness in the two matched case communities according to community defined indicators.[5]

At this point it is important to discuss what I consider constitutes a substantive difference between communities. The findings presented in this chapter are based primarily on the results of survey questions generated from the everyday peace indicators and ranked by respondents on a 1–5 Likert-type scale ranging from "never" to "always." Yet, at what point is the difference between indicator averages, categories or individual indicators important and when is it not? There is no commonly held standard for establishing substantive difference or determining how much and

---

[2] See Chapter 3 for more information on sample size and survey procedures. See Chapter 4 for more information on the research design in Uganda and Colombia.

[3] The difference in means is statistically significant at 95 percent confidence. There is a significant difference in the mean of everyday peace indicators for Atiak R1 ($M = 3.74$, $SD = .44$) and Odek R1 ($M = 3.59$, $SD = .37$); $t(200) = 2.63$, $p = 0.009$ (for round 1), a significant difference in the mean of indicators for Atiak R2 ($M = 3.79$, $SD = .52$) and Odek R2 ($M = 3.57$, $SD = .34$); $t(256) = 4.33, p = .000$ (for round 2), and a significant difference in the mean of indicators for Atiak R3 ($M = 3.81$, $SD = .37$) and Odek R3 ($M = 3.66$, $SD = .41$); $t(383) = 3.98, p = .000$ (for round 3). There is a significant difference in the mean of everyday peace indicators for El Salado ($M = 2.54$, $SD = .53$) and Don Gabriel ($M = 2.12$, $SD = .30$); $t(496) = 12.29$, $p = .000$. Full statistical results are available from the author by request.

[4] Since the indicators differed across communities, they are, technically, not directly comparable. However, the use of secondary level dimensions (as explained in Chapter 5) allows us to compare categories directly even though those categories are measured by different indicators in each of the communities.

[5] There is a very slight margin of error in Colombia since we surveyed all households in both El Salado and Don Gabriel. In Uganda, there is a 6 percent margin of error for Atiak and a seven percent margin of error for Odek. In order to calculate the margin of error I used population figures of adults ages 18 and above in those sub-counties from the 2014 Ugandan census.

when something matters on a statistical scale, nor does substantive difference ensure statistical significance or causality.[6] Essentially, this is done by placing it in perspective and making relatively subjective decisions about whether or not the difference demonstrates something substantive or not. Therefore, for the purposes of this study I will establish substantive difference at 0.5 on the Likert-type scale. Half a point difference on a 5 point scale gives us a sense that there was a real change or difference in perception between surveys or between communities. This becomes only more substantive as that point difference grows. In addition, 0.5 represents a shift of 1/10 on the Likert-type scale and it would be hard to claim that any smaller difference is substantively meaningful. It is, however, important to keep in mind that although there may be a substantive difference in particular categories or related to specific indicators, this difference is still relatively small. In none of the cases studied did the overall average of the indicators differ more than 1 point on the Likert-type scale. Therefore, although it is important to note the differences and discuss them, the findings still indicate that there was little overall difference between perceptions of peacefulness across the in-country comparison cases.

Using these parameters for substantive difference, when I disaggregate for individual indicators and categories of peace we see a more checkered record of success. Communities with little intervention across the study perceive more security than those with a lot of intervention. In comparison, according to the survey data, daily security in particular is an issue of increased concern for those communities that have received more external intervention.[7] In development, another dimension of peace, the communities that have received high levels of assistance report significantly higher levels of development. These results indicate that development interventions have an effect on community perceived changes; however, and in contrast to leading theories of change in the peacebuilding literature, they also suggest that development comes with the cost of higher perceived insecurity among residents.[8]

In the dimension of social relations, results in communities with assistance are on average only slightly higher than those in low-intervention communities, suggesting that communities with large amounts of external interventions lack an appropriate amount of *small-p* peacebuilding interventions in post-conflict communities. This is particularly important when taking into consideration the finding presented in Chapter 5 that communities with more intervention prioritize indicators of social relations when defining peace.

The next section takes a more detailed look at findings in each country context. It examines the kinds of external interventions being implemented in the surveyed

---

[6] Miller 2015: 56–9.
[7] Residents of those communities in Uganda perceived a substantively meaningful difference in security, whereas the difference in Colombia, while statistically significant, was too small to be substantively meaningful.
[8] Bachmann and Schouten 2018.

communities to determine whether or not they complement community needs and perceptions of peace. An analysis of the indicators gives context and nuance to what communities affected by violence use to measure their own everyday peace and how their indicators compare to the measures of those external actors implementing programs. Conducting such a gap analysis gives us a better understanding of why community-level interventions have often fallen short in addressing community level concerns. It demonstrates that in large part the constituents and distribution of many interventions after war are not in tune with the specific needs and priorities of communities. The actual everyday indicators selected by communities and complemented by qualitative data collected through interviews and focus groups, give us insight into the survey results and reveal how interveners are sometimes disconnected from community needs. By looking at the kinds of interventions being implemented in the selected communities, especially in the communities with high levels of intervention, and comparing types of intervention to community indicators, I generate a new gap analysis that can reveal whether interventions are designed to succeed or fail, according to community definitions of peace.

Why Do Local Level Interventions Often Fail to Significantly Increase Everyday Peace?

Colombia

On average, during two annual surveys in Colombia, Don Gabriel answered that they "never" perceived positive indicators of peace and El Salado answered that they "rarely" perceived positive indicators of peace based on a 1–5 Likert-type scale.[9] Peace perception improved slightly for El Salado between 2016 and 2017, whereas it decreased for Don Gabriel during the same time period. El Salado, the community with higher levels of intervention, had a slightly (0.45 point) higher peace perception than Don Gabriel in the first round of surveys. In the second round, that gap grew to 0.826 (see Figures 6.1 and 6.2). Overall, people in El Salado have a higher peace perception than in Don Gabriel as seen below in Figures 6.1 and 6.2, with a substantive difference in peace perception between the two communities after the peace accord was put into place in November of 2016 as demonstrated by the second survey.

Although average overall levels of peacefulness are relatively close between the two communities, upon conducting a disaggregated analysis of peace indicators, unique profiles for each community emerge. As seen in Figures 6.3 and 6.4, when analyzing the indicators by category and indicator question, inhabitants of El Salado

---

[9] Questions were all phrased positively, such as "Does the local government have a good attitude?" In those cases where this was not possible, the data scale was reversed for measurement purposes. For example, "Is there consumption of drugs?"

Key Findings

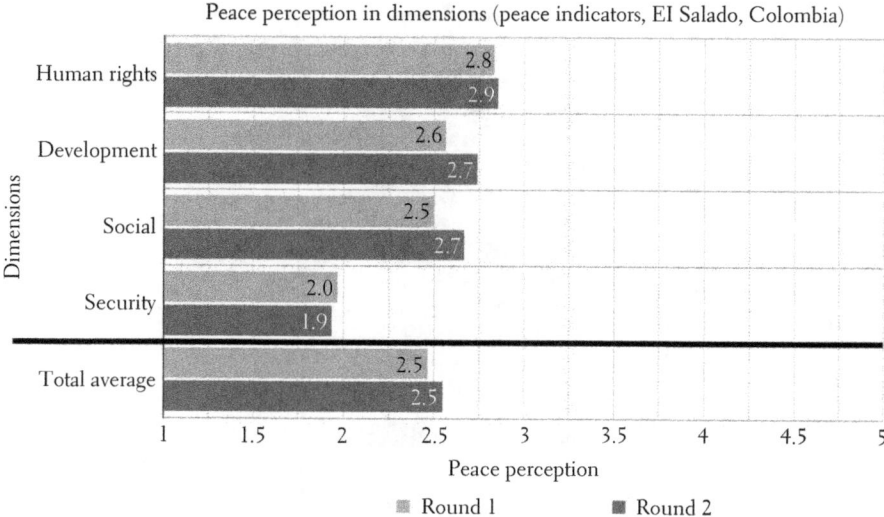

FIGURE 6.1. Dimensional analysis of survey results – El Salado

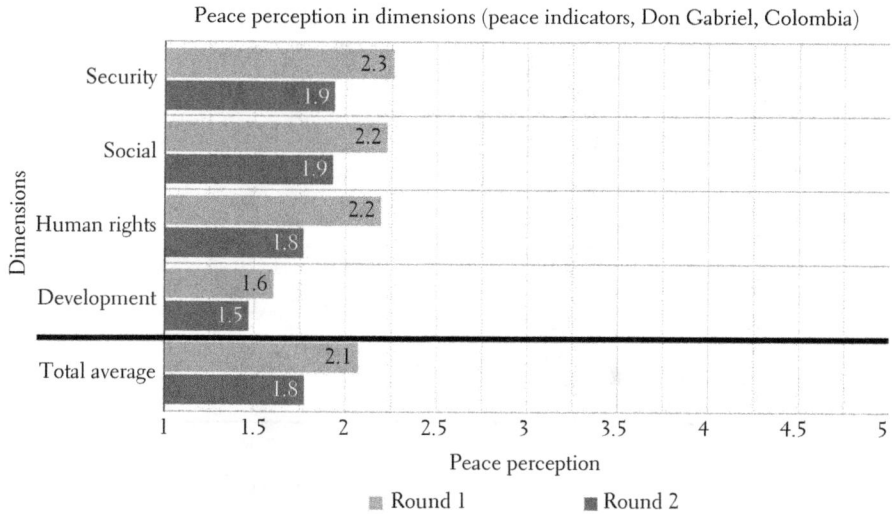

FIGURE 6.2. Dimensional analysis of survey results – Don Gabriel

feel significantly more freedom than in Don Gabriel and this gap only grows more substantive over time. They also have significantly higher levels of food and agricultural security, feel more economic security, and are more comfortable with their leadership. There are positive indications that relations between communities neighboring El Salado continue to improve, with residents answering on average that they sometimes have joint activities with other communities. In Don Gabriel,

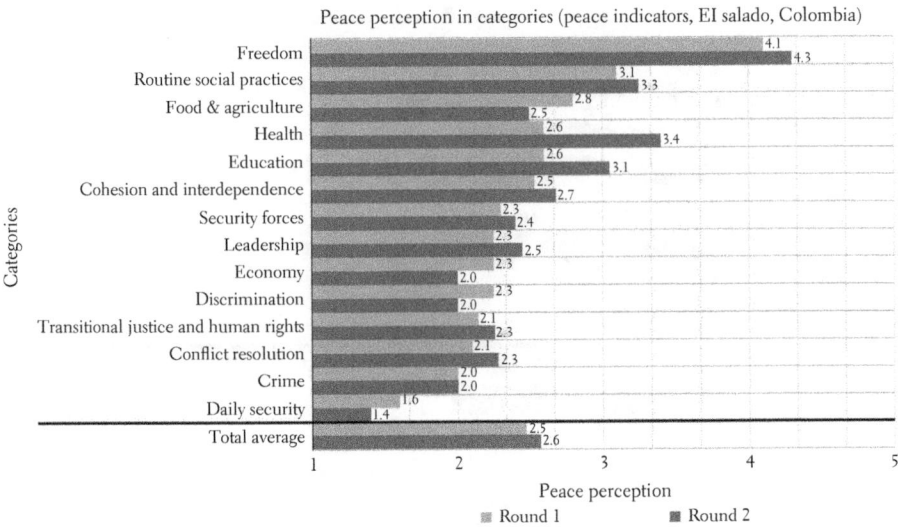

FIGURE 6.3. Category analysis of survey results – El Salado[a]
[a]Residents of El Salado did not choose any peace indicators in the category of "Infrastructure."

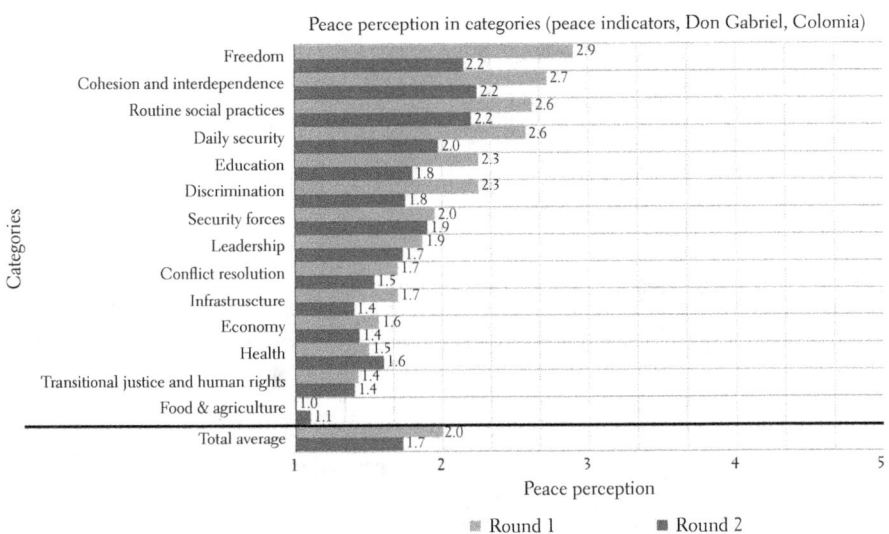

FIGURE 6.4. Category analysis of survey results – Don Gabriel[a]
[a]Residents of Don Gabriel did not choose any peace indicators in the category of "Crime."

neighboring relations seem to have declined between survey rounds. Respondents felt in the first round that they often had good relations with neighboring communities, but in the second round this went down about 1 point from "sometimes" to "rarely" having good relations, although they continue to rarely have joint activities.

Key Findings

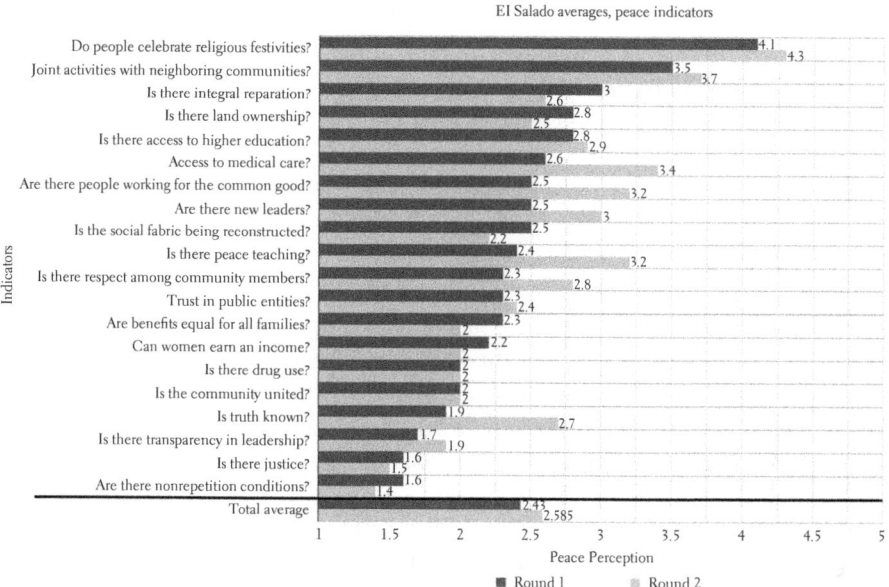

FIGURE 6.5. El Salado average survey responses – peace indicators

In fact, residents of El Salado overall have a higher peace perception than Don Gabriel in all categories except for daily security. This is despite the fact that El Salado (with a population of approximately 1,500 inhabitants) is protected by a police post staffed with ten police officers in addition to a military outpost on a hill above the community that is staffed at all times by two soldiers. Yet, inhabitants in El Salado continued to feel more or equally insecure in comparison to Don Gabriel, which does not have any police post or military presence nearby, suggesting that communities with higher levels of intervention perceive higher levels of insecurity.

It is evident from the survey data that residents of these villages struggle to come to terms with past injustices. As we can see in Figure 6.5, villagers fear that war will return to the region and feel that justice has never been done and that the truth of what happened there is not known. Considering the significant amount of security provided to El Salado in the form of police and military protection in comparison to Don Gabriel, it seems important that when asked, "In El Salado, are there conditions in place that ensure that the victimizing events will not repeat themselves?," 75 percent said *never* and 4 percent replied *rarely*, and the percentage of people responding negatively increased in the second round of surveys. In fact, confidence levels went down by 0.2 points between the first and second rounds. This "nonrepetition indicator," along with the indicator measuring perceptions of justice, was ranked the lowest among the peace perception spectrum for El Salado.

Although residents of El Salado have higher opinions of whether or not their human rights are being respected, the average response remains only *rarely* (as opposed to *never* in Don Gabriel). Residents responded overwhelmingly negatively to questions on the status of human rights and transitional justice. Such a low average response for human rights related indicators may be relevant for El Salado since significant efforts at documentation, reparations and human rights capacity training has taken place in the village, including a book published about the events of the massacres.[10] When asked, "In El Salado, does one know the truth about the victimizing events?" 60 percent responded *never* and 10 percent *rarely*. When asked, "In El Salado, has justice been achieved regarding the victimizing events?" 69 percent replied *never* and 8 percent replied *rarely*. Respondents' confidence in reparations decreased in the second round of surveys even though El Salado has received significant attention regarding both individual and collective reparations and was also one of the original pilots of the government's first collective reparations program (PIRC).[11]

While these findings are initially puzzling, a closer analysis shows that community needs for justice have not been directly addressed. The great majority of interventions that El Salado has received have been focused on development, health and education as reconstruction efforts after the violence and displacement, many in the form of collective reparations. Of the large amount of intervention El Salado has absorbed, only a small percentage has been *small-p* peacebuilding work. In fact, as demonstrated in Chapter 4, there have only been three main interventions that would be categorized as such: the documentation and publication of the massacre in El Salado,[12] the psychosocial support given through a court order to the community by the *Fundación Mi Sangre*[13] and, most recently, a process of dialogue, mourning and reconstruction of the community's social fabric called *Entrelazando*, conducted by the Unidad para las Víctimas.[14] These have been complemented by some public memorialization activities in the community.

Similarly, in Don Gabriel the lowest ranked indicators (sometimes as low as 0.1) dealt with issues of justice for victims, alongside access to clean water and medical care (although the latter indicator had markedly improved by the second round) (see Figure 6.6). In contrast to El Salado, however, Don Gabriel has still not received reparations as of 2017 so this result is not as surprising. However, the government has recently started visiting the community and has held some initial meetings and information sessions, which may actually have contributed to the decrease in peace perception in the second round. Don Gabriel has experienced an increase in access

---

[10] Machado et al. 2009.
[11] Firchow 2013b.
[12] Grupo de Memoria Histórica. "La Masacre de El Salado: Esa Guerra no era nuestra (The El Salado Massacre: That war was not ours")" 2009, www.centrodememoriahistorica.gov.co/descargas/informes2009/informe_la_masacre_de_el_salado.pdf
[13] For the judgment in Spanish, see: www.corteconstitucional.gov.co/relatoria/2010/t-045-10.htm
[14] This process was only started within the last year. For more about *Entrelazando* in Spanish, see: www.unidadvictimas.gov.co/sites/procesos_caracterizados/38.%20PROCEDIMIENTO%20ENTRELAZANDO%20v3.pdf

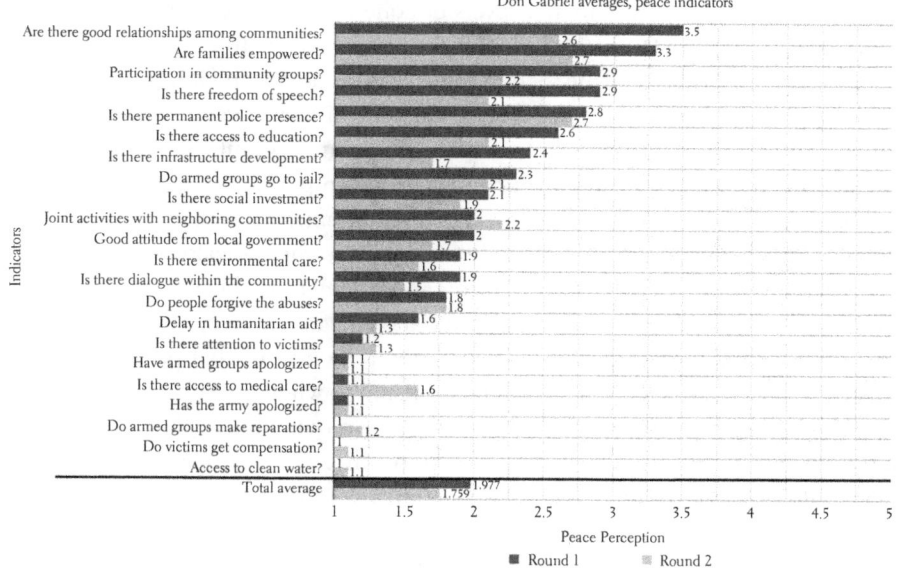

FIGURE 6.6. Don Gabriel average survey responses – peace indicators[a]

[a] Questions in these figures are abbreviated. Please see Chapter 5 for the complete list of indicators.

to information and contact with the government in the last year, which has also raised expectations. In addition, the peace process has also brought more attention to government benefits for victims and those displaced, and people are more informed about what neighboring communities are receiving. Evidence that people are much better informed in Don Gabriel is demonstrated by the striking difference in responses to the question "Has Don Gabriel received Collective Reparations?" In the first round of surveys, 53.8 percent of respondents answered that they had received collective reparations. A year later, in the second round of surveys, only 2.6 percent responded affirmatively to this question![15] This change in capacitation and exposure may in part explain why levels of peace perception have gone down in Don Gabriel, since people are more informed and responding with higher expectations than they did previously.

Demonstrating the difference in interventions between the two communities, when looking at dimensions of peace, residents of the two villages report significant, substantive differences in the area of development. Villagers in El Salado rate development-related indicators significantly higher than those in Don Gabriel, with a 1 point difference between the two villages. This reflects the reality that El Salado has received significantly more development and reconstruction intervention than Don Gabriel.

[15] The surveys in the two rounds were identical and the question was asked in the same order and phrasing as in the first round of surveys. Answers to this question in El Salado remained around the same for both survey rounds.

Don Gabriel has slightly higher levels of cohesion and interdependence in the first round, indicating that people were more at harmony with one another than in El Salado. This changed by the second round with residents in Don Gabriel experiencing less social cohesion. El Salado also tends toward low perceptions of cohesion, which is important since El Salado community members ranked indicators in the category of cohesion and interdependence as most important in the indicator analysis presented in Chapter 5. People in El Salado define peace overwhelmingly in terms of cohesion and interdependence according to the indicator analysis, which is unfortunately precisely the kind of programming that has been neglected in the community. As previously discussed, although El Salado has received an enormous amount of outside support, little of that support attends to what people prioritize most and look to on a daily basis when determining whether they are more or less peaceful. These findings indicate that without symbolic and socially related programming in communities, development interventions by themselves do not lead to peace. Although El Salado has received significantly more intervention in terms of material assistance than Don Gabriel, the latter indicates only slightly lower levels of average social cohesion and social relations in general (according to the dimensional analysis in Figures 6.1 and 6.2).

Possibly a sign of more unity and consensus in Don Gabriel, there was more agreement there than in El Salado about levels of peace and a lower rate of response dispersion in both rounds of surveys. In round one in Don Gabriel there was a consensus in responses to questions about seven peace indicators: police presence, attention to victims, health services, water, military apology, compensation and armed group apology. In contrast, in El Salado, there was only majority consensus about non-repetition, with the overwhelming majority of villagers being uncertain about whether violence will return to the village or whether there are conditions preventing recurrence of victimizing events. Other categories of indicators in El Salado showed a high dispersion of responses, reflecting a diversity of views about various indicators of peace.

These results are perhaps not surprising since many of the interventions that have been put in place have caused conflict in El Salado, pitting certain groups against others – in particular beneficiaries against non-beneficiaries. This has been particularly the case in the implementation of reparations schemes.[16] Reparations schemes in El Salado have had a disproportionate emphasis on assistance and compensation and have not integrated enough *small-p* peacebuilding and reconciliation programming in order to help increase the impact of reparations on peace.[17]

A focus on the payment of individual reparations in the form of compensation has created resentment within El Salado. The perception is that certain people

---

[16] For more details on the effect of reparations on this community in comparison to Don Gabriel, see Firchow, 2017.
[17] Firchow 2017.

are favored in the participation of programs and the payment of benefits. Those who see themselves as most vulnerable feel isolated because they have not received compensation from the state. This is part of the strategy of the Colombian government, which follows the subsistence model of ensuring basic needs before paying reparations.[18] But because the strategy is poorly implemented and communicated to beneficiaries it has caused rancor in the community. Before paying reparations to anyone in a community, implementers should work to bring everyone in a village or community to a place where they are ready to receive reparations.

Feelings of resentment within the community also extend to benefits and assistance beyond reparations and are clearly illustrated in the indicators chosen by community members. Community members in El Salado chose "parity of benefits for families" and "the community is united" as indicators of peace. As one male community member complained: "they always give to the same ones – that's the fight" demonstrating the frustration of the community in the unequal distribution of assistance.[19] Another female community member explained to me: "when they [external actors] come here, they need to look closely at the internal dynamics. If you give something to one neighbor and not to the other – why? That causes conflict."[20] This was a resounding theme in the interviews I conducted in El Salado. When looking at peace indicators disaggregated demographically, for those who self-identified as project beneficiaries in El Salado there was only a very slight difference (<0.2) in their responses from those who identified as non-beneficiaries. Non-beneficiaries were only slightly less optimistic when responding to questions based on the peace indicators. In other words, receiving benefits does not seem to alter peace perception and being a beneficiary of a project did not make a community member significantly more or less optimistic about peace in their village, perhaps because beneficiaries perceive themselves as targets of non-beneficiaries.[21] This was also the case for Don Gabriel and remained consistent throughout both rounds of surveys.

From the outside, the external intervention in El Salado can be seen as highly participatory with accompaniment by the Fundación Semana and continuous consultation with community members, as demonstrated by my interviews with Fundación Semana and the government actors working in the village. Yet, clearly from the inside, external intervention has caused conflict and rancor among community members, in particular for those who have felt excluded and marginalized. Disagreements about who has been consulted, who has benefited and who has a right to benefits cause community members to feel less at peace. This indicates that although a participatory approach in planning and implementing external

---

[18] Dixon 2016; Unidad de Víctimas Staff 1, Cartagena, March 4, 2016.
[19] Interview, El Salado, March 1, 2016.
[20] Interview, El Salado, February 23, 2016.
[21] The self-identifying question was: Have you received some kind of project assistance in relation to the violence in your community?

interventions is important, it is also important to think about the politics of community participation – who is included, as well as who is excluded, and what kinds of consequences unequal distribution of benefits may have for community cohesion. Uneven implementation and participation can have detrimental consequences for sustainable peace by creating further divides in a community.

Uganda

"With the amount of actors we have received here, we should be the most peaceful and well off place, but our spirit is not there. People do not want to do as they are told, they do not want to work. The camps were a place for staying and waiting and if you get used to that then you don't understand how the world works" (Community Leader, **Atiak** (November 24, 2016)).

"People in the camps were idle, when they returned from the camps they continued this, but now people are working hard again" (Community Leader, **Odek** (November 25, 2016)).

In both communities in Uganda, residents answered on average that they "sometimes" perceived positive indicators of peace in their communities, with an overall average of 3.5 in Odek and 3.67 in Atiak over all three rounds of surveys (see Figures 6.9 and 6.10). Reflecting the same trend as in Colombia, the community with higher levels of interventions, Atiak, demonstrated a marginally higher level of peacefulness according to community-defined indicators. In the first round of surveys, there was a 0.15 difference between Atiak and Odek, with Atiak demonstrating a mean of 3.7 in peacefulness and Odek a mean of 3.55 (see Figures 6.9 and 6.10). Levels of peacefulness remained stable for all three years, although in year two they decreased slightly (0.1) in Odek.

Survey results suggest that although Atiak has received significantly more intervention than Odek, average perceived levels of peacefulness over three years of surveys remain similar to those in Odek. The reasons for this can be traced back to the impact of war and displacement, as well as subsequent external assistance. The two contrasting quotations above, from conversations with community leaders in Odek and Atiak, demonstrate the problems Acholi are facing in returning to their traditional lifestyles after being displaced. In refugee camps IDPs received assistance to satisfy their basic needs from external organizations, and could not work or farm. Living in the camps broke the social ties and community responsibilities and traditions that were ingrained in the Acholi culture. As a result, when the displaced returned to their villages, many had grown accustomed to receiving benefits such as food and housing from external actors, without needing to work. They no longer had a culture of pride and hard work, something that was especially true for the youth that had grown up in the camps. What interveners did not think about enough was how to effectively transition people from camp to village and what kind of programming was needed to address issues related specifically to years of idleness in a camp setting.

Key Findings

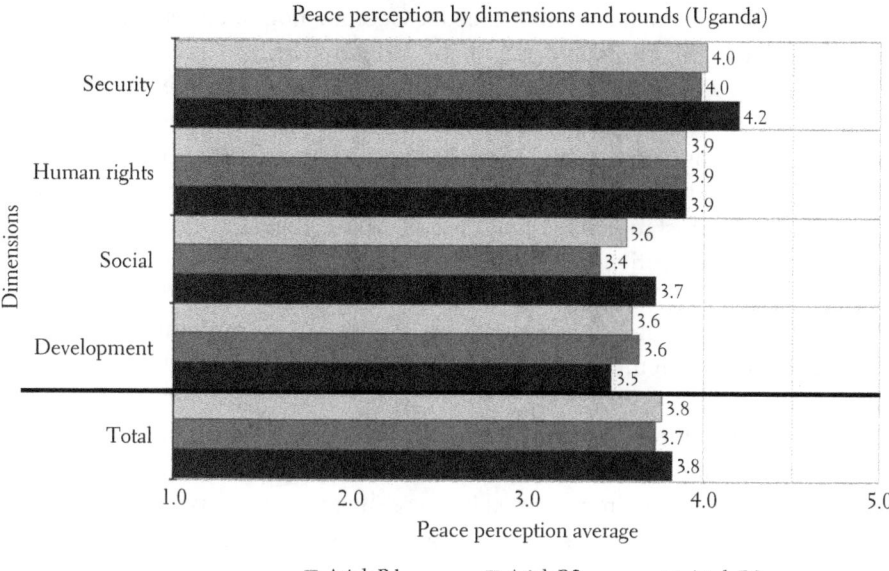

FIGURE 6.7. Peace perception by dimension – Atiak

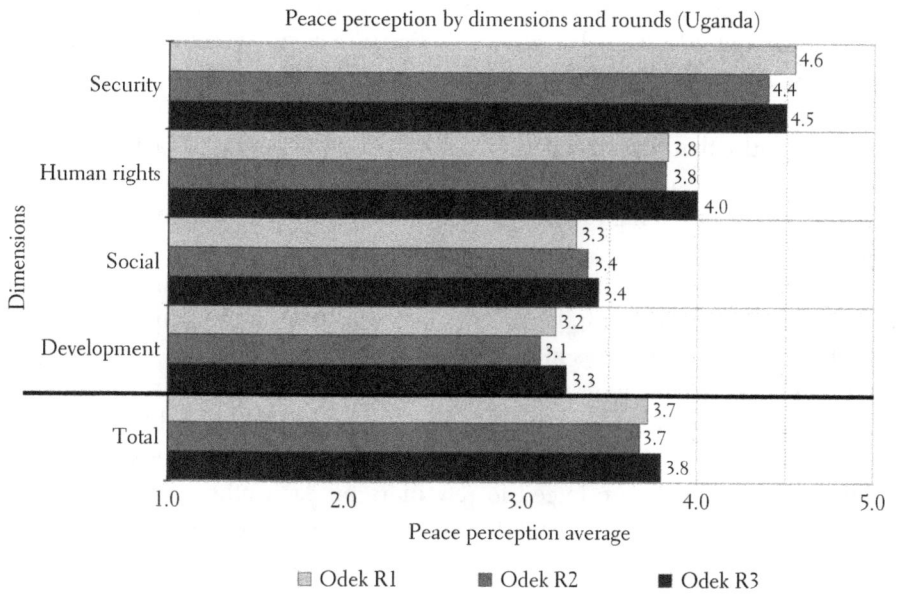

FIGURE 6.8. Peace perception by dimension – Odek

Until 2011, the United Nations Office for Coordination of Humanitarian Affairs (UNOCHA) coordinated interventions in northern Uganda. External actors, all coordinated by UNOCHA, worked mainly in the camps and on the reconstruction and return of IDPs around 2009. By 2004 almost everyone in northern Uganda lived either in an IDP camp or in a city.[22] During this time, most assistance projects lasted a maximum of three years. As one NGO worker who has been working in the area of humanitarian assistance since that time told me, "If you are going to assess the impact of their interventions from before, you can hardly feel that they were there."[23] Clearly, interventions during the conflict and displacement had little to no sustainable impact on community welfare and only attended to the most immediate needs.

Once people had returned to their villages and reconstructed their homes, the government of Uganda took over from UNOCHA and relegated the responsibility of coordination to the respective sub-counties or districts. Since then, all external organizations wanting to work in a sub-county should register with the sub-county or district, but often this is circumvented because the process is very bureaucratic and corrupt.[24] Therefore, records kept by the government are usually not an accurate reflection of what is happening on the ground. In addition, according to a representative of the Office of the Prime Minister, the government is now less interested in tracking what NGOs are doing in the area because sufficient resources are not available for the level of monitoring required.[25]

The fact that there has been little tracking or coordination of assistance in the region has resulted in an uneven distribution of benefits. Outside agencies working on the return of IDPs focused on reconstruction, but did not focus enough on issues pertaining to the social and psychological effects of camp displacements such as community cohesion, conflict resolution and psycho-social factors such as depression and apathy that have resulted in alcohol and drug abuse. A lack of focus on community needs was especially prevalent in high profile areas such as Atiak, which continued to receive a high level of outside assistance for development and reconstruction, but very little for activities focused on community cohesion and social issues. Survey results indicate slightly more unity and consensus in Odek. There was more agreement about indicators in Odek than in Atiak and an overall higher rate of dispersion of responses in Atiak over all three rounds. Odek had little to no intervention overall due to its remote location and the stigma associated with being the birthplace of Joseph Kony. This meant that people had to fend for themselves once they returned to their farming and daily routines. Without external assistance, community members were forced to rely more on each other when they found themselves in difficulty. As a result, the community seems to have slightly stronger

---

[22] Interview, former UNOCHA staff, Gulu, November 25, 2016.
[23] Interview, International NGO staff, Gulu, December 1, 2016.
[24] Interview, International NGO staff, Atiak, November 24, 2016.
[25] Interview, OPM staff, Gulu, November 25, 2016.

bonds than in Atiak as suggested by the levels of dispersion in the survey questions as well as interviews with community members. By pure necessity, people in Odek had to find ways to work together to overcome the extreme poverty they confronted and continue to confront today. Again, similar to Colombia, this indicates more consensus in communities with less intervention. In Atiak, there was only majority consensus about the presence of gunshots in the first round with the overwhelming majority infrequently hearing gunshots. In subsequent rounds, we see a decrease of dispersion as people in Atiak begin to agree more about the possibility of digging in their gardens (farming) and safely sleeping at home. Odek starts out in the first round with more consensus in responses to three peace indicators: sleeping safely at home, freedom of religion and the availability of electricity. These remain stable for the subsequent two rounds of the survey.

The situation in Odek is in contrast to Atiak, where outside assistance and external opportunities have been much more available. Many people in Atiak no longer feel they must rely on traditional forms of livelihood such as digging and farming in order to survive, since other opportunities for income have arisen through assistance and training programs and the recently paved Juba road running through Atiak. Since the road was completed in 2016, Atiak has become a strategic place for South Sudanese relations. The status of a larger trading center and business opportunities brought improvements with it, but also more problems, such as prostitution and crime. Although overall people in Odek and Atiak prioritized indicators of positive peace when identifying their everyday peace in categories such as cohesion and interdependence, routine social practices and conflict resolution, people in Atiak were especially concerned with issues of daily security when looking for signs of everyday peace (e.g. walking freely at night), as demonstrated by the indicator analysis in Chapter 5. Insecurity and crime are much more prevalent now in Atiak than they are in Odek, in part due to Atiak's proximity to South Sudan and its location along the Juba road. This is reflected in survey results indicating Atiak has lower scores for indicators in the security categories than Odek, suggesting that people in Atiak feel more insecure and exposed to crime and violence. This is consistent with the findings in Colombia that communities with more external intervention experience more perceived insecurity and suggests that the extra attention provided to communities, as well as additional infrastructure (such as roads) leads to additional security concerns (Figures 6.7 and 6.8). This finding is in contrast to the prevalent theory of change in the *Big-p* Peacebuilding community that large-scale infrastructure programs lead to peace, even at the local level.[26] Also, consistent with the findings in Colombia, Atiak indicated higher levels of development than Odek over all three rounds of surveys, due to the construction of the Juba road and other development and infrastructure-related interventions in that community.

---

[26] Bachmann and Schouten 2018: 3.

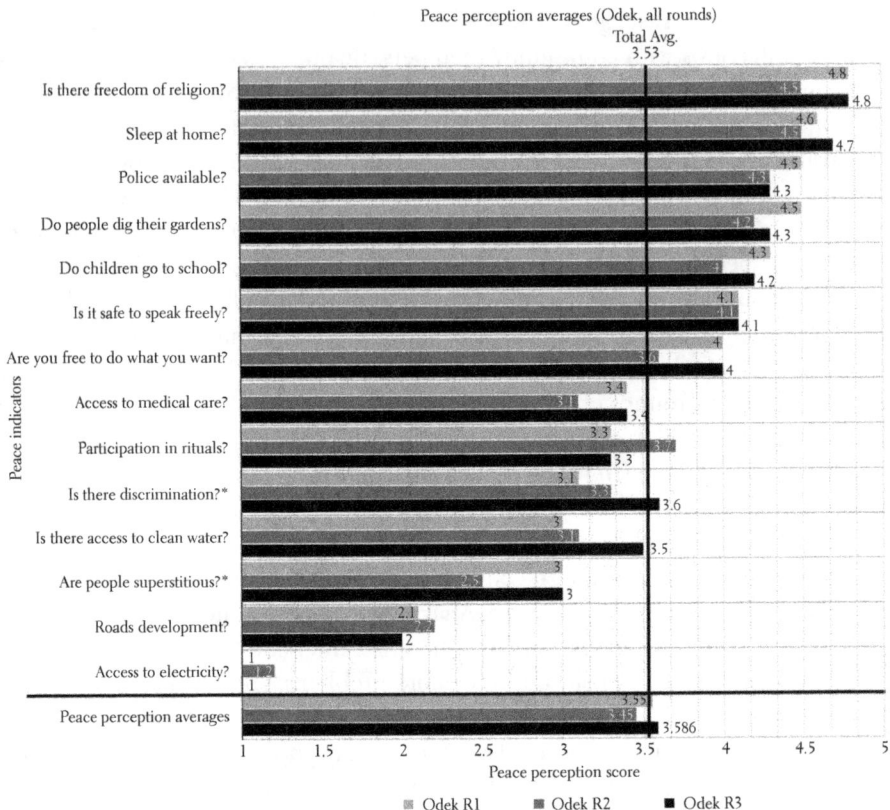

FIGURE 6.9. Odek average survey responses – peace indicators
*For questions that indicate less peace, we have used an inverted scale

Although both communities have received some *small-p* peacebuilding interventions, in the form of dialogue, community cohesion work, psycho-social support and memorialization, such interventions have been relatively minimal in comparison to reconstruction, economic development and humanitarian aid. The government approach has been to focus on reconstruction and assistance with little *small-p* peacebuilding elements integrated into its programming. As one local government official in Atiak explained to me: "From what I understand peacebuilding or reconciliation work to be, I have only seen this done by NGOs. The government funding is entirely focused on development-related work."[27] In fact, the Peace Recovery and Development Program (PRDP), the main government program related to peacebuilding in northern Uganda, is "not really peace-related"[28] and is not "so close to the

[27] Interview, Local Government Official, Atiak, November 24, 2016.
[28] Ibid. There have been three phases of the PRDP since 2007. The first focused on reconstruction (health, water, education and roads); the second expanded to eight areas with the above areas of focus

Key Findings

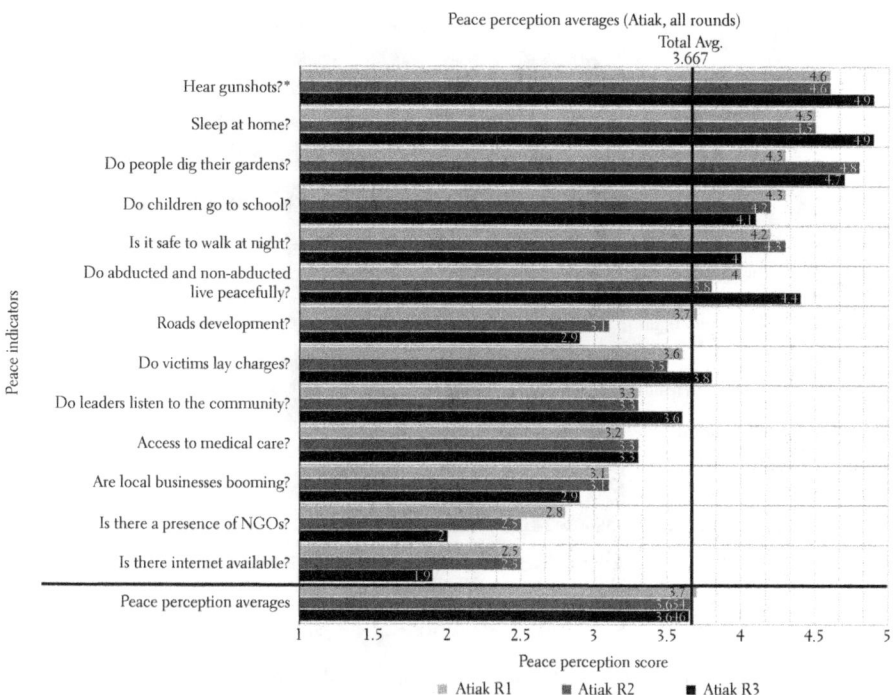

FIGURE 6.10. Atiak average survey responses – peace indicators
*For questions that indicate less peace, we have used an inverted scale

communities on the ground. It doesn't work with the community members directly."[29] In addition, neither symbolic nor compensatory reparations have been paid to any of the survivors, victims or displaced of northern Uganda. Little effect on beneficiaries is reflected by looking at peace indicators disaggregated demographically. We can see that there was a slightly higher (>0.2) perception of peacefulness among beneficiaries in Odek than non-beneficiaries (no difference in Atiak), although the difference was not substantive enough to make any conclusions about whether increased perceptions of peace can be associated with project beneficiary status.

As a consequence, the results from this study suggest that external interventions have failed to comprehensively address the difficulties of readjusting to normal life after living in the camps. In Atiak, this has been compounded by a quickly growing sub-county that now has many non-traditional sources of income, allowing its citizens to continue with a life more similar to the camps than to their previous existence. That is not say that Odek has not struggled with cultural norms being

---

adding capacity building environment and DDR; the third continues to focus on reconstruction, but has redirected most of its resources to focus on livelihoods (job trainings and increased incomes).

[29] Interview, Office of the Prime Minister, Gulu, November 25, 2016.

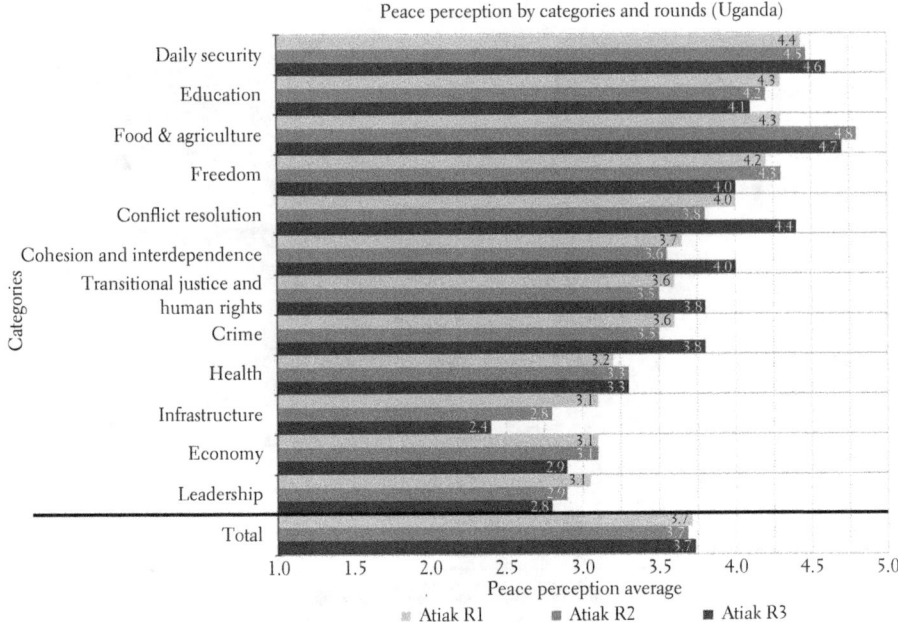

FIGURE 6.11. Peace perception by category – Atiak

disintegrated by the war; however, community cohesion is greater out of necessity and the community has had to come together to find ways to survive with very limited external assistance.

The comparison of Atiak and Odek suggests that it is fundamental to integrate programming to attend to community cohesion and the social aspects of transitions from war more aligned to *small-p* peacebuilding initiatives (see Figures 6.11 and 6.12). This is even more important if a community – such as in the case of Atiak – receives high levels of development and humanitarian assistance than if it receives none at all. The introduction of external assistance programs allows for dynamics to develop in communities that are not as relevant when they are left to fend for themselves. For example, as seen in Figure 6.11, in 2015, people in Atiak demonstrated a substantive increase in perceiving non-abducted and abducted persons living together peacefully (3.8–4.4 between 2014 and 2015). Formerly abducted persons often live with stigma in northern Uganda as they are sometimes implicated in the activities of the LRA, having been child soldiers or wives of LRA commanders. The fact that there was an increase in perceived harmony between the two groups is interesting and relevant considering our partner, the Justice and Reconciliation project, spent 2014 conducting a year-long community truth-telling project in Atiak called "Bearing Witness, Dealing with the Past to Create a Better Future." The project created forums for community members in Atiak to share their experiences of conflict, through story-telling

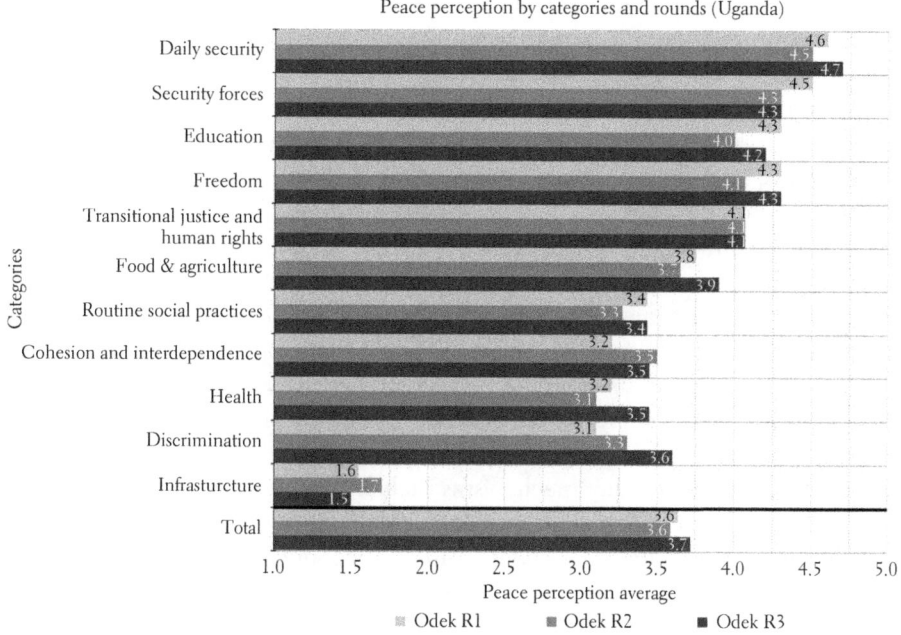

FIGURE 6.12. Peace perception by category – Odek

sessions and truth-telling dialogues. In addition, that year JRP led a community-led documentation project through which a small committee, known as the Community Reconciliation (CORE) team, led the documentation of conflict events in the lives of the people in Atiak. 2014 was the first time JRP conducted a continuous year of activities in Atiak, suggesting that the work on dealing with the past could have possibly had an effect on community perceptions of the formerly abducted.[30]

CONCLUSION

The community-generated indicators of peace provided the basis of surveys conducted longitudinally in the communities. The results of the surveys complement the indicator analysis presented in the previous chapter by allowing us to measure community perceptions of everyday indicators over time. The findings indicate that overall there is low substantive average difference between the two communities chosen in each country in the matched case research design, despite significant differences in external intervention received. The result suggests that there are disparities

---

[30] Report of JRP's work in Atiak and Odek prepared by Oryem Nyeko, July 2016, and communication by email with Oryem Nyeko, February 14, 2017.

between what communities need and prioritize when defining peace and the interventions external actors prioritize in peacebuilding and reconstruction efforts.

Although the survey results indicate more nuanced findings for the individual communities surveyed, some overarching trends can be identified when disaggregating by category and dimension. Perhaps most importantly, I found that development interventions, including large-scale infrastructure projects, seem to have a positive effect on community perceived changes; however, I also found that development interventions come with the significant cost of higher perceived insecurity among residents. In other words, my findings suggest that an increase in development and infrastructure does not always lead to peace in war-affected contexts. This is in contrast to much of the academic and policy literature that advocates for increased economic development and infrastructure as a path toward stabilization, extension of state authority and the achievement of security.[31] Although development and infrastructure are sorely needed in these contexts, they are not enough to build peace effectively and, without other mechanisms such as increased community networks, social cohesion and relationships, they can actually do more harm than good. Aid for development also often supersedes *small-p* peacebuilding efforts, giving priority to infrastructure and economic development over more socially focused interventions. As Bachman and Schouten conclude in their article on infrastructure and peacebuilding, "such efforts often end up substituting the building of a road for real engagement with the root causes of conflict."[32] This may be mitigated in part if interventions find ways to build social relationships through infrastructure development, such as building community centers or other common spaces that bring together parties in conflict.

The survey and indicator analysis suggest that a focus on community level social and political relationships is key for efforts at building peace, in particular in communities that have received high levels of assistance. Currently, many national and international efforts at peacebuilding operate under the flawed assumptions that reconstruction, development and statebuilding efforts with some minor social programming are enough to rebuild relationships and work toward peace at a local level. This chapter suggests that interventions focused on bringing together communities in villages and neighborhoods are especially important to emphasize (and fund accordingly) when conducting other, more large-scale, interventions in conflict-affected contexts.

---

[31] Bachmann and Schouten 2018; Doyle and Sambanis 2006.
[32] Bachmann and Schouten 2018: 16.

Conclusion

In a follow-up focus group in Atiak, I found myself debating with the participants about an indicator they wanted to eliminate from the original indicators list developed by the community three years prior and used in this study.[1] I was in Uganda to reconvene community members from Atiak and Odek to test and update the initial list of selected indicators. This particular group in Atiak was insisting that one of their previously selected peace indicators was no longer relevant. Incidentally, the indicator in question was the only indicator used by EPI that is included in the measurement of SDG 16: walking alone safely at night. I argued to the group that actually this would be a good measurement of peace in their community, but the villagers did not agree. They insisted that this particular indicator was now obsolete since no one in the community felt safe to walk alone at night any longer due to increased insecurity. Therefore, it could no longer be considered an everyday measure of peace. With recent crime waves precipitated in part by the large influx of South Sudanese refugees to camps near Atiak, the perceived insecurity of villagers had increased dramatically, so much so that they no longer dared leave their homes alone in the evenings. Therefore, the indicator had lost its utility for helping villagers to assess whether they felt more or less at peace.

The resistance on the part of the villagers to keeping this indicator three years after they had selected it for their final lists demonstrates the organic nature of indicators in daily life. Indicators do not remain stagnant. They change over time in response to emerging circumstances and shifting lived experience of concepts such as peace that are difficult to measure. Measurement systems therefore need to adjust to changing circumstances as well to consistently identify meaningful outcomes. Peace and thus peacebuilding effectiveness are relative, and fluctuate over time.

---

[1] Focus Group, Atiak, November 29, 2016.

Conclusion

This study presents several main empirical findings about local level peacebuilding effectiveness, but three main findings stand out. First, localities with more intervention reported higher levels of development in comparison to the communities with little intervention. However, they also reported higher levels of insecurity. These findings suggest that development interventions are effective, but may come with the cost of higher perceived insecurity. The analysis of the everyday indicators suggests that this may be because not enough is done to accompany communities in the healing process and reconstruction of social ties after war, since localities with high levels of intervention prioritize social issues such as community cohesion, interdependence and conflict resolution mechanisms when identifying their everyday peace. This finding is in contrast to much of the academic and policy literature that advocates for increased economic development and infrastructure as a path toward stabilization, extension of state authority, the achievement of security and, consequently, the building of peace. Second, localities saturated with high levels of interventions do not have substantively higher levels of peacefulness according to community-generated indicators of everyday peace. This result also suggests that there are disparities between what communities need and prioritize when defining peace and the interventions external actors prioritize in peacebuilding and reconstruction efforts. Third, the majority of indicators selected in the matched case studies were overwhelmingly indicators of improved welfare and positive peace, which aligns with findings in the literature that localities further away from violent conflict prioritize factors related to social ties and relationships when determining peace in their communities. The study also found that peace, as defined locally, is a multidimensional, context-based and dynamic concept. The variability of peace indicators from context to context demonstrates that people define peace according to their circumstances as well as their experiences during wartime. This also has significant implications for peacebuilding design and implementation and measurement – template approaches won't work. Therefore, the first step toward determining what works best is to actively include communities not only as sources of data in measurement but also as partners in the design of the tools used to evaluate them. If the international community wants to improve its impact in conflict-affected contexts, the Everyday Peace Indicators approach offers a data-driven path to align international and local priorities and increase the chances of success from the perspective of all stakeholders. This conclusion proceeds to give more context and depth to these three main conclusions, as well as a summary of the rest of the arguments made in the book.

LOCAL PEACE: MULTIDIMENSIONAL, CONTEXTUAL AND DYNAMIC

This study finds that peace as defined locally is a multidimensional, context-based, and dynamic concept. People look to multiple categories of indicators to measure their everyday peace, including positive measures that refer to improved welfare and negative measures of peace that refer to violence reduction. The majority of indicators selected in the matched case studies were overwhelmingly indicators of improved welfare and positive peace, which aligns with the findings that communities further away from violent conflict prioritize factors related to social ties and relationships when determining peace in their communities. The latter is relevant for empirical measurement since the majority of top-down attempts at measuring peace use indicators that focus primarily on violence reduction. The communities in this study prioritized social- and development-related indicators when defining everyday peace. People looked primarily toward things such as cohesion and interdependence, conflict resolution and leadership in their communities, as well as infrastructure, education and health related indicators. The multidimensionality of community-defined peace consequently requires local level interventions to be multi-dimensional, which is frequently not the case.

Another main conclusion of this study is that factors contributing to the successes and failures of local level interventions after war are highly specific to individual contexts and situations. From this analysis of participatory, community-sourced indicators of peace, I find that local level everyday indicators of peace, as well as being highly multidimensional, are variable according to context. The variability of peace indicators from context to context demonstrates that people define peace according to their circumstances as well as their experiences during wartime. Although indicators in the matched case designs were similar when coded into categories, individual indicators differed in important ways to reflect the realities of each community. Everyday indicators of peace vary from village to village and neighborhood to neighborhood, depending on current events and histories of violence. As we see from the discussion in Atiak, mentioned at the beginning of this chapter, locally defined peace is a dynamic and evolving concept that develops in response to changing circumstances and proximity to violence.

The findings of this study have major implications for how we measure peace conceptually, as well as how we measure peacebuilding effectiveness on a project level. The everyday indicators have a high utility in articulating the nuances between communities and informing effective local interventions that address the specific needs of a community at a specific point in time. They demonstrate how template or universal approaches to designing interventions are insufficient to address the complex ontological understandings of peace.

TOWARD DESIGNING AND EVALUATING MORE EFFECTIVE INTERVENTIONS

The findings in this study support Adam Moore's rejection of the capacity argument put forward by Michael Doyle and Nicholas Sambanis.[2] Doyle and Sambanis assert that an increase in international assistance at the national level has a positive effect on

---

[2] Moore 2013.

sustainable peace, as defined by international actors.[3] My findings suggest that there is much more complexity required than an increase in aid and personnel to ensure sustainable peace at the local level, at least according to the communities themselves.

The analysis of the everyday indicators and the survey results in the matched case studies presented in this book suggest that the psychological and social aspects of community healing must be attended to after war. Such an approach is especially important in communities that are receiving significant support in sectors such as development and humanitarian assistance, as evidenced by the survey data results in Atiak and El Salado. At the same time, the distribution of the assistance programs would benefit from additional attention paid by implementers on equitable administration, which should be decided through a community process representative of all groups in situations where everyone cannot be a beneficiary. In other words, community politics should not be forgotten in efforts to reconstruct after war. Finally, as demonstrated in Chapter 1, there is a lack of coordination and transparency among international peacebuilders in conflict-affected contexts. Therefore, it is important for governments, donors, NGOs and agencies implementing interventions to more adequately coordinate and share information. Donors should encourage active collaboration by rewarding transparency and information sharing. This is already being encouraged by some donors, but needs to be expanded upon significantly.

This study suggests that localities saturated with high levels of interventions do not have significantly higher levels of peacefulness according to community-generated indicators of everyday peace. The everyday indicators suggest that communities with high levels of intervention prioritize social issues such as community cohesion, interdependence, and conflict resolution mechanisms when identifying their everyday peace. Yet, such issues are rarely attended to comprehensively in these communities, since interveners prioritize reconstruction and development. However, when surveyed, these communities reported higher levels of development in comparison to the communities with little intervention. Study results indicate that development interventions have an effect on community perceived changes, but that development interventions may come with the cost of higher perceptions of insecurity. Although communities that received higher levels of intervention didn't prioritize security when identifying everyday peace in their communities (as demonstrated in Chapter 5), they experienced much higher levels of perceived insecurity when compared to communities with little intervention (as demonstrated in Chapter 6).

Communities without much intervention also prioritized social issues, but had higher or comparable survey scores in areas related to social dynamics, indicating a higher or comparable level of social cohesion in comparison to communities with significantly more intervention. They also had lower levels of dispersion in their responses to survey questions, indicating more consensus in communities with less

---

[3] Doyle and Sambanis 2006: 4.

intervention. Perhaps this is because in the absence of state, NGO or INGO assistance, people engage in pragmatic coping mechanisms that may include tolerance, reconciliation, conflict avoidance, and conscious forgetting. This "everyday peace" speaks of a gradual and locally-grounded series of micro-processes that rely on emotional intelligence and decision-making by individuals who are forced to make do without external assistance.[4] Beneficiaries in all of the communities studied did not have significantly higher levels of peace perception than non-beneficiaries. Overall, receiving benefits did not alter individual peace perception.

Considering the disappointing outcomes of the study, it may be fair to ask why I do not encourage international actors to dismiss the international peacebuilding enterprise altogether, as other scholars have done. Adam Branch, for example, advocates for "disintervention" on the grounds that intervention crowds out the political space that allows Africans to "exercise their political agency in a meaningful way" and that, in contrast to intervention, "can promote political accountability and responsibility."[5] To some extent, my findings are in accordance with his argument. In both Odek and Don Gabriel, community members have taken reconstruction and reconciliation efforts into their own hands. They have had to overcome significant hurdles in order to rebuild their homes and their communities by themselves and to find ways to help each other move on after the devastating effects of war and displacement.

Yet retreating from communities in need is not the solution. As Séverine Autesserre explains, "it would deprive people in conflict zones of all the advantages and assistance that expatriates offer."[6] The data from this study concurs. As discussed above, high-intervention communities score higher on development-related indicators, demonstrating the value and effectiveness of those interventions in achieving a narrow scope of objectives. The good news is that development-oriented interventions do achieve development-related outcomes. The takeaway for policymakers, however, is that development often comes at the cost of social cohesion and security, and that more effort must be made to attend social needs and insecurity in communities with high levels of intervention. The advantages of external intervention are potentially significant if implemented together with partner communities and with a clear understanding of their priorities and needs. Of course, such an approach is easier said than done considering the political economy of the peacebuilding and aid industries.[7] If the international community wants to improve its impact in conflict-affected contexts, the Everyday Peace Indicators approach offers a data-driven path to align international and local priorities and increase the chances of success from the perspective of all stakeholders.

---

[4] Mac Ginty 2014.
[5] Branch 2011a: 247.
[6] Autesserre 2014: 254.
[7] de Waal 1997; Uvin 1998; Duffield 2014.

Constituents and Distribution

I conclude that external actors must pay more attention to the constituent parts and distribution of the assistance programs they administer in communities affected by war. External interveners must seek vigorous inclusion of and participation by the communities affected by the interventions. International actors should move beyond elite level relationship-building in capital cities to work together with community members from all sectors to carefully consider the effects of what is being done in a community and who is receiving benefits. Implementers should resist temptations to introduce donor-driven projects unrelated to community concerns since community ownership of projects can only be accomplished by communities themselves, sometimes through the assistance of external interveners. Additionally, communities must establish their own priorities, contribute to their own projects and determine their own outcomes, which means they need to be actively involved in the design, monitoring and evaluation of any external interventions.

As illustrated in Chapter 6, programs in communities saturated with interventions do not necessarily reflect the needs or concerns that people consider when determining their everyday peace. The majority of interventions being implemented in the communities in this study focused on development, infrastructure, agricultural, and reconstruction efforts, whereas communities looked primarily to social factors to determine their daily peace. Although some interventions addressed social cohesion, such programming was by far the least prevalent and least funded. Also, state activities were less likely to focus on social concerns and instead were concentrated on more structural activities such as reconstruction and livelihood interventions. Such an approach was particularly the case in Uganda, where little attention was paid to the social fabric of communities after refugees returned from IDP camps. The government of Uganda continues to neglect victim needs and requests, refusing to pay reparations or fund victim-centered programming. Residents of Atiak have not yet recovered from displacement and community members, especially the youth, have become complacent and accustomed to outside assistance. Little effort has been made to address these issues in a holistic way, apart from generic jobs programs and interventions directed toward "livelihoods." While such programs are important, they are not effective without the additional *small-p* peacebuilding work that is necessary to sustain them through focused community building and psycho-social attention after war and displacement. Currently, programming neglects the legacies of war and displacement that the community has experienced.

In Colombia, more attention has been paid to victims. Yet, most of that attention has again been through formal means of compensation or development projects in the form of individual and collective reparations. Only more recently have social programs been introduced to deal with the collective and individual traumas experienced by the communities affected by the war. El Salado has seen an enormous amount of interventions, yet only a fraction of those attend to *small-p* peacebuilding concerns of relationship building and inclusion. Families feel isolated and alienated by external assistance programs that attend to their neighbors, but not to them, which has caused unintended conflict in the communities. In particular, the payment of individual reparations in the form of compensation has created resentment within El Salado. The perception is that certain people are favored in the participation of programs and the payment of benefits. Those who see themselves as most vulnerable feel isolated because they have not received compensation from the state. Of course, this is also a part of the strategy of the government, which follows the subsistence model of ensuring basic needs before paying reparations.[8] But because this strategy is poorly communicated to beneficiaries it has caused competition in the community. Although a participatory approach in planning and implementing reparations programs is important,[9] it is also important to think about the politics of community participation – who is included, as well as who is excluded, and what kinds of consequences this may have for community cohesion. Before introducing peacebuilding initiatives to anyone in a community, implementers should work together with communities to bring everyone in a village or community to a place where they are ready to receive assistance and there is greater consensus about who receives aid and why.

Communities saturated with interventions also indicate higher levels of security concerns than those without intervention. Clearly, the introduction of outside actors, regardless of their intentions, bring problems for those communities, which might not otherwise be of concern. Both El Salado and Atiak indicate less confidence in their security situations than Don Gabriel and Odek, although none of the communities prioritized security related indicators. The high level of attention to these communities has also exposed them more to the outside world, which has in turn introduced an increased sense of insecurity – whether real or imagined. Increased sense of insecurity may also be related to the lower levels of social cohesion and conflict resolution in communities and a lack of trust amongst neighbors.

Participation and Inclusion

Determining the constituent parts of large-scale interventions to support local peace requires a concerted effort by interveners to listen to communities. Third parties have widely recognized the importance of local participation and the necessity of giving communities a voice in the implementation process. However, elites continue to set the agendas of *what* those outside interventions can be and only use community input to tailor a pre-existing repertoire of interventions to a particular context. Besides offering victims some redress, the historically dominant liberal

---

[8] Dixon 2016; Interview Unidad de Víctimas Staff 1, Cartagena, March 4, 2016.
[9] Laplante 2015.

peacebuilding paradigm has mainly been justified regarding its goal of consolidating a liberal democratic order with a strong focus on security.[10] As discussed in depth in Chapters 1 and 2, such an approach has tended to privilege elites, the state, and the international over the local and the everyday.

In order to change the existing paradigm, international interveners must begin to seriously embed themselves in the contexts in which they work. International organizations must prioritize contextual knowledge over technical knowledge so that staff can understand the contexts in which they are working. It also means that in most cases qualified local staff should be given equal status to international staff and local NGOs should be prioritized, with external support where appropriate, when funding peacebuilding work at the local level. Local staff should be recruited as organizational and project leaders when possible, and recognized as important resources and partners for understanding the context. Local staff and NGOs should be prioritized for leadership development and advancement. While this embedded approach is advocated by other experts on local level peacebuilding effectiveness, such as Béatrice Pouligny and Adam Moore,[11] I argue that embeddedness must be taken a step further to actively include participatory approaches that include communities in the decision-making of the "what, when and how" of the interventions taking place in their communities. Participatory numbers such as the everyday peace indicators are a step in that direction, but there are many other possibilities that allow for an engaged effort in the peacebuilding enterprise. The goal should no longer be to understand peacebuilding as a purely external exercise – instead the recognition that peacebuilders are usually local is fundamental to peacebuilding's success.

Embeddedness is also critical to ensure meaningful and representative participation of communities in assistance programs. Without contextual knowledge and experience in a locality, external interveners fail to see community-level politics and divisions that are important to identify in order to more accurately represent diverse community interests when doing participatory work. The lack of representation and genuine inclusiveness of some participatory approaches is criticized by those scholars who argue that participation is used in name only and constricted to the confines of the roles and identities provided by the intervention.[12] Truly participatory programs are designed to empower people and therefore give them a place at the decision-making table, at least in terms of what is being done in their own communities. Participatory numbers allow for the needs and priorities of communities to be communicated to policymakers by using numbers and statistics that are increasingly required by governments to justify their decisions. Questions of broader structural changes in the institutions and government of a conflict-affected context are beyond the scope of community participation, although the empowerment that participatory approaches

---

[10] Sharp 2013.
[11] Moore 2013: 168; Pouligny 2006: 87–95.
[12] Branch 2011a: 150.

can contribute to can often lead to collective action. For example, in Colombia, some of the communities working with civil society actors on issues important to them have successfully lobbied the government to pay attention to their rights.[13]

Many participatory approaches that aim to establish the collective goals of a community are designed to be representative and elicitive.[14] The everyday indicator approach is designed to complement participatory approaches that empower through the collection of data and indicators based on community priorities. An approach using local people's knowledge to empower local people's capabilities is one that can lead to sustainable local action and institutions, as demonstrated by past efforts at creating indigenous technical knowledge.[15] In this study, we have found that communities who have experienced relative recent stability prioritize social issues that deal with community ties, conflict resolution and freedom of movement. These issues are stressed particularly in communities that have received generous external intervention, since many interventions rarely deal with social issues. Using community-generated indicators to identify community priorities is helpful to interveners designing participatory interventions. Since there are often competing claims about what is most important in a community and who is being represented, it is necessary to find ways to simplify the decision-making processes. However, this must be done with utmost care and quality assurance, avoiding bad practices as they pertain to participatory action work and the generation of participatory numbers whenever possible.[16]

Transparency and Cooperation

During the fieldwork for this project, I also found that quality local interventions are not only dependent on increased emphasis on quality local participation and collaboration between international interveners and local communities, but also among the international interveners themselves. Competition for funding and territory prevent many NGOs from being more transparent and cooperative. There is little incentive to share local level information, unless organizations are working together in explicit cooperatives with other organizations, often funded by the same donors. As discussed in Chapter 1, this situation often creates duplicative extra work for staff who need to do baselines and evaluations on projects for their own organizations when they could be done for multiple organizations operating in the same contexts with similar projects. Of the fifteen organizations we interviewed in Gulu, none were willing to share their monitoring and evaluation reports and conflict assessments that were not already made public. NGO staff responded that they did not have the mandates or were not allowed to share requested reports as they

---

[13] Mampujan is one such example.
[14] Chambers 1997: 115.
[15] For more see Chapter 3.
[16] Chambers 1997: 211; Holland 2013.

were for internal use only. For example, the International Criminal Court Outreach Section explained to us: "This is confidential for outreach only. It's just basic. It's not sensitive, but we try to keep it confidential."[17] The sharing of data, monitoring and evaluation reports and even mapping of interventions is a highly guarded affair. When I tried to access a simple mapping of actors in Odek sub-county from World Vision, I was told, "Area Program design is purely an internal document, it can only be utilized within the World Vision Family."[18] Because of the lack of transparency and communication, agencies often double-up and receive funding for similar programming in a community that they identified as necessary during the same funding cycles. Because of the guarded nature of the sharing of documents and reports among agencies, the government is typically the default for information on existing programming, which is often unavailable and incomplete. Ultimately, this kind of uncoordinated, highly opaque process makes it difficult for third parties or communities themselves to assess what programs have already been done, are ongoing, or the kinds of outcomes other organizations have had with certain kinds of programming. A lack of transparency also has consequences for participatory interventions as there is little possibility for interveners to recall what worked and what did not in past interventions when working with communities to design programs.

In addition, donors ask organizations individually to come up with project indicators and goals. These are not meaningfully integrated into a larger picture of what change should happen in a community, and frequently NGOs do not feel as though they are part of a larger coordinated effort. Also, the number of governments with competing agendas in a country means that work funded by one country can be duplicated (or at cross purposes) with the work done by another country or donor. Funders must get together to coordinate so that they do not put out Requests for Proposals (RFPs) for overlapping work. This is notoriously hard to do and largely depends upon the geo-political considerations of each country or donor.

THREADING THE NEEDLE BETWEEN LOCAL, STATE AND INTERNATIONAL NEEDS

Using the power of indigenous technical knowledge and participatory numbers, we can find ways to more effectively empower communities to work together with government and international actors who espouse normative goals of peace. The onus is on the international community to ensure that with every project we remember Robert Chambers' words of inclusion:

- "Whose knowledge counts?
- Whose values?

---

[17] Interview, Gulu, January 20, 2016.
[18] Email communication, January 3, 2017.

- Whose criteria and preferences?
- Whose appraisal, analysis and planning?
- Whose action?
- Whose monitoring and evaluation?
- Whose learning?
- Whose empowerment?
- Whose *reality* counts?
- "Ours" or "Theirs"?

What can and should we ... do to make our realities count less, and the realities of ... the poor, weak and vulnerable – count more?"[19]

Paying attention to the needs and priorities of all levels – local, state and international – is important for working toward sustainable peace. The likelihood of sustainability is higher if the responsibility is placed on communities to work together with national and international actors to establish peace at the local level. It is arguably worthwhile to keep Robert Chambers' words in mind when acting at any level, but communities are often the least empowered to advocate for their interests. The lack of community representation is particularly detrimental when projects and actors purport to be building peace in a locality. Therefore, Chambers' questions are particularly important when working at the community level.

This study is based on the assertion that the formation and construction of a concept such as peace matters when trying to formulate policies and evaluate outcomes. International, state, and civil society actors can be better informed about local concerns through measurement that takes into consideration the needs and circumstances of localities. What remains to be tested, however, is how capturing local priorities in measures such as everyday indicators can produce data that can influence local decision makers. How might local governments use measurement data in their decision-making processes, how might they process and interpret local level data and what implications would access to more representative data have for peacebuilding effectiveness? How might civil society activists use local data to increase pressure on political actors to address community needs? How might communities self-organize to promote their own needs through participatory statistics? More research needs to be done in order to get a better understanding of what happens to bottom-up, community information once it reaches a municipal or ministerial office. What are the political barriers to using local level data effectively? How do local governments use data and how can data about communities be most effectively communicated? Does improved local data help policymakers or communities themselves advocate in a sharper way or donors spend their money in more efficient ways? Such questions are fundamental to understanding whether the exercise of measurement at a local level is purely academic or also has policy implications.

[19] Chambers 1997: 101.

Serious work to support peace requires sustained, long-term efforts that rarely yield instant success. Ultimately, change requires committed local people partnering with embedded nationals and internationals to develop strategies to effectively communicate and advocate for community needs. The approaches presented in this book help us strive to continue to actively listen to concerned parties, advance knowledge about their circumstances and reflect on the most effective steps for international interveners to work together with communities toward sustainable peace.

APPENDIX 1

Accounting of interventions in Atiak & Odek, Uganda and El Salado & Don Gabriel, Colombia

The tables in Uganda were compiled through interviews conducted in Gulu, Odek and Atiak from 2012 to 2017. The tables were vetted by Isaac Odiya from the Justice and Reconciliation Project. The tables are incomplete due to missing information and a lack of accounting, but they are representative of the majority of projects conducted in Atiak and Odek since the massacres and displacement occurred.

The tables in Colombia were compiled through interviews conducted in Don Gabriel and El Salado from 2012 to 2017. In addition, Fundación Semana kept records of most of their collaborations with other actors in El Salado. These documents helped inform the tables and were later vetted by Fundación Semana staff. As in Uganda, they do not account for absolutely every intervention in each village, but are an accurate overview of the majority of projects conducted in Don Gabriel and El Salado since the massacres and displacement took place.

TABLE 1. INTERVENTIONS IN ATIAK, UGANDA

Implementing organization	Source of funding	Years	Type of activities
WFP	N/A	1996	Food distribution Opening community access roads; food for work Cassava cuttings multiplication; training farmers on value addition
NRC	Norwegian Ministry of Foreign Affairs, UNHCR, WFP	1998	School construction Provision of scholastic materials Drilling deep boreholes Psychosocial support
Lwani Memorial College Head Teacher	AVSI, Window Trust, Restore International, Government	1999	Secondary school
CARE International	N/A	2004	Supply of seedlings and other farm equipment Training farmers on value addition
JRP	Lui Institute for Global Studies, University British Columbia; Norwegian Embassy-Kampala; USAID-SAFE; J.D MacArthur Foundation	2005–2016	Dialogue, truth telling, documentation, memorialization, capacity building on advocacy and TJ-related issues Peace building Psychosocial support Trainings in advocacy and conflict analysis, community-led documentation, exchange visits between survivor groups, community-based truth telling, conflict memory and reconciliation
International Criminal Court (ICC)	N/A	2005	Indictment of Vincent Otti, but not for massacre in Atiak due to statute of limitations

International Criminal Court (ICC)	USAID-SAFE	2007–2008	Outreach, facilitate victims' participation
Uganda Amnesty Commission	USAID-SAFE	2009–2015	Counseling for reporters, tree planting, agriculture interpersonal group therapy for reporters and community members, vocational skill training
Peace Recovery and Development Plan PRDP	Government of Uganda through the Office of the Prime Minister	2011–ongoing	Reconstruction assistance: Livestock, schools and roads constructed, oxen and grinding machines for farming, twenty boreholes drilled in 2012/2013
Japan International Cooperation Agency; World Bank	Government of Japan	2012–2016	Juba-Nimule Road construction – wasn't completed in Atiak until 2015
Atiak Massacre Survivors Association	Justice and Reconciliation Project (JRP), ACORD (in kind)	2011–2015	Story telling, truth telling, memorial prayers, community theatre
UNOHCHR	UNOHCHR	2012	Sensitization for transitional justice for community leaders
Grassroots Reconciliation Group	German embassy, individual funding, charitable organization	2012–2013	Livestock, community theatre, solar dryer project, psychological support
Refugee Law Project	DFID	2012–2014	Training in basic counseling to survivors of the massacre, training in group dynamics, training on lobbying and advocacy, video documentary
African Youth Initiative Network	Uganda Fund	2013–2014	Access to justice – legal aid services, meditation and dialogues, access to land

(continued)

TABLE 1 (Continued)

Implementing organization	Source of funding	Years	Type of activities
ACORD	USAID-SAFE	2013–2015	Peace model – capacity building in peacebuilding, capacity building of local structures, women's participation (UN Resolution 1325), income generation, small loans, program. Micro-peace project (1) mediation, dialogues with community, Micro-peace project (2) building school, fixing a road, community mobilization
African Youth Initiative Network	Trust Africa Funding	2014	National War Victims' Conference
Office of the President	Office of the President	2014	President Museveni gave 50 m Uganda shillings (US$14,000) to survivors of Atiak massacre
African Youth Initiative Network	Trust Africa Funding	2015	Memorial prayers
Acholi Religious Leaders Peace Initiative	USAID	2015–2016	Land conflict: mediation, reconciliation, community debate, sensitization and land security, tree planting, radio talk show
Center for Victims of Torture	N/A	2016	Psychosocial support; individual psychological counseling
UNICEF	UNICEF	N/A	Classroom construction Provision of sanitation facilities; training of traditional birth attendance and village health team; provision of scholastic materials – books, school bags; drilling of deep boreholes and protected springs; training water-use committees

ACORD	N/A	N/A	Supplementary feeding to children; provision of oxen and ox plough; peace building
Chafford	N/A	N/A	Food security
War Child	N/A	N/A	Informal and vocational training
AVSI	N/A	N/A	Orphan and vulnerable case management and IDPs; economic support; psychosocial support (counseling)
Save the Children	N/A	N/A	Voluntary counseling and testing, school support (school construction and provision of scholastic materials like books); school construction; bore-hole drilling; supply of oxen and ox plough
			Trainings on gender-based violence; skills training on building and carpentry, hair salon, motor vehicle mechanics
World Vision	N/A	N/A	Drilling boreholes; training water-use committees; supply of seedlings, oxen and ox plough; sanitation facilities; psychosocial support
Mosquito Nets	Ministry of health – Uganda	N/A	Provision of mosquito nets to families

TABLE 2. INTERVENTIONS IN ODEK, UGANDA

Implementing organization	Source of funding	Years	Activities
International Criminal Court (ICC)	ICC	2005; 2015	Indictment of Dominic Ongwen; outreach, community mobilization, training of trainees, facilitation of victims in ICC registration
Grassroots Reconciliation Group	N/A	2007–2012	Trainings: Entrepreneurship, VSLA concepts, community theatre Participatory development project: Animal husbandry, crop production, psychological support
World Vision	World Vision international offices	2007–2012	Medical rehabilitation, replacement of artificial limbs, interpersonal therapy; psychosocial and reintegration support through its Children of War Rehabilitation Center
Peace Recovery and Development Plan PRDP	Government of Uganda through the Office of the Prime Minister	2011–ongoing	Security sector reforms, infrastructural development, provision of clean water and educational reforms (construction of schools and siting facilities)
UNOHCHR	UNOHCHR	2008	Research on Transitional Justice Juba Peace Process Consultation
Formerly Amnesty Commission	N/A	2009–2015	Counseling for reporters, tree planting, agriculture, interpersonal group, vocational skill training
Center for Reparation and Rehabilitation	MacArthur Foundation	2010–2013	Access to justice, redress to sexual and gender based violence, psychological support, narrative exposure therapy
Acholi Religious Leaders Peace Initiative	Mensen met een Missie	2010–2015	Community sensitization, mediation in land conflict
Gulu Support the Children Organization (GUSCO)	N/A	2012	Resettlement of IDPs and formerly abducted persons; facilitated a dialogue between community and the formerly abducted in 2012 and a traditional cleansing ceremony at Te-olam

Organization	Funder	Year	Project
JRP	Norwegian Embassy Kampala	2013	Community-level reconciliation
ACORD	USAID, SAFE	2013–2014	Social peace and recovery model – capacity enhancement of local structures, dialogues, mediation, micro peace projects, MDD youth project – music, dance and drama
African Youth Initiative Network	Uganda Fund, MacArthur Foundation	2013–2014	Access to justice–legal aid services, mediation and dialogues, access to land
African Youth Initiative Network	Uganda Fund, MacArthur Foundation UNHCR	2014–2015	Address sexual and gender-based violence, legal mobile clinics
African Youth Initiative Network	Uganda Fund, MacArthur Foundation UNHCR	2014–2015	Medical and psychosocial rehabilitation
	USAID-SAFE	2014	Across ethnic boundaries: fostering regional reconciliation, the case of Acholi and Lango sub regions
Refugee Law Project	DGF	2015–ongoing	Community views and video documentation, physical rehabilitation of victims
ICC	ICC	2016–ongoing	Dominic Ongwen detained by ICC; Trial is in progress (as of May 8, 2018)

TABLE 3. INTERVENTIONS IN EL SALADO, COLOMBIA

Implementing organization	Source of funding	Years	Type of activities
Círculo de Obreros San Pedro Claver/CORSOC Asvidas	Acción Social, CHF	2009–2010	House improvement
Fundación Carvajal/Fundación Semana	Fundación Bavaria	2009	Shopkeeper's capacitation program
Fundación SER	Femsa, Fundación Alpina, Fundación Santa Fe de Bogota, Mutual Ser, Profamilia	2010	Microcredit program
Fundación Semana, Fundación MIMA	Acción Social, Gobernación de Bolívar, Fundación Alpina	2010–ongoing	Establishment of a school farm
OIM, PBA	OIM, Ayuda en Acción, Incoder, Ministerio de Agricultura, Colombia Responde	2010–ongoing	Support for displaced peasants
Fundación Carvajal	Programa Cimientos (USAID); Alcaldía del Carmen de Bolívar, Fundación Carvajal	January–March 2010	Infrastructure (building school restaurant)
SENA	USAID, DPS, SENA	June–December 2010	Strengthening productive unit of bee-keepers
Fundación Carvajal	Acción Social, Fundación Carvajal, PAVCO, Fundación Bolívar Davivienda	June–December 2010	Sewer construction
Electricaribe	Electricaribe	July–September 2010	Improvement of the electrical networks
Fundación Carvajal	Eternit	September–December 2010	Installation of sanitation in common housing
CIREC	CIREC/Fair Tunes	2010–2011	Capacitation of Coco Salado
Fundación SER	Protección y Fundación Sura	2010–2011	Food Security Program
Fundación Antioquia Presente	Argos	2010–2011	Young Producers Project
Fundación SER	Fundación Saldarriaga Concha	2010–2013	Economic recovery and microcredit project

UT Montes de María	Invías, Gobernación de Bolívar	2010–2013	Road improvement
IETA Carmen de Bolívar	Ministerio de Educación	2011–ongoing	High school support (creation of 10th and 11th grade)
Fundación Carvajal, Fundación Semana	Acción Social	June–December 2011	Provision of resources for the Workshop – house for welders Assistance to weavers and welders
Fundación Carvajal	OIM, Fundación Carvajal, Fundación Semana	2011–2012	Construction of wastewater treatment plant
Fundación REI	OIM, Fundación Mi Sangre	2011–2012	Psychosocial Care Program
Fundación Carvajal, Fundación Semana (Lanzamiento), Caira	Coltabaco, ING, Autogalias, Fundacion John Ramírez Moreno, Chevron, Hybrytec, Aceral, Argos, Corona, Eternit, Simón Hosie/ Casa del Pueblo, Gaira, C Vilar	2011–2013	Construction house of culture
Fundación Carvajal, Fundación Semana	Ministerio de Justicia	2012	Memory house
Fundación Semana	Fundación Restrepo Barco	January–April 2012	Establishment of a health office and improvement of service quality
FundaciónCarvajal	Gobernación de Bolívar, Fundación Carvajal	May–June 2012	Police station construction
Fundación Semana	ICBF	June–December 2012–2013	Implementation of the program *Familias Con Bienestar*
Pintuco	Pintuco, Fundación Mundial	December 2012	House and public places improvement
Fundación Arraigo	Local Government – Bolívar	2012	Economic development – small business support
Fundación Semana	Surtigas, Fundación Antonio Restrepo Barco	2012–2013	Leadership courses

(*continued*)

TABLE 3 (Continued)

Implementing organization	Source of funding	Years	Type of activities
Fundación Semana	Protección y Fundación Sura	2012–2014	Food Security Program – Veredas de El Salado
Fundación Carvajal, Fundación Semana	Fundación Saldarriaga Concha, Fundación Ramirez Moreno, Fundación Protección	2012–2015	Support for senior citizens (building of senior citizens' house. Creation of Adult Literacy Program)
N/A	Surtigas, Fundación Ayuda en Acción	2012–2015	Local capacity-building program
Fundación Semana	OEA Trust	2012–2015	Digital Literacy Program
NUWA/Escuela de Futbol Nueva Generacion	Pacific Rubiales	2012–2015	Construction of School of Sports
Fundación Semana	BID - FOMIN	2012–2017	BID IADB economic development projects – "Recuperación del desarrolloeconómico local en regiones de posconflicto"
Fundación Semana	Pacific Rubiales	January–December 2013	Donation of space to build a soccer field
Consorcio TECAS	Unidad Nacional de Gestión y Prevención del Riesgo	June–October 2013	Infrastructure (channeling of the stream and canal improvement)
Ibicol Company	Ibicol Company	September–October 2013	Water purification
Fundación Semana	Pacific Rubiales	2013–2014	Project to recover local economy in post-conflict regions in partnership with IADB
Fundación Carvajal	ANSPE, Fundación Carvajal, Fundación Semana	2013–2015	Housing development

Fundación Semana	Incoder	January–December 2014	Productive Incentives for Rural Development (IPDR)
Fundación Semana	Fundación Ayuda en Acción, Fundación John Ramirez Moreno	2014–2015	Music school
UNOPS	DPS	2014–2015	House improvement
Fundación Semana	UNODC, Fundación SURA	2014–2015	Strengthening welders, group
N/A	Argos Company	2014–2015	Road pavement
Fundación Semana	Patrimonio Natural, Fundación Crecer en Paz	2014–2015	Natural Heritage and Growing Up in Peace: IADB Projects
NUWA	Pacific Rubiales	March–June 2015	School construction
Fundación Semana	Fundación Ayuda en Acción	March–June 2015	Water program "Ayuda en Acción"
Fundación Semana	Argos Company	June–December 2015	Installation of toilets
CCI	Fundación Clinton, Ministerio de Agricultura	June–December 2015	Productive development project – Clinton Foundation
Fundación Semana	Fundación Ayuda en Acción	July–September 2015	Solar panel and refrigerators for schools
Fundación James Rodríguez, Fundación Colombia Somos Todos, Fundacion Tecnoglass, Fundación Pacific, Fundación Lead	Fundación James Rodríguez, Fundación Colombia Somos Todos, Fundacion Tecnoglass, Fundación Pacific, Fundación Lead	2015–2016	"Colombia, un campo parasoñar y crecer" – children's soccer programming, education and clothing
Fundación Semana	Fundación Ayuda en Acción	2015–ongoing	Promotion of children and adolescent's rights
Fundación Semana	Fundación Ayuda en Acción	2015–ongoing	Strengthening tobacco farming and tobacco organization

(continued)

TABLE 3 (*Continued*)

Implementing organization	Source of funding	Years	Type of activities
Toms Shoes	Toms Shoes	2016	Toms shoes donated to village of El Salado
Fundación Semana	Fundación Ayuda en Acción – Fer roviales	2017	Aqueduct improvement
Fundación Semana	Fundación Ayuda en Acción – APC (agencia colombiana de cooperación internacional)	2017	Water solutions for the surrounding Veredas
Fundación Semana	Pacific Rubiales – Presidencia de la republica	2017	Construction and inauguration of soccer field
IOM	Ayuda en Acción – DPS	2017	Donation of housing for women tobacco workers
Fundación Semana	Fundación Saldarriaga Concha	18 months	Program working with senior citizens
Fundación Carulla	Fundación Carulla, ICB, Fundación Ayuda en Acción	Permanent	Early Childhood Program
Ministerio de Salud/ANSPE	Ministerio de Protección Social, DPS	Permanent	"Familias en su Tierra" Program: Support for displaced families
SENA	SENA	2-month training cycle	Higher Education programs (technical and technological)
Telefónica	Telefónica	N/A	Installation of communication antenna
OIM/Fundación Semana	OIM, Fundación Ayuda en Acción	N/A	Strengthening productive unit tobacco rollers
Hocol	Hocol	N/A	Road improvement
BE TV	BE TV, Caracol TV	N/A	Documentary "El Salado"

TABLE 4. INTERVENTIONS IN DON GABRIEL, COLOMBIA

Implementing organization	Source of funding	Years	Type of activities
Colombia responde	N/A	2014	Leadership and Participation Program
Unidad de Restitución de Tierras	Government	2017	Infrastructure (new homes)
Departamento para la Prosperidad Social	Government	Irregular	Support for agricultural families
Institute Colombiano de Desarollo Rural	Government	Irregular	Support to the Peasant Reserve Zone Enhancing Committee
Unidad de Víctimas	Government	2017	The Unidad de Victimas has started the social process to provide reparations
Centro Nacional de Memoria Histórica	Government	Irregular	Projects to reconstruct what happened in Don Gabriel. Production of the documentary, "La tierra ya no es pa'l que trabaja"
Mayor's Office	Local Government	N/A	Infrastructure (road and day-care center improvement)
Fundación Red de Desarrollo y Paz de los Montes de Maria	N/A	N/A	Productive projects, youth employment

APPENDIX 2

List of Interviews by Location

WASHINGTON, DC

Peacebuilding NGO M&E Staff, 19 January 2016.
Alliance for Peacebuilding M&E Staff, 19 January 2016.
United States Institute for Peace M&E Staff, 11 February 2016
Peacebuilding NGO M&E Staff, 15 February 2016.
Peacebuilding NGO M&E Staff, 18 February 2016.
United States Institute for Peace M&E Staff, 21 March 2016
Search for Common Ground M&E Staff, 19 April 2016.
USAID OTI Staff, 3 May 2016
Former Institute for Economics and Peace (IEP) Staff member, 20 July 2016.
Search for Common Ground Staff, 27 July 2016.
Former Office of US Foreign Assistance Resources Staff member, 5 November 2016.

NEW YORK CITY

Independent Peacebuilding M&E Consultant, 26 April 2016.
Henk-Jan Brinkman, Chief Policy, Planning and Application in the Peacebuilding Support Office of the United Nations, 10 March 2017.
Staff Member 1, United Nations Development Program (UNDP), 10 March 2017.
Staff Member 2, United Nations Development Program (UNDP), 10 March 2017.

EL SALADO, COLOMBIA

Focus Group with community members, 7 July 2012.
Male Community Member, 23 February to 1 March 2016 (various).
Female Community Member, 23 February to 1 March 2016 (various).
Community Leader, 23 February to 1 March 2016 (various).
Focus Group with adult male community members, 24 February 2016.

Focus Group with adult female community members, 24 February 2016.
Focus Group with youth community members, 25 February 2016.
Community Leader, 1 March 2016 (various).
Verification Focus Group with community members, 2 March 2016.
Fundación Semana staff, March 2016 (various).

DON GABRIEL, COLOMBIA

Male Community Member, 23 February to 1 March 2016 (various).
Female Community Member, 23 February to 1 March 2016 (various).
Community Leader, 23 February to 1 March 2016 (various).
Focus Group with adult male community members, 26 February 2016.
Focus Group with adult female community members, 26 February 2016.
Focus Group with youth community members, 27 February 2016.
Verification Focus Group with community members, 3 March 2016.

CARTAGENA, COLOMBIA

Unidad de Víctimas Staff 2, 29 February 2016.
Unidad de Víctimas Staff 1, 4 March 2016.
International Organization of Migration Staff, 4 March 2016.

BOGOTA, COLOMBIA

Claudia García, 16 July 2012.
UNDP Colombia Staff, 18 July 2012.
Unidad de Victímas Staff, 20 July 2012.

ATIAK, UGANDA

Focus Group with adult male community members, 4 October 2013.
Focus Group with adult female community members, 4 October 2013.
Focus Group with youth community members, 4 October 2013.
Verification Focus Group with community members, 12 November 2013.
LCIII village chief, 5 March 2014.
Atiak Massacre Survivors Association, 18 July 2016.
Lwani Memorial College Head Teacher, 20 July 2016.
Community Leader, 24 November 2016 (various).
International NGO staff, 24 November 2016.
Local Government Official, 24 November 2016.
Community Development Officer, 24 November 2016.
Focus Group with community members, 29 November 2016.
LCIII village chief, 29 November 2016.

ODEK, UGANDA

Focus Group with adult male community members, 8 October 2013.
Focus Group with adult female community members, 8 October 2013.
Focus Group with youth community members, 8 October 2013.
Verification Focus Group with community members, 6 December 2013.
LCIII village chief, 11 March 2014.
Community Development Officer, 11 March 2014.
Community Development Officer, 30 July 2015.
LCIII village chief, 25 November 2016.
Community Development Officer, 25 November 2016.
Community Leader, 25 November 2016 (various).
Focus Group with community members, 30 November 2016.

GULU, UGANDA

Justice and Reconciliation Staff, March 2014 (various).
African Youth Initiative Network Staff, 19 January 2016.
ICC Outreach Section Staff, 20 January 2016.
Centre for Reparations and Rehabilitation (CRR) Staff 1, 20 January 2016.
ACORD Staff members, 20 January 2016.
Former Amnesty Commission Staff, 20 January 2016.
UNOHCHR Staff, 21 January 2016.
Grassroots Reconciliation Group Staff, 1 July 2016.
Justice and Reconciliation Staff, July and November 2016 (various).
Refugee Law Project Staff, 23 August 2016.
Acholi Religious Leaders Peace Initiative (ARLPI) Staff 2, 30 August 2016.
Acholi Religious Leaders Peace Initiative (ARLPI) Staff 1, 24 October 2016.
Centre for Reparations and Rehabilitation (CRR) Staff 2, 25 October 2016.
World Vision Staff, 27 October 2016.
Isaac Odiya, Justice and Reconciliation Project, 23 November 2016.
International NGO staff, 24 November 2016.
Former UNOCHA staff, 25 November 2016.
Office of the Prime Minister (OPM) Staff, 25 November 2016.
International NGO staff, 1 December 2016.
World Vision Staff, 1 December 2016.

KIGALI, RWANDA

Tutsi Genocide survivor focus group participants, 21 December 2015.

Bibliography

Adcock, R., Collier, D., (2001). Measurement validity: a shared standard for qualitative and quantitative research. *The American Political Science Review*, 95(3), 529–46.

Agrawal, A. (1995). Dismantling the divide between indigenous and scientific knowledge. *Development and Change*, 26(3), 413–39.

Anderson, M. B., Brown, D., & Jean, I. (2012). *Hearing People on the Receiving End of International Aid*. Cambridge, MA: CDA Collaborative Learning Projects.

Andreas, P., & Greenhill, K. M. (2010). *Sex, Drugs, and Body Counts: The Politics of Numbers*. Ithaca, NY: Cornell University Press.

Andrews, M., Pritchett, L., & Woolcock, M. (2013). Escaping capability traps through problem driven iterative adaptation (PDIA). *World Development*, 51(Supplement C), 234–44. https://doi.org/10.1016/j.worlddev.2013.05.011

Arriaza, L., & Roht-Arriaza, N. (2008). Social repair at the local level: the case of Guatemala. *Transitional Justice from Below: Grassroots Activism and the Struggle for Change*, 143–66. Portland, OR: Hart Publications.

Austen, S., Jefferson, T., & Thein, V. (2003). Gendered social indicators and grounded theory. *Feminist Economics*, 9(1), 1–18. https://doi.org/10.1080/1354570032000063065

Autesserre, S. (2010). *The Trouble with the Congo: Local Violence and the Failure of International Peacebuilding*. (Vol. 115). Cambridge: Cambridge University Press.

 (2014). *Peaceland: Conflict Resolution and the Everyday Politics of International Intervention*. New York, NY: Cambridge University Press.

Avruch, K. (1998). *Culture and Conflict Resolution*. (Vol. 31). Washington, DC: US Institute of Peace Press.

Babst, D. V. (1964). Elective governments: a force for peace. *The Wisconsin Sociologist*, 3(1), 9–14.

Bachmann, J., & Schouten, P. (2018). Concrete approaches to peace: infrastructure as peacebuilding. *International Affairs*, 94(2), 381–98.

Backer, D. (2009). Cross-national comparative analysis. In H. Van der Merwe, V. Baxter, & A. R. Chapman (Eds.), *Assessing the Impact of Transitional Justice: Challenges for Empirical Research* (pp. 23–90). Washington, DC: US Institute of Peace Press.

Baines, E. K. (2007). The haunting of Alice: local approaches to justice and reconciliation in Northern Uganda. *The International Journal of Transitional Justice*, 1(1), 91–114.

Baines, E. (2010). Spirits and social reconstruction after mass violence: rethinking transitional justice. *African Affairs*, 109(436), 409–30.

Barma, N. H., Levy, N., & Piombo J. (2017). Disentangling aid dynamics in statebuilding and peacebuilding: a causal framework, *International Peacekeeping*, 24(2), 187–211. DOI: 10.1080/13533312.2016.1252677

Barnett, M. (2002). *Eyewitness to a Genocide: The United Nations and Rwanda*. Ithaca, NY: Cornell University Press.

Barnett, M., Kim, H., O'Donnell, M., & Sitea, L. (2007). Peacebuilding: what is in a name? *Global Governance: A Review of Multilateralism and International Organizations*, 13(1), 35–58. https://doi.org/10.5555/ggov.2007.13.1.35

Bell, C., & O'Rourke, C. (2009). *Counting Peace Agreements: The Transitional Justice Peace Agreement Database* (Transitional Justice Institute Research Paper No. 09-12.). Retrieved from https://ssrn.com/abstract=1504709

Bell, C. (2009). Transitional justice, interdisciplinarity and the state of the "field or non-field". *International Journal of Transitional Justice*, 3(1), 5–27.

Blum, A. (2011). *Improving Peacebuilding Evaluation* (Special Report No. 280) (p. 16). Washington, DC: United States Peace Institute. Retrieved from https://usip.org/publications/2011/06/improving-peacebuilding-evaluation

——— (2016). *Gauging What Works and What Doesn't in Peacebuilding: Reflections on Monitoring and Evaluation from a Departing "M&E Guy"* (Analysis and Commentary). Washington, DC: United States Peace Institute. Retrieved from https://usip.org/publications/2016/06/gauging-what-works-and-what-doesnt-peacebuilding

Bonta, B. D. (1996). Conflict resolution among peaceful societies: the culture of peacefulness. *Journal of Peace Research*, 33(4), 403–20.

Bouvier, V. (2015). Q&A: Colombia Breakthrough a World Model for Peace Talks; Transitional Justice for Victims Breaks New Ground. https://vbouvier.wordpress.com/2015/09/25/qa-colombia-breakthrough-a-world-model-for-peace-talks-transitional-justice-for-victims-breaks-new-ground/ (accessed April 28, 2016).

Branch, A. (2008). Against humanitarian impunity: rethinking responsibility for displacement and disaster in Northern Uganda. *Journal of Intervention and Statebuilding*, 2(2), 151–73.

——— (2011a). *Displacing Human Rights: War and Intervention in Northern Uganda*. New York, NY: Oxford University Press.

——— (2011b). Neither liberal nor peaceful? Practices of "Global Justice" by the ICC. In S. Campbell, D. Chandler, & M. Sabaratnam (Eds.), *A Liberal Peace? The Problems and Practices of Peacebuilding* (pp. 121–38). London: Zed Books.

Briggs, J. (2005). The use of indigenous knowledge in development: problems and challenges. *Progress in Development Studies*, 5(2), 99–114.

Broome, A., & Quirk, J. (2015). Governing the world at a distance: the practice of global benchmarking. *Review of International Studies*, 41(5), 819–41.

Burton, J. (1990). *Conflict: Resolution and Prevention (Vol. 1)*. London: Macmillan.

——— (1993). *Conflict: Human Needs Theory*. Basingstoke: Palgrave Macmillan.

Call, C. T. (2008a). *Building States to Build Peace*. Boulder, CO: Lynne Rienner Publishers Inc.

——— (2008b). The fallacy of the "failed state." *Third World Quarterly*, 29(8), 1491–507. https://doi.org/10.1080/01436590802544207

——— (2012). *Why Peace Fails: The Causes and Prevention of Civil War Recurrence*. Washington, DC: Georgetown University Press.

Call, C. T., & Cousens, E. M. (2008). Ending wars and building peace: international responses to war-torn societies. *International Studies Perspectives*, 9(1), 1–21.

Carpenter, A. C. (2014). *Conflict Drivers: In Community Resilience to Sectarian Violence in Baghdad* (pp. 41–52). New York, NY: Springer.

Carruth, L. (2018). The data hustle: how beneficiaries benefit from continual data collection and humanitarian aid research in the Somali Region of Ethiopia. *Medical Anthropology Quarterly*.

Catley, A., Burns, J., Abebe, D., Suji, O. (2013). *Participatory Impact Assessment: A Design Guide*. Somerville: Feinstein International Center, Tufts University.

Catley, A., Lind, J., & Scoones, I. (2013). Development at the Margins: Pastoralism in the Horn of Africa. In A. Catley, J. Lind, & I. Scoones (Eds.), *Pastoralism and Development in Africa: Dynamic Change at the Margins* (pp. 1–27). London: Routledge.

Chambers, R. (1997). *Whose Reality Counts?: Putting the First Last*. London: Intermediate Technology Publications.

(2007a). *Poverty Research: Methodologies, Mindsets and Multidimensionality* (Working Paper No. 293) (p. 59). Brighton: Institute of Development Studies. Retrieved from https://opendocs.ids.ac.uk/opendocs/bitstream/handle/123456789/4149/Wp293.pdf

(2007b). *Who Counts? The Quiet Revolution of Participation and Numbers* (Working Paper No. 296) (p. 43). Brighton: Institute of Development Studies. Retrieved from https://www.ids.ac.uk/files/Wp296.pdf

(2010). A revolution whose time has come? The win–win of quantitative participatory approaches and methods. *IDS Bulletin*, 41(6), 45–55.

(2013). *Rural Development: Putting the Last First* (First published 1983 by Pearson Education Limited). London: Routledge.

Chenoweth, E., & Stephan, M. J. (2011). *Why Civil Resistance Works: The Strategic Logic of Nonviolent Conflict*. New York, NY: Columbia University Press.

Chigas, D., Church, M., & Corlazzoli, V. (2014). *Evaluating Impacts of Peacebuilding Interventions: Approaches and Methods, Challenges and Considerations (Practice Product)* (p. 51). London: DFID. Retrieved from http://cdacollaborative.org/wordpress/wp-content/uploads/2016/02/Evaluating-Impacts-of-Peacebuilding-Interventions.pdf

Christia, F. (2012). *Alliance Formation in Civil Wars*. Cambridge: Cambridge University Press.

Clark, P. (2010). *The Gacaca Courts, Post-Genocide Justice and Reconciliation in Rwanda: Justice without Lawyers*. Cambridge: Cambridge University Press.

Cole, E. & Firchow, P. (2018). Reconciliation Barometers: Tools for Post-Conflict Policy Design. Working Paper.

Collier, P. (2008). *The Bottom Billion: Why the Poorest Countries Are Failing and What Can Be Done About It*. New York, NY: Oxford University Press, USA.

Cooke, B., & Kothari, U. (2001). *Participation: The New Tyranny?* London: Zed Books.

Croke, K., Dabalen, A., Demombynes, G., Giugale, M., & Hoogeveen, J. (2013). *Collecting High-Frequency Data Using Mobile Phones: Do Timely Data Lead to Accountability?* Washington, DC: World Bank.

Cyr, J. (2015). The pitfalls and promise of focus groups as a data collection method. *Sociological Methods & Research*, 45(2), 231–59. https://doi.org/10.1177/0049124115570065

Daly, S. Z. (2012). Organizational legacies of violence: conditions favoring insurgency onset in Colombia, 1964–1984. *Journal of Peace Research*, 49(3), 473–91.

Davenport, C., & Stam, A. C. (2009). What Really Happened in Rwanda? *Miller-McCune*, October, 6, 2009.

Davidov, E., Meuleman, B., Cieciuch, J., Schmidt, P., & Billiet, J. (2014). Measurement equivalence in cross-national research. *Annual Review of Sociology*, 40.

De Coning, C., & Romita, P. (2009). *Monitoring and Evaluation of Peace Operations*. New York, NY: International Peace Institute (IPI).

De Juan, A., & Pierskalla, J. H. (2014). Civil war violence and political trust: microlevel evidence from Nepal. *Conflict Management and Peace Science*, 33(1), 67–88. https://doi.org/10.1177/0738894214544612

De Waal, A. (1997). *Famine Crimes: Politics and the Disaster Relief Industry in Africa*. Bloomington, IN: Indiana University Press.

Demombynes, G., Gubbins, P., & Romeo, A. (2013). *Challenges and Opportunities of Mobile Phone-Based Data Collection: Evidence from South Sudan*.

Denskus, T. (2007). Peacebuilding does not build peace. *Development in Practice*, 17(4–5), 656–62.

Desvousges, W. H., and J. H. Frey. (1989). "Integrating focus groups and surveys: examples from environmental risk studies." *Journal of Official Statistics* 5, 349–63.

Diehl, P. F., & Druckman, D. (2010). *Evaluating Peace Operations*. Boulder, CO: Lynne Rienner Publishers.

Dixon, J. (2016). *Social Welfare in Africa*. London: Routledge.

Dixon, P. J. (2016). Reparations, assistance and the experience of justice: lessons from Colombia and the Democratic Republic of the Congo. *International Journal of Transitional Justice*, 10(1), 88–107. https://doi.org/https://doi.org/10.1093/ijtj/ijv031

Doran, G. T. (1981). There's a S.M.A.R.T. way to write management's goals and objectives. *Management Review*, 70(11), 35–6.

Doyle, M. W., & Sambanis, N. (2006). *Making War and Building Peace: United Nations Peace Operations*. New Jersey, NJ: Princeton University Press.

Duffield, J. S. (2001). Transatlantic relations after the Cold War: theory, evidence, and the future. *International Studies Perspectives*, 2(1), 93–115.

Duffield, M. (2014). *Global Governance and the New Wars: The Merging of Development and Security*. London: Zed Books Ltd.

Dunning, T. (2008). Improving causal inference: strengths and limitations of natural experiments. *Political Research Quarterly*, 61(2), 282–93.

  (2012). *Natural Experiments in the Social Sciences: A Design-Based Approach*. Cambridge: Cambridge University Press.

Duursma, A., Firchow, P., & Levy, N. (2018). Advancing Peace Measurement: The Scalability of Locally-Sourced Indicators. Working Paper.

Dwyer, L. (2012). 'Don't disturb the peace': post-conflict politics in Aceh, Indonesia. *Global Studies Review*, 8(2).

Dwyer, L. and D. Santikarma (2018) *A World in Fragments': Aftermaths of Mass Violence in Bali, Indonesia*. University of Pennsylvania Press.

Economic, U. N., & Council, S. (2015). Report of the friends of the Chair Group on broader measures of progress. February 2015. E/CN.

Edington, S., & Hughes, C. (2016). Refugees and peacebuilding: "poor country problems" in Cambodia and Bosnia-Herzegovina. In P. Firchow & H. Anastasiou (Eds.), *Practical Approaches to Peacebuilding: Putting Theory to Work* (pp. 109–26). Boulder, CO: Lynne Rienner Publishers.

Escobar, A. (2011). *Encountering Development: The Making and Unmaking of the Third World*. New Jersey, NJ: Princeton University Press.

Esser, D. E., & Vanderkamp, E. E. (2013). Comparable and yet context-sensitive? Improving evaluation in violently divided societies through methodology. *Journal of Peacebuilding & Development*, 8(2), 42–56. https://doi.org/10.1080/15423166.2013.820103

Fabbro, D. (1978). Peaceful societies: an introduction. *Journal of Peace Research*, 15(1), 67–83.

Ferguson, J. (1990). *The Anti-politics Machine: 'Development', Depoliticization and Bureaucratic Power in Lesotho*. Cambridge: Cambridge University Press Archive.

Finnström, S. (2008). *Living with Bad Surroundings: War, History, and Everyday Moments in Northern Uganda*. Durham, NC: Duke University Press.

Firchow, P. (2013a). A Cuban Spring? The use of the internet as a tool of democracy promotion by United States Agency for International Development in Cuba. *Information Technology for Development*, 19(4), 347–56.

(2013b). Must our communities bleed to receive social services? Development projects and collective reparations schemes in Colombia. *Journal of Peacebuilding & Development*, 8(3), 50–63.

(2014). The implementation of the Institutional Programme of Collective Reparations in Colombia. *Journal of Human Rights Practice*, 6(2), 356–75.

(2017). Do reparations repair relationships? Setting the stage for reconciliation in Colombia. *International Journal of Transitional Justice*, 11(2): 315–38.

Firchow, P. and R. Mac Ginty. (2017a) Including hard to access populations using mobile phone surveys and participatory indicators. *Sociological Methods and Research*, DOI: 0049124117729702.

(2017b) The practicalities and ethics of mobile phone surveys in conflict-affected contexts. *International Studies Perspectives*, 18(1): 4–42.

(2017c). Measuring peace: comparability, commensurability and complementarity using bottom-up indicators. *International Studies Review*, 19(1): 6–27.

Firchow, P., & Mac Ginty, R. (2018). Indivisibility as a way of life: transformation in microprocesses of peace in Northern Uganda [Forthcoming]. In P. Gready & S. Robins (Eds), *From Transitional Justice to Transformative Justice*. Cambridge: Cambridge University Press.

Firchow, P. & Tilton, Z. (2018). Everyday peace indicators: renegotiating rigor for peacebuilding evidence [forthcoming]. *International Journal on Conflict Engagement and Resolution*.

Fortna, V. P. (2008). *Does Peacekeeping Work?: Shaping Belligerents' Choices after Civil War*. New Jersey, NJ: Princeton University Press.

Freire, P. (2000). *Pedagogy of the Oppressed* (30th Anniversary Edition. Originally Published in 1968). New York, NY: Bloomsbury Academic.

Fritzen, S. A. (2007). Can the design of community-driven development reduce the risk of elite capture? Evidence from Indonesia. *World Development*, 35(8), 1359–75.

Fuller, T. D., Edwards, J. N., Vorakitphokatorn, S., & Sermsri, S. (1993). *Using Focus Groups to Adapt Survey Instruments to New Populations: Experience from a Developing Country*. In D. L. Morgan (Ed.), *Sage Focus Editions, Vol. 156. Successful Focus Groups: Advancing the State of the Art* 89–104. Thousand Oaks, CA: Sage Publications, Inc.

Geertz, C. (1975). On the nature of anthropological understanding: not extraordinary empathy but readily observable symbolic forms enable the anthropologist to grasp the unarticulated concepts that inform the lives and cultures of other peoples. *American Scientist*, 63(1), 47–53.

Gibson, J. L. (2003). The legacy of apartheid: racial differences in the legitimacy of democratic institutions and processes in the New South Africa. *Comparative Political Studies*, 36(7), 772–800.

Goertz, G. (2005). Necessary condition hypotheses as deterministic or probabilistic: Does it matter? *Qualitative Methods*, 3(1), 22–7.

(2006a). Assessing the trivialness, relevance, and relative importance of necessary or sufficient conditions in social science. *Studies in Comparative International Development*, 41(2), 88–109. https://doi.org/10.1007/BF02686312

(2006b). *Social Science Concepts: A User's Guide*. Princeton, NJ: Princeton University Press.

(2016). Multimethod research. *Security Studies*, 25(1), 3–24.

Goertz, G., & Mahoney, J. (2012). *A Tale of Two Cultures: Qualitative and Quantitative Research in the Social Sciences*. Princeton, NJ: Princeton University Press.

Goetschel, L. (2009). Conflict transformation. In V. Chetail (Ed.), *Post-Conflict Peacebuilding: A Lexicon*. (pp. 92–104). Oxford: Oxford University Press.

Goetschel, L., & Hagmann, T. (2009). Civilian peacebuilding: peace by bureaucratic means? *Conflict, Security & Development*, 9(1), 55–73. https://doi.org/10.1080/14678800802704911

Gullette, D., & Rosenberg, D. (2015). Not just another box to tick: conflict-sensitivity methods and the role of research in development programming. *Development Policy Review*, 33(6), 703–23.

Guillermoprieto, A. (2018). After five decades of Civil War, Colombia's healing begins. *National Geographic Magazine*, January 2018.

Harbom, L., Högbladh, S., & Wallensteen, P. (2006). Armed conflict and peace agreements. *Journal of Peace Research*, 43(5), 617–31.

Harlacher, T., Okot, F. X., Obonyo, C. A., Balthazard, M., & Atkinson, R. R. (2006). *Traditional Ways of Coping in Acholi: Cultural Provisions for Reconciliation and Healing from War*. Kampala: Caritas Gulu Archdiocese.

Hegre, H. (2001). Toward a democratic civil peace? Democracy, political change, and civil war, 1816–1992. *American Political Science Review*, 95(1), 33–48.

Heideman, L. (2013). The vulnerable protecting the vulnerable. In A. M. Tripp et al. (Eds.), *Gender, Violence, and Human Security: Critical Feminist Perspectives* (pp. 214–37). New York, NY: New York University Press.

Heideman, L. J. (2016). *Institutional Amnesia: Sustainability and Peacebuilding in Croatia* (Vol. 31, pp. 377–96). Presented at the Sociological Forum, Wiley Online Library.

Hinton, A. (2004a). The poetics of genocidal practice: violence under the Khmer Rouge. In N. Whitehead (Ed.), *Violence* (pp. 157–84). Santa Fe, NM: School of American Research.

Hinton, A. L. (2004b). *Why Did You Kill?: The Cambodian Genocide and the Dark Side of Face and Honor*. Berkeley, CA: University of California Press.

Hirsch, S. F. (2010). The victim deserving of global justice: power, caution, and recovering individuals. *Mirrors of Justice: Law and Power in the Post-Cold War Era*, 149–70.

Holland, J. (Ed.). (2013). *Who Counts?: The Power of Participatory Statistics*. Practical Action Publishing.

Hood, C. (1991). A public management for all seasons? *Public Administration*, 69(1), 3–19.

Howard, L. M. (2008). *UN Peacekeeping in Civil Wars*. Cambridge: Cambridge University Press

Howes, M., & Chambers, R. (1979). Indigenous technical knowledge: analysis, implications and issues. *IDs Bulletin*, 10(2), 5–11.

Hudson, V. M., Ballif-Spanvill, B., Caprioli, M., & Emmett, C. F. (2012). *Sex and World Peace*. New York, NY: Columbia University Press.

Irmer, C. (2009). *A Systems Approach and the Interagency Conflict Assessment Framework (ICAF)*. Presented at the Cornwallis Group XIV Workshop: Analysis of Societal Conflict and Counter-Insurgency.

Jackson, R. (2015). How resistance can save peace studies. *Journal of Resistance Studies*, 1(1), 18–49.

Jensen, S. (2010). The security and development nexus in Cape Town: war on gangs, counterinsurgency and citizenship. *Security Dialogue*, 41(1), 77–97.

Joshi, M., Quinn, J. M., & Regan, P. M. (2015). Annualized implementation data on comprehensive intrastate peace accords, 1989–2012. *Journal of Peace Research*, 52(4), 551–62.

Justino, P., Brück, T., & Verwimp, P. (2013). *A Micro-level Perspective on the Dynamics of Conflict, Violence, and Development*. Oxford: Oxford University Press.

Kagan, S. (2011). Do I make a difference? *Philosophy & Public Affairs*, 39(2), 105–41. https://doi.org/10.1111/j.1088-4963.2011.01203.

Kaldor, M. (1999). *New and Old Wars: Organized Violence in a Global Era*. Cambridge: Polity.

Kalyvas, S. N. (2006). *The Logic of Violence in Civil War*. Cambridge: Cambridge University Press.

Kapiszewski, D., MacLean, L. M., & Read, B. L. (2015). *Field Research in Political Science: Practices and Principles*. Cambridge: Cambridge University Press.

Keele, L., & Titiunik, R. (2016). Natural experiments based on geography. *Political Science Research and Methods*, 4(1), 65–95.

Kelley, J. G., & Simmons, B. A. (2015). Politics by number: indicators as social pressure in international relations. *American Journal of Political Science*, 59(1), 55–70. https://doi.org/10.1111/ajps.12119

Keohane, R. O., & Nye Jr, J. S. (1998). Power and interdependence in the information age. *Foreign Affairs*, 77(5), 81–94. https://doi.org/10.2307/20049052

Kihika, K. S., & Regué, M. (2015). Pursuing accountability for serious crimes in Uganda's courts. International Center of Transitional Justice. Retrieved from https://ictj.org/sites/default/files/ICTJ-Briefing-Uganda-Kwoyelo-2015.pdf

King, G., Murray, C. J. L., Salomon, J. A., & Tandon, A. (2004). Enhancing the validity and cross-cultural comparability of measurement in survey research. *American Political Science Review*, 98(1), 191–207. https://doi.org/10.1017/S000305540400108X

Kreutz, J. (2010). How and when armed conflicts end: introducing the UCDP conflict termination dataset. *Journal of Peace Research*, 47(2), 243–50.

Labonte, M. T. (2011). From patronage to peacebuilding? Elite capture and governance from below in Sierra Leone. *African Affairs*, 111(442), 90–115.

Laplante, L. J. (2015). Just repair. *Cornell International Law Journal*, 48 (3), 513–578.

Lederach, J. P. (1999). Justpeace – the challenge of the 21st century. *People Building Peace. 35 Inspiring Stories from Around the World*, 27–36. http://homepage.univie.ac.at/silvia.michal-misak/justpeace.htm

   (2005). *The Moral Imagination: The Art and Soul of Building Peace*. New York, NY: Oxford University Press.

Lederach, J. P., Culbertson, H., & Neufeldt, R. (2007). *Reflective Peacebuilding: A Planning, Monitoring and Learning Toolkit*. Notre Dame, IN: Joan B. Kroc Inst. for International Peace Studies, University of Notre Dame and Catholic Relief Services.

Lemanski, C. (2004). A new apartheid? The spatial implications of fear of crime in Cape Town, South Africa. *Environment and Urbanization*, 16(2), 101–12.

Lemay-Hébert, N. (2009). Statebuilding without nation-building? Legitimacy, state failure and the limits of the institutionalist approach. *Journal of Intervention and Statebuilding*, 3(1), 21–45.

Levine, C., & Grino, L. (2015). *Local Ownership in Evaluation: Moving from Participant Inclusion to Ownership in Evaluation and Decision Making*. Briefing Paper, Interaction.

Linde, P. (2014). Un laboratorio de paz en Colombia. El País (8 Abril, 2014). https://elpais.com/elpais/2014/04/08/planeta_futuro/1396972680_950665.html

Luengo-Cabrera, J. & Butler, T. (2017). Reaping the Benefits of Cost-Effective Peacebuilding. International Peace Institute Global Observatory. https://theglobalobservatory.org/2017/07/peacebuilding-expenditure-united-nations-sustaining-peace/

Lund, J. F., & Saito-Jensen, M. (2013). Revisiting the issue of elite capture of participatory initiatives. *World Development*, 46(Supplement C), 104–12. https://doi.org/10.1016/j.worlddev.2013.01.028

Mac Ginty, R. (2008). Indigenous peace-making versus the liberal peace. *Cooperation and Conflict*, 43(2), 139–63.

(2011a). Hybrid peace: how does hybrid peace come about. In S. Campbell, D. Chandler, & M. Sabaratnam (Eds.), *A Liberal Peace: The Problems and Practices of Peacebuilding* (209–25). London: Zed Books.

(2011c). *International Peacebuilding and Local Resistance: Hybrid Forms of Peace*. Basingstoke: Palgrave Macmillan.

(2012a). Between resistance and compliance: non-participation and the liberal peace. *Journal of Intervention and Statebuilding*, 6(2), 167–87.

Mac Ginty, R. M. (2012b). Routine peace: technocracy and peacebuilding. *Cooperation and Conflict*, 47(3), 287–308.

Mac Ginty, R. (2013a). Indicators+: a proposal for everyday peace indicators. *Evaluation and Program Planning*, 36(1), 56–63.

(2013b). Introduction: the transcripts of peace. Public, hidden or non-obvious? *Journal of Intervention and Statebuilding*, 7(4: Everyday Peace Indicators), 423–30. https://doi.org/ http://dx.doi.org/10.1080/17502977.2012.727535

(2013c). *Routledge Handbook of Peacebuilding*. London: Routledge.

(2014). Everyday peace: bottom-up and local agency in conflict-affected societies. *Security Dialogue*, 45(6), 548–64.

(2015). Where is the local? Critical localism and peacebuilding. *Third World Quarterly*, 36(5), 840–56.

Mac Ginty, R., & Firchow, P. (2016). Top-down and bottom-up narratives of peace and conflict. *Politics*, 36(3), 308–23.

Mac Ginty, R., & Richmond, O. (2016). The fallacy of constructing hybrid political orders: a reappraisal of the hybrid turn in peacebuilding. *International Peacekeeping*, 23(2), 219–39.

Machado, A., Suarez, A., Camacho, A. Gonzalez S. J., F. et al. (2009). *La masacre de El Salado. Esa guerra no era nuestra*. Bogota, Colombia: Grupo de Memoria Histórica.

MacLean, L. M. (2010). *Informal Institutions and Citizenship in Rural Africa: Risk and Reciprocity in Ghana and Cote d'Ivoire*. Cambridge: Cambridge University Press.

MacQueen, K. M., McLellan, E., Metzger, D. S., et al. (2001). What is community? An evidence-based definition for participatory public health. *American Journal of Public Health*, 91(12), 1929–38.

Mahoney, J., & Goertz, G. (2006). A tale of two cultures: contrasting quantitative and qualitative research. *Political Analysis*, 14(3), 227–49.

Maslow, A. H. (1943). A theory of human motivation. *Psychological Review*, 50(4), 370.

Mazurana, D., Jacobsen, K., & Gale, L. A. (2013). *Research Methods in Conflict Settings: A View from Below*. Cambridge: Cambridge University Press.

McCandless, E. (2013). Wicked problems in peacebuilding and statebuilding: making progress in measuring progress through the new deal. *Global Governance: A Review of Multilateralism and International Organizations*, 19(2), 227–48.

McTaggart, R. (1991). Principles for participatory action research. *Adult Education Quarterly*, 41(3), 168–87.

(1994). Participatory action research: issues in theory and practice. *Educational Action Research*, 2(3), 313–37.

Melko, M. (1971). Discovering peace. *Peace Research*, 3(12), 16–17.

(1973). *52 Peaceful Societies*. Oakville: Canadian Peace Research Institute Press.

Mercer, J., Kelman, I., Suchet-Pearson, S., & Lloyd, K. (2009). Integrating indigenous and scientific knowledge bases for disaster risk reduction in Papua New Guinea. *Geografiska Annaler: Series B, Human Geography*, 91(2), 157–83.

Merry, S. E. (2016). *The Seductions of Quantification: Measuring Human Rights, Gender Violence, and Sex Trafficking*. Chicago, IL: University of Chicago Press.

Merry, S. E., Davis, K. E., & Kingsbury, B. (2015a). The local-global life of indicators: law, power, and resistance. In S. E. Merry, K. E. Davies & B. Kingsbury (Eds.), *The Quiet Power of Indicators: Measuring Governance, Corruption and the Rule of Law, Cambridge Studies in Law and Society*, pp. 1–24. Cambridge: Cambridge University Press.

(2015b). *The Quiet Power of Indicators: Measuring Governance, Corruption, and Rule of Law*. Cambridge: Cambridge University Press.

Merry, S. E., Rottenburg, R., Park, S.-J., & Mugler, J. (2015). *The World of Indicators: The Making of Governmental Knowledge through Quantification*. Cambridge: Cambridge University Press.

Merry, S. E., & Wood, S. (2015). Quantification and the paradox of measurement: translating children's rights in Tanzania. *Current Anthropology*, 56(2), 205–29. https://doi.org/10.1086/680439.

Miller, J. E. (2015). *The Chicago Guide to Writing about Numbers*. University of Chicago Press.

Minow, M. (1998). Between vengeance and forgiveness: South Africa's truth and reconciliation commission. *Negotiation Journal*, 14(4), 319–55.

Mohan, G., & Stokke, K. (2000). Participatory development and empowerment: the dangers of localism. *Third World Quarterly*, 21(2), 247–68.

Moore, A. (2013). *Peacebuilding in Practice: Local Experience in Two Bosnian Towns*. Ithaca, NY: Cornell University Press.

Morgan, V. (1996). *Women and the Peace Process in Northern Ireland*. Durham, NC: Center for International Studies, Duke University.

Natsios, A. (2011). *The Clash of the Counter-Bureaucracy and Development*. Center for Global Development.

Nee, A., & Uvin, P. (2010). Silence and dialogue: Burundians' alternatives to transitional justice. In R. Shaw & L. Waldorf (Eds.), *Localizing Transitional Justice: Interventions and Priorities after Mass Violence*. (pp. 157–82). Stanford, CA: Stanford University Press.

Newman, J. (2013). An (unintentional) façade of democratic debate. BACUP – British Academics for a Colombia under peace. Retrieved from http://sro.sussex.ac.uk/46619/

Nordstrom, C. (1992). The Dirty War: civilian experience of conflict in Mozambique and Sri Lanka. In K. Rupesinghe (Ed.), *Internal Conflict and Governance*. New York, NY: St. Martin's Press in association with the International Peace Research Institute, Oslo.

Nordstrom, C., & Martin, J. (1992). *The Paths to Domination, Resistance, and Terror*. Berkeley, CA: University of California Press. Retrieved from Table of contents http://catdir.loc.gov/catdir/toc/ucal041/91004767.html

Nordstrom, C., & Robben, A. C. (1995). *Fieldwork under Fire: Contemporary Studies of Violence and Survival*. Berkerley, CA: University of California Press.

Nygren, A. (1999). Local knowledge in the environment–development discourse: from dichotomies to situated knowledges. *Critique of Anthropology*, 19(3), 267–88.

O'Brien, K. (1993). *Improving Survey Questionnaires through Focus Groups*. Presented at the an earlier version of these findings was presented at the conference on Focus Groups and Group Interviews: Advancing the State of the Art. Portland, OR: Sage Publications, Inc., October 4–6, 1990.

O'Neill, C. (2016). *Weapons of Math Destruction. How Big Data Increases Inequality and Threatens Democracy*. New York, NY: Crown.

O'Reilly, M., Súilleabháin, A. Ó., & Paffenholz, T. (2015). *Reimagining Peacemaking: Women's Roles in Peace Processes*. New York, NY: International Peace Institute, 11–13.

Ostrom, E. (2015). *Governing the Commons*. Cambridge: Cambridge University Press.

Paris, R. (2004). *At War's End: Building Peace after Civil Conflict*. Cambridge: Cambridge University Press.

Parkins, J. R., Stedman, R. C., & Varghese, J. (2001). Moving towards local-level indicators of sustainability in forest-based communities: a mixed-method approach. *Social Indicators Research*, 56(1), 43–72.

Parkins, J. R., Varghese, J., & Stedman, R. (2001). *Locally Defined Indicators of Community Sustainability in the Prince Albert Model Forest* (Vol. 379). Edmonton, AB: Canadian Forest Service.

Pinnock, D. (1984). *The Brotherhoods: Street Gangs and State Control in Cape Town*. Cape Town: David Philip.

Platteau, J. (2004). Monitoring elite capture in community-driven development. *Development and Change*, 35(2), 223–46.

Pouligny, B. (2006). *Peace Operations Seen from Below: UN Missions and Local People*. London: Hurst.

Pugh, M. (2013). The problem-solving and critical paradigms. In R. Mac Ginty, (Ed.), *Routledge Handbook of Peacebuilding*. New York, NY: Routledge.

Quaker Council for European Affairs (2018). *Building Peace Together: A Practical Resource*. UK: Creative Commons.

Reed, M. S., Dougill, A. J., & Baker, T. R. (2008). Participatory indicator development: what can ecologists and local communities learn from each other. *Ecological Applications*, 18(5), 1253–69.

Riaño-Alcalá, P., & Baines, E. (2011). The archive in the witness: documentation in settings of chronic insecurity. *International Journal of Transitional Justice*, 5(3), 412–33.

Richmond, O. (2012). *A Post-Liberal Peace*. London: Routledge.

Richmond, O. P. (2005a). *The Transformation of Peace*. Basingstoke: Palgrave Macmillan.

  (2009). Becoming liberal, unbecoming liberalism: liberal-local hybridity via the everyday as a response to the paradoxes of liberal peacebuilding. *Journal of Intervention and Statebuilding*, 3(3), 324–44.

  (2014). *Failed Statebuilding: Intervention, the State, and the Dynamics of Peace Formation*. New Haven, CT: Yale University Press.

Ricigliano, R. (2012). *Making Peace Last: A Toolbox for Sustainable Peacebuilding*. Boulder, CO: Paradigm.

Rieff, D. (2003). *A Bed for the Night: Humanitarianism in Crisis*. New York, NY: Simon and Schuster.

Roberts, D. (2011a). Beyond the metropolis? Popular peace and post-conflict peacebuilding. *Review of International Studies*, 37(5), 2535–56.

  (2011b). *Liberal Peacebuilding and Global Governance: Beyond the Metropolis*. London: Taylor & Francis.

  (2011c). Post-conflict peacebuilding, liberal irrelevance and the locus of legitimacy. *International Peacekeeping*, 18(4), 410–24.

Rohter, L. (2000). Colombians Tell of Massacre, as Army Stood By. *The New York Times* (July 14, 2000).

Rogers, M., Chassy, A., & Bamat, T. (2010). *Integrating Peacebuilding into Humanitarian and Development Programming: Practical Guidance on Designing Effective, Holistic Peacebuilding Projects*. Baltimore, MD: Catholic Relief Services.

Rogers, P. J. (2012). Introduction to impact evaluation. *Impact Evaluation Notes* (1) March. Washington, DC: InterAction.

Rosenfeld, F. (2010). Collective reparation for victims of armed conflict. *International Review of the Red Cross*, 92(879), 731–46. https://doi.org/10.1017/S1816383110000494

Sarkin, J. (2014). Providing reparations in Uganda: substantive recommendations for implementing reparations in the aftermath of the conflicts that occurred over the last few decades. *African Human Rights Law Journal*, 14(2), 526–52.

Sartori, G. (1970). Concept misformation in comparative politics. *American Political Science Review*, 64(4), 1033–53.

Schaffer, F. C. (2014). Thin descriptions: the limits of survey research on the meaning of democracy. *Polity*, 46(3), 303–30.

(2016). *Elucidating Social Science Concepts: An Interpretivist Guide*. New York, NY: Routledge.

Scharbatke-Church, C. (2011). *Evaluating Peacebuilding: Not Yet All It Could Be*. In M. Fischer, B. Austin & H. J. Giessmann (Eds.), *Advancing Conflict Transformation. The Berghof Handbook II* (pp. 459–82). Opladen: Barbara Budrich Publishers.

Sekhon, J. S., & Titiunik, R. (2012). When natural experiments are neither natural nor experiments. *American Political Science Review*, 106(1), 35–57.

Sen, A. (2002). Health: perception versus observation: self reported morbidity has severe limitations and can be extremely misleading. *BMJ: British Medical Journal*, 324(7342), 860–1.

Sharp, D. N. (2013). Beyond the post-conflict checklist: linking peacebuilding and transitional justice through the lens of critique. *Chicago Journal of International Law*, 14, 165.

Sillitoe, P. (1998). The development of indigenous knowledge. *Current Anthropology*, 39(2), 223–52. https://doi.org/10.1086/204722

Skaar, E., García-Godos, J., & Collins, C. (2015). *Reconceptualizing Transitional Justice: The Latin American Experience*. London: Routledge.

Skaar, E., Malca, C. G., & Eide, T. (2015). *After Violence: Transitional Justice, Peace, and Democracy*. London: Routledge.

Skocpol, T. (1979). *States and Social Revolutions: A Comparative Analysis of France, Russia and China*. Cambridge: Cambridge University Press.

Sriram, C. L., García-Godos, J., Herman, J., & Martin-Ortega, O. (2012). *Transitional Justice and Peacebuilding on the Ground: Victims and Ex-combatants*. London: Routledge.

Summers, N. (2012). Colombia's victims' law: transitional justice in a time of violent conflict? *Harvard Human Rights Journal*, 25(1), 219–35.

Sylvester, C. (2002). *Feminist International Relations: An Unfinished Journey* (Vol. 77). Cambridge: Cambridge University Press.

Tandon, R. (1988). Social transformation and participatory research. *Convergence*, 21(2), 5.

Theidon, K. (2012). *Intimate Enemies: Violence and Reconciliation in Peru*. Pennsylvania, PA: University of Pennsylvania Press.

Thiessen, Chuck. (2017). *United Nations Peacebuilding Impact in Kyrgyzstan: A Final Report on the Baseline And Endline Assessment of the Kyrgyzstan Peacebuilding Priority Plan (PPP)*.

Thomson, S. (2013). *Whispering Truth to Power: Everyday Resistance to Reconciliation in Postgenocide Rwanda*. Wisconsin, WI: University of Wisconsin Press.

Tomlinson, M., Solomon, W., Singh, Y., et al. (2009). The use of mobile phones as a data collection tool: a report from a household survey in South Africa. *BMC Medical Informatics and Decision Making*, 9(1), 51.

United Nations. (2015). *Report of the High-level Panel on Peace Operations (HIPPO) Convened by the Secretary-General to Undertake a thorough Review of the Current United Nations Peace Operations and the Emerging Needs of the Future* (No. Doc. a/70/95-s/2015/446) (p. 104). New York, NY: United Nations. Retrieved from http://www.un.org/en/ga/search/view_doc.asp?symbol=S/2015/446

UNHCR. (2007). *The Global Report 2006*. New York, NY: UNHCR (30 June 2007). Retrieved from www.unhcr.org/en-us/publications/fundraising/501f7d2e2/global-report-2006.html

Uvin, P. (1998). *Aiding Violence: The Development Enterprise in Rwanda*. Kumarian Press.

(2013). *Life after Violence: A People's Story of Burundi*. Zed Books Ltd.

Van Heerden, A. (2014a). *Evidence for the Feasibility, Acceptability, Accuracy and Use of Electronic Data-Collection Methods for Health in KwaZulu-Natal.* Pretoria: Human Science Research Council. Retrieved from: http://repository.hsrc.ac.za/bitstream/handle/20.500.11910/2453/8197.pdf?sequence=1
  (2014b). *Pervasive Computing and Public Health Research in Africa: Mobile Phones in the Collection, Analysis and Dissemination of Health Research.* (Doctoral dissertation) University of the Witwatersrand: Johannesburg South Africa.
Van Heerden, A. C., Norris, S. A., Tollman, S. M., & Richter, L. M. (2014). Collecting health research data: comparing mobile phone-assisted personal interviewing to paper-and-pen data collection. *Field Methods*, 26(4), 307–21.
Van Metre, L. (2016). *Community Resilience to Violent Extremism in Kenya.* Washington, DC: United States Institute of Peace.
Vinck, P., & Pham, P. (2008). Ownership and participation in transitional justice mechanisms: a sustainable human development perspective from eastern DRC. *The International Journal of Transitional Justice*, 2(3), 398–411.
Walker, H. A., & Cohen, B. P. (1985). Scope statements: imperatives for evaluating theory. *American Sociological Review*, 288–301.
Wallensteen, P. (2011). The origins of contemporary peace research. In K. Hoglund & M. Oberg (Eds.), *Understanding Peace Research: Methods and Challenges* (pp. 14–32). London: Routledge.
  (2015). *Quality Peace: Peacebuilding, Victory and World Order.* Oxford: Oxford University Press.
Wallensteen, P., & Axell, K. (1994). Conflict resolution and the end of the Cold War, 1989–93. *Journal of Peace Research*, 31(3), 333–49.
Walter, B. F. (2002). *Committing to Peace: The Successful Settlement of Civil Wars.* New Jersey, NJ: Princeton University Press.
  (2004). Does conflict beget conflict? Explaining recurring civil war. *Journal of Peace Research*, 41(3), 371–88. https://doi.org/10.1177/0022343304043775
Willis, G. (2017). Before the body count: homicide statistics and everyday security in Latin America. *Journal of Latin American Studies*, 49(1), 29–54. doi:10.1017/S0022216X16000407
Willis, G. D. (2015). *The Killing Consensus: Police, Organized Crime, and the Regulation of Life and Death in Urban Brazil.* University of California Press.
Wittgenstein, L. (2010). *Philosophical Investigations.* Chicester: Wiley-Blackwell.
Wolff, B., Knodel, J., & Sittitrai, W. (1993). Focus groups and surveys as complementary research methods: A case example. In D. Morgan (Ed.), *Successful Focus Groups: Advancing the State of the Art* (pp. 118–36). Thousand Oaks, CA: Sage Publications, Inc.
World Bank. (2011). World development report 2011: Conflict, security, and development. World Bank.
Zürcher, C., Manning, C., Evenson, K. D., Hayman, R., & Roehner, N. (2013). *Costly Democracy: Peacebuilding and Democratization after War.* Palo Alto, CA: Stanford University Press.

Index

accountability
  cost, 37
  disintervention and, 151
  evaluation and, 13, 29, 50
  government, 42
  indicators and, 22, 37
  local level programming and, 24, 31
  mechanisms, 39
  small-p peacebuilding and, 48
Afghanistan, 64, 72
Afrobarometer, 40, 41
Alliance for Peacebuilding, 51, 59
Area Development Program (ADP), 102
Autesserre, Séverine, 18, 57, 151

Babst, Dean, 39
Baines, Erin, 80
basic needs. See Maslow, Abraham
benchmarking, 6, 8, 36
big-P Peacebuilding, 4, 5–6, 32–3, 34, 35, 54, 93, 141
Block, Jan Gotlib, 38
Bosnia, 16, 19
Boulding, Kenneth, 38
Branch, Adam, 18, 151
Brazil, 42
Broome, Andre, 8
businessification, 36

Chambers, Robert, 62–4, 65, 82–3, 156–7
change agents, 50
Chenoweth, Erica, 40
civil resistance, 40

civil society
  Colombia and, 79–80, 94, 104, 155
  everyday peace indicators and, 69, 71, 78–9, 157
  institutional memory and, 97
  mobile phone-assisted personal interviewing and, 75
  New Deal for Engagement in Fragile States and, 46
  peacebuilding and, 17, 31, 35
  small-p peacebuilding and, 99
  Uganda and, 80–1, 92, 93, 118
  use of indicators, 38
  Virtual Network for the Development of Indicators for Goal 16 and, 46
Collaborative Learning Project (CDA), 19, 59
collective harm, 24
collective victimhood, 24
Colombia
  Don Gabriel, 11, 76–7, 77, 103–4, 106, 118–20, 130–8, 153
  El Salado, 11, 76–7, 77, 102–4, 104–6, 115, 118–20, 125, 130–8, 150, 152–3, 153
  Entrelazando process, 106
  everyday peace indicators and, 10, 71, 87–8, 115, 118–20, 122, 125, 126, 130–8
  external interventions in, 104–6
  FARC (Revolutionary Armed Forces of Colombia), 92, 95, 102, 103–4
  Fundación Red de Desarrollo y Paz de los Montes de Maria, 106
  Fundación Semana and, 79–80, 104–5, 137

Colombia (cont.)
  Integrated Plan of Collective Reparations (PIRC), 105, 134
  internally displaced persons in, 11, 91
  Justice and Peace Law (Law 975), 94–5
  Laboratory for Peace, 104
  levels of intervention in, 26, 127–8, 152–3
  National Reparations and Reconciliation Commission (CNRR), 105
  National Victims registrar, 94
  paramilitary violence in, 11, 90–1, 102–4
  reconciliation and, 10, 61, 94, 107, 115, 126, 136, 151
  reconciliation barometers and, 39
  reconstruction and, 105, 120, 134–6, 151
  religion and, 77, 91
  reparations and, 71, 94–5, 105–6, 133–5
  small-p peacebuilding in, 106, 126, 152–3
  Sustainable Development Goal 16 and, 60–1
  transitional justice and, 92, 94–5, 134
  Unidad de Víctimas, 106
  Unidad para las Víctimas, 105, 106, 135
  United Self-Defense Forces (AUC), 94–5, 103
  Victim's Law of 2011 (Law 1448), 94
  Workers Revolutionary Party of Colombia (PRT), 103
Community Reconciliation team (CORE), 145
community-defined indicators, 2, 19, 127, 138
community-defined peace, 26, 84, 87, 127, 128, 149
conflict resolution
  big-P Peacebuilding and, 6
  Colombia and, 115, 118, 126
  elites and, 31
  everyday peace indicators and, 118, 120, 124, 148, 149, 150, 153, 155
  Sustainable Development Goal 16 and, 60
  Uganda and, 115, 120, 126, 140, 141
conflict sensitivity, 33
conscientization, 83
contact hypothesis, 13
coordination, 2, 16–17, 51, 54–5, 125, 150
  United Nations Office for Coordination of Humanitarian Affairs and, 140
Correlates of War, 38
Curle, Adam, 38

data revolution, 10, 29
demobilization
  Colombia and, 90, 95, 103
  Uganda and, 90, 95
democratic peace theory, 32, 39, 40. *See also* liberal peace model

Democratic Republic of Congo (DRC), 18, 95, 122
Department for International Development (DFID), 17
design, monitoring and evaluation (DME), 152
development. *See also* Sustainable Development Goal 16; Sustainable Development Goals
  as dimension of peace, 14
  as everyday peace indicator, 26, 67, 69, 78, 82, 84, 109, 110, 111, 121, 122, 126, 129, 149, 150–2
  as indicator, 38, 109
  big-P Peacebuilding and, 6, 33
  Colombia and, 80, 103, 104, 106, 118, 120, 134, 135–6, 152
  conflict sensitvity and, 33
  evaluation and, 6, 12, 29, 30, 36, 50, 52
  experimental research design and, 95
  fragile states and, 31
  indigenous knowledge and, 58
  indigenous technical knowledge and, 65
  institutional memory and, 97
  local perception of, 21
  peacebuilding and, 2, 16, 146, 148, 152
  Rapid Rural Appraisal and, 83
  small-p peacebuilding and, 34
  Uganda and, 93, 99–100, 101, 106, 115, 122, 140, 141–3
disintervention, 18, 151
donors
  coordination and, 16–17, 150, 155
  empathetic cooperation and, 56
  evidence-based approach and, 29, 36–7
  funding for peacebuilding, 3, 12, 15, 16
  indicators and, 48, 121, 156
  monitoring and evaluation and, 13, 52, 53, 157
  participatory statistics and, 66
  small-p peacebuilding and, 34
  transparency and, 16–17, 150, 155

economic liberalization, 16, 32. *See also* democratic peace theory; liberal peace model
elite capture, 24, 35, 78, 126
elites. *See also* elite capture
  Colombian, 80
  hybridity and, 25, 54, 56, 57
  participatory research and, 21, 82
  peacebuilding and, 17, 35, 53, 152, 153
empathetic cooperation, 56
evaluand, 48
evaluation
  challenges to, 54
  donors and, 12, 16

ethics of, 24
evaluand, 48
experimental research designs and, 49, 95
harmonization and, 22–3
hybridity and, 66–7
impact, 49, 51, 96
interpretivist approach to, 36
local ownership in, 31, 68, 84
monitoring and, 3, 5, 6, 13, 79, 152, 155
Most Significant Change (MSC), 50
Outcome Harvesting, 50
Outcome Mapping, 50
participatory approaches to, 50–1
quantitative approach to, 29–30, 35–7
Rapid Rural Apprasial and, 83
small-p peacebuilding and, 48–50, 51–2
technocratic approaches to, 53
everyday indicators. *See* everyday peace indicators
everyday peace indicators, 10–11, 14–15, 25–6, 108–9, 125–6, 148
as advocacy, 23
categorization of, 109–15, 120–2, 129, 148–9
Colombia and, 14, 115, 118–20, 120, 125, 126, 25–6, 153
decision-makers and, 157
development of, 69–73
external interventions and, 107
indigenous technical knowledge and, 3–4, 25, 65–6
Likert-type scale and, 125–6
local partners and, 78–9
Masolow's hierarchy of needs and, 122–4
methodology, 25
participatory research and, 81–2, 83–4, 155
program design and, 125
South Africa and, 123–4, 125
South Sudan and, 124
theoretical foundations of, 25, 54
Uganda and, 14, 115–18, 121, 122–3, 126, 138–45, 147, 153
evidence-based approach, 29
experience-distant
concept of, 9, 59
indicators, 60, 61, 111–15
experience-near
concept of, 9, 59
indicators, 60, 61, 111–15, 125
experimental research design, 95, 96

FARC (Revolutionary Armed Forces of Colombia), 92, 95, 102, 103–4
F-indicators (Standard Foreign Assistance Indicators), 48
Finnström, Sverker, 115–16

focus groups
everyday peace indicators and, 68–73, 81, 120
measurement validity and, 73–4
most significant change and, 50
Participatory Tracking and, 65
foreign direct investment (FDI), 56
Fragile States Index, 40
Freire, Paulo, 83
Fundación Mi Sangre, 106, 135
Fundación Red de Desarrollo y Paz de los Montes de Maria, 106
Fundación Semana, 11, 79–80, 104–5, 105, 137
funding
Colombia and, 11, 80
cooperation and, 155
coordination and, 3
donors and, 15–16, 16, 34
evaluation and, 36
indicators and, 7, 48
SDG 16 and, 42
transparency and, 155, 156
Uganda and, 93, 142

g7+, 32, 46
García, Claudia, 79–80
Geertz, Clifford, 9, 59
gender
indicators and, 8, 38, 41, 121, 127
justice, 80
surveys and, 76
violence, 121
Global Integrity, 59
Global Peace Index (GPI), 22, 40, 41, 46
Goal 16. *See* Sustainable Development Goal 16
Goertz, Gary, 7–8
governance reform, 6, 15, 41

harmonization, 3, 22, 43, 94
historical memory, 5
Human Development Index (HDI), 22, 40
human rights
as dimension of peace, 14
as everyday peace indicator, 26, 109, 110, 111, 121–2, 126
big-P Peacebuilding and, 32, 34
Colombia and, 90, 92, 95, 115, 118, 133–4
evaluation and, 6, 29, 36
International Criminal Court and, 12
liberal peace model and, 32
Rwanda and, 1
small-p peacebuilding and, 34
Uganda and, 90, 92, 93, 118

Human Terrain Systems (HTS), 64
humanitarian assistance. *See also* international assistance
  big-P Peacebuilding and, 6
  Colombia and, 106, 150
  Uganda and, 99, 140, 144, 150
hybridity, 18, 25, 54, 56–7, 67

impact evaluations, 49–50, 51, 96
in gear
  concept of, 59, 61
INCORE (International Conflict Research Institute), 39
indicators
  bottom-up, 22
  community-defined, 2–3, 10–11, 15, 19, 107, 108, 127–8, 145, 150
  conceptual challenges to, 6–10, 52–3
  definition of, 6
  ethics of, 24
  experience-distant, 59–60, 61, 111–15
  experience-near, 59–60, 61–2, 111–15, 125
  experts and, 5
  external development of, 3, 4, 5
  external interventions and, 2–3
  F- (Standard Foreign Assistance Indicators), 48
  global, 6, 22, 48
  Human Development Index and, 40
  local ownership in, 57–8
  measurement validity and, 62
  New Public Management and, 37
  paradox of measurement and, 7–9
  political uses of, 38
  power and, 7, 10, 22
  qualitative, 7
  quantitative, 5, 37–8
  SDG 16 and, 43–8, 60–1
  SDGs and, 42
  small-p peacebuilding and, 48
  time and, 147
  universal, 40–2
Indigenous Technical Knowledge (ITK), 3, 25, 54, 62–5, 67, 69, 155, 156
  Rapid Rural Apraisal and, 83
Institute for Economics and Peace (IEP), 46–7
institutional memory, 24, 51, 97
Integrated Plan of Collective Reparations (PIRC), 105, 134
Interagency Conflict Assessment Framework, 59
Internally Displaced Persons (IDPs), 11, 91, 98, 110, 123, 138–41, 152

international aid. *See* humanitarian assistance; international assistance
international assistance, 14, 31, 47, 149. *See also* humanitarian assistance
International Criminal Court (ICC), 12, 92–3, 95, 98–9, 101, 118
interpretivism, 8, 9, 36, 65
Iraq, 20, 64
isomorphic mimicry, 3

Justice and Reconciliation Project (JRP), 80–1, 100–01, 145

Kant, Immanuel, 32
Kwoyelo, Thomas, 92

Latinobarometro, 40
liberal peace model, 30, 31–2, 33, 34, 54–6. *See also* democratic peace theory
Listening Project, 88
logframes, 51
Lord's Resistance Army (LRA), 12, 92–3, 93, 95, 97–9, 118, 144
Lukwiya, Raska, 92

Mac Ginty, Roger, 18, 56
Making All Voices Count, 59
Maslow, Abraham
  hierarchy of needs, 109, 122
matched case research design, 11, 25, 26, 88, 95–6, 127, 128, 145, 148–9
measurement, 2, 5. *See also* monitoring and evaluation
  bias in, 69
  challenges to, 25, 54
  critique of, 24–5
  everyday peace indicators and, 10, 25, 58, 109, 111
  indicators and, 4, 8, 22, 37–8, 41, 60, 69
  language and, 59
  local ownership in, 31, 148, 157
  paradox of, 8–9, 62
  participatory numbers and, 65–6
  quantitative, 29, 36–7, 40, 42, 51
  SDG 16 and, 43, 46, 147
  small-p peacebuilding and, 48, 52
  technocratic approaches to, 53
  validity, 61–2, 73–4, 96
Mercy Corps, 59
Merry, Sally Engle, 6, 7–8
Millennium Development Goal (MDG), 43
mobile phone–assisted personal interviewing (MPAPI), 74–6
mobilizations, 35, 50, 80

Index

monitoring and evaluation (M&E), 5–6, 13, 50, 51, 79. *See also* measurement
  output, 13
  process, 13
  transparency and, 155
most significant change (MSC), 50
Museveni, Yoweri, 11, 92

National Reparations and Reconciliation Commission (CNRR), 105
National Resistance Army (NRA), 98
National Science Foundation, 36
negative peace, 39
  everyday peace indicators and, 25
  indicators, 15, 18–19, 41, 109, 121, 123
  indicators in South Africa, 123–4
  indicators in Uganda, 115
New Deal for Engagement in Fragile States, 46
New Public Management, 10, 36–7
non-governmental organizations (NGOs)
  Colombia and, 104
  coordination and, 150, 156
  evaluation and, 35
  institutional memory and, 97
  international (INGOs), 35, 51
  local, 154
  New Public Management and, 36
  participatory statistics and, 66
  small-p peacebuilding and, 34, 48
  transparency and, 155
  Uganda and, 101, 117, 140, 142
Nonviolent and Violent Conflict Outcomes (NAVCO), 40

Odhiambo, Okot, 92
Ongwen, Dominic, 92–3, 98–9, 118
Organization for Economic Cooperation and Development (OECD), 32, 40
Organization for International Migration, 105
Otim, Michael, 80
Otti, Vincent, 12, 92, 97–8, 98–9
Outcome Harvesting, 50
Outcome Mapping, 50

paramilitary groups, 11, 90–1, 95, 102–4, 105. *See also* FARC; Lord's Resistance Army; National Resistance Army; United Self-Defense Forces
Participatory Action Research (PAR), 68, 81–4, 96
participatory impact assessments, 50, 69, 82, 96
participatory numbers, 25, 54, 65–6, 81, 154–5, 156

participatory research approach, 58–9, 81–4, 155. *See also* Participatory Action Research; participatory numbers; Rapid Rural Appraisal
Participatory Rural Appraisal (PRA), 82. *See also* Participatory Action Research; Rapid Rural Appraisal
participatory statistics, 66, 81, 157
Participatory Tracking, 65
Peace Accords Matrix (PAM), 39
Peace Recovery and Development Plan (PRDP), 93, 142
peacebuilding. *See big-P* Peacebuilding; peacebuilding effectiveness; *small-p* peacebuilding
Peacebuilding and Statebuilding Goals (PSGs), 46
peacebuilding effectiveness
  community-generated indicators and, 81
  conceptual challenges, 5
  evaluation and, 35, 49, 52
  hybrid approach to, 57
  local level, 3, 4, 6, 24, 68, 148, 154, 157
  local standards of, 21
  project level, 149
  theoretical explanations of, 4, 17–21
Peacebuilding Evaluation Consortium, 58
peacefulness
  levels of, 2, 30, 53, 126, 128, 130, 138, 148, 150
peacekeeping, 17–18, 19, 33
Political Settlements Research Programme at the University of Edinburgh the Peace Agreements Database (PA-X), 39
positive peace, 38–9
  big-P Peacebuilding and, 33
  everyday peace indicators and, 25
  indicators, 15, 19, 41, 109, 121, 122, 123, 148, 149
  indicators in Colombia, 130–2
  indicators in Uganda, 115, 116, 138, 141
positivism, 8–10, 36, 51, 65
power dynamics, 31, 55
problem-solving approach, 55
program design, 67, 125

Rapid Rural Appraisal (RRA), 65, 83–4. *See also* Participatory Action Research; Participatory Rural Appraisal
reconciliation, 5, 30, 151. *See also* Justice and Reconciliation Project
  as everyday peace indicator, 125
  Colombia and, 10, 61, 94, 107, 115, 126, 136, 151
  funding for, 15

reconciliation (*cont.*)
  indicators, 40–2
  Rwanda and, 4–5, 5
  small-p peacebuilding and, 34
  Uganda and, 93, 95, 100–01, 115, 118, 126, 142, 151
reconciliation barometers, 39, 41
reconstruction, 2, 14, 17, 61, 126, 146, 148, 150
  Colombia and, 105, 120, 134–6, 151
  Uganda and, 93, 99, 140–2, 142, 151, 152
reification, 8–9
reintegration, 80, 92, 93, 101, 118
Richardson, Lewis Fry, 38
Richmond, Oliver, 18, 56, 121
rule of law, 6, 17, 32, 33, 47
  United Nations and, 46
Rwanda, 88
  genocide in, 1–2
  reconciliation and, 4–5, 5

Santos, Juan Manuel, 95
Schaffer, Fred, 8, 9, 53, 66
scientific knowledge
  evaluation and, 36–7
  indigenous technical knowledge and, 63–5, 67
SDG 16 Data initiative, 47. *See also* Sustainable Development Goal 16
Search for Common Ground (SFCG), 34, 51, 59
security
  as dimension of peace, 14
  as everyday peace indicator, 15, 26, 109, 110, 111, 121, 122–4, 126, 125–6, 147–8, 150
  as indicator, 61, 109, 129
  big-P Peacebuilding and, 6, 32, 33
  Brazil and, 42
  Colombia and, 80, 103, 104, 118, 130–3, 153
  food and, 99, 110
  peacebuilding effectiveness and, 17
  sector reform, 17
  small-p peacebuilding and, 34
  Uganda and, 99, 116–18, 141, 153
  women and, 40
segmentation, 69. *See also* focus groups
Semana, 79. *See also* Fundación Semana
Sen, Amartya, 23
sensitization, 35, 93
  workshops, 50
small-p peacebuilding, 4, 5–6, 14, 32, 34, 33–5, 35–6, 54, 93, 99, 129, 146
  evaluation and, 48–9, 51–2
  in Colombia, 106, 134, 136, 152
  in Uganda, 142–5, 152
  Justice and Reconciliation Project as, 81, 101
  United Nations and, 34

social relations
  as dimension of peace, 14
  as everyday peace indicator, 110
Sorokin, Pitirim, 38
South Africa, 88
  everyday peace indicators and, 11, 61, 111, 122, 123–4, 125
South African Barometer Survey, 39
South Sudan
  everyday peace indicators and, 11, 122, 124
  Internally Displaced Persons and, 91, 123
  Lord's Resistance Army and, 12, 95, 97–8
  Uganda and, 141, 147
structural violence, 19
Subject Matter Experts (SMEs), 48
surveys. *See also* reconciliation barometers
  evaluation and, 50
  everyday peace indicators and, 10, 25, 76–8, 88, 96, 97, 128–30
  in Colombia, 77, 135, 130–8
  in Uganda, 74, 77, 138–45
  indicators and, 53
  measurement validity and, 73–4
  mobile phone, 74–6
  panel, 74
  Verification Focus Groups and, 71, 72
Sustainable Development Goal 16 (SDG 16), 40, 46, 48, 60–1, 111, 147
Sustainable Development Goals (SDGs), 42–3, 47, 61

theories of change, 13–14, 15, 51, 52, 129
transitional justice
  Colombia and, 94–5, 118, 134
  peacebuilding and, 6
  Uganda and, 80, 93, 95, 100, 118, 120
transparency, 2, 14, 16–17, 24, 37, 150, 155–6

Uganda
  Amnesty Act, 92
  Area Development Program (ADP), 102
  Atiak, 11–12, 77, 81, 97–8, 98–9, 99–102, 115–18, 138–40, 140–5, 147, 150, 152, 153
  big-P Peacebuilding in, 93, 141
  Community Reconciliation team (CORE), 145
  everyday peace indicators and, 87–8, 115–18, 122–3, 125, 126, 138–45, 147
  external interventions in, 18, 99–102
  internally displaced persons in, 91, 98, 140, 152
  International Crimes Division (ICD), 92
  International Criminal Court and, 92–3, 95, 98–9, 118
  Justice and Reconciliation Project (JRP), 80–1, 100–01, 145

levels of intervention in, 26, 128
Lord's Resistance Army and, 11–12, 92–3, 95, 97–9, 144–5
National Resistance Army (NRA), 98
Odek, 11–12, 77, 98–9, 99–102, 115–18, 138–40, 140–5, 153
paramilitary violence in, 90–1
Peace Recovery and Development Plan (PRDP), 93, 142
Peoples' Defence Forces (UPDF), 98
reconciliation and, 93, 95, 115, 118, 126, 142, 151
reconstruction and, 93, 99, 140–2, 142, 151, 152
reintegration and, 93
religion and, 91
reparations and, 94
small-p peacebuilding in, 99–100, 101, 126, 142–3, 152
transitional justice and, 92–3, 95, 100, 118, 120
Uganda Peoples' Defence Forces (UPDF), 98
Unidad de Víctimas, 106
Unidad para las Víctimas, 105, 106, 135
United Kingdom
  Department for International Development (DFID), 17
United Nations (UN)
  Children's Fund (UNICEF), 99
  Committee on the Rights of the Child, 7
  Development Program (UNDP), 46
  High Commissioner for Refugees (UNHCR), 91
  Inter-Agency Expert Group (IAEG-SDG), 47
  Millennium Development Goal (MDG), 43
  Office for Coordination of Humanitarian Affairs (UNOCHA), 140
  Office on Drugs and Crime, 46
  peace operations, 21
  peacebuilding and, 17, 18, 33
  Peacebuilding Support Office, 46, 47
  Rule of Law Unit, 46

Sustainable Development Goal 16 (SDG 16), 40, 43–8
Sustainable Development Goals (SDGs), 42–3, 47, 61
Sustainable Development Solutions Network, 40
Technical Support Team (TST), 46
Virtual Network for the Development of Indicators for Goal 16, 46
United Self Defense Forces (AUC), 91, 94–5, 103
United States
  Agency for International Development (USAID), 17, 48, 51, 80, 105
  Army, 64
  Institute of Peace (USIP), 59
  State Department, 48, 59
Uppsala Conflict Data Program, 38, 41

validity
  conceptual, 5, 7
  internal, 111
  measurement, 62, 73–4, 96
Verification Focus Groups (VFGs), 71–3
victimhood
  collective, 24
  in Rwanda, 5
Virtual Network for the Development of Indicators for Goal 16, 46

Wittgenstein, Ludwig, 59
WomenStats Project, 40
Workers Revolutionary Party of Colombia (PRT), 103
World Bank, 17, 32
  Participatory Tracking, 65
World Happiness Report, 40
World Vision, 99, 101, 102, 156
Wright, Quincy, 38

Zimbabwe
  everyday peace indicators and, 11, 122–3